HUNGER IN AMERICA

The Physician Task Force on Hunger in America
was sponsored by
the Harvard School of Public Health
and directed by
J. Larry Brown, Ph.D.

HUNGER IN AMERICA

The Growing Epidemic

Physician Task Force on Hunger in America

WESLEYAN UNIVERSITY PRESS
Middletown, Connecticut

Research and related activities of the Physician Task Force on Hunger in America were made possible by grants to the Harvard School of Public Health from the following foundations:

The Field Foundation, New World Foundation, Villers Foundation, Boston Globe Foundation, Jessie Cox Trust, Permanent Charity Fund of Boston, Norman Foundation, Mary Reynolds Babcock Foundation, Hartford Foundation, Hyams Trust, Sherwood Forest Fund, Polaroid Foundation

The research, analysis, conclusions and recommendations are those of the Task Force as a body, and do not necessarily imply that they represent the views of individual members, foundations, or Harvard University.

The Physician Task Force expresses deep gratitude to persons and organizations around the nation who cooperated with its research activities, and acknowledges great respect for their quiet and persevering efforts to respond to the crisis of hunger in America.

LIBRARY OF CONGRESS CATALOGING-IN-PUBLICATION DATA

Physician Task Force on Hunger in America.
    Hunger in America.
    Includes index.
    1. Nutrition policy—United States. 2. Hunger.
3. Malnutrition—United States. 4. Nutritionally
induced diseases—United States. I. Title.
TX360.U6P49   1985   363.8'0973   85-17824
ISBN 0-8195-5150-3 (alk. paper)
ISBN 0-8195-6158-4 (pbk.: alk. paper)

Distributed by Harper & Row Publishers, Keystone Industrial Park, Scranton, Pennsylvania 18512.

Manufactured in the United States of America

FIRST EDITION

Contents

List of Tables and Figures

Tables

Figures

Members of the Physician Task Force on Hunger in America

J. Larry Brown, Ph.D., *Chairman*
Harvard School of Public Health, Boston, Massachusetts

William R. Beardslee, M.D.
Harvard Medical School; Children's Hospital Medical Center,
Boston, Massachusetts

Stephen Berman, M.D.
Head, Section of General Pediatrics, University of Colorado
Health Sciences Center, Denver, Colorado

Reverend Craig Biddle III
Director, IMPACT (National Interreligious Network),
Washington, DC

James P. Carter, M.D.
Chairman and Professor, Department of Nutrition, Tulane
University School of Public Health, New Orleans, Louisiana

Amos Christie, M.D.
Chairman Emeritus, Department of Pediatrics, Vanderbilt University School of Medicine, Nashville, Tennessee

Reverend Kenneth Dean
Pastor, First Baptist Church, Rochester, New York

Catherine DeAngeles, M.D., M.P.H.
Director, Pediatric and Adolescent Medicine, Johns Hopkins School
of Medicine, Baltimore, Maryland

Kenneth Dodgson, M.D.
Surgeon, University of Rochester Memorial Hospital, Rochester,
New York

Gordon P. Harper, M.D.
Harvard Medical School, Children's Hospital Medical Center,
Boston, Massachusetts

Judith A. Kitzes, M.D., M.P.H.
Maternal and Child Health Consultant, Albuquerque Area Indian
Health Service, Albuquerque, New Mexico

Stanley N. Gershoff, Ph.D.
Dean, School of Nutrition, Tufts University; Chairman, 1969 White
House Conference on Nutrition, Panel on Food Delivery

Fernando Guerra, M.D.
Founder and Medical Director, Barrio Health Center, San Antonio,
Texas; former Chairman, Community Health Services Committee,
American Academy of Pediatrics

Joyce C. Lashof, M.D.
Dean, School of Public Health, University of California at Berkeley,
Berkeley, California

Agnes Lattimer, M.D.
Director, Division of Ambulatory Pediatrics, Cook County
Hospital, Chicago, Illinois

John C. MacQueen, M.D.
Professor of Pediatrics, University of Iowa College of Medicine,
Iowa City, Iowa; former President, American Academy of Pediatrics

C. Arden Miller, M.D.
Chairman and Professor, Department of Maternal and Child Health,
University of North Carolina School of Public Health, Chapel Hill,
North Carolina

George Pickett, M.D., M.P.H.
Associate Dean and Professor, University of Alabama School of
Public Health, Birmingham, Alabama; former President, American
Public Health Association

Julius B. Richmond, M.D.
Director, Division of Health Policy, Research and Education,
Harvard Medical School, Boston, Massachusetts; U.S. Surgeon General (1977–1981)

Aaron Shirley, M.D.
Chairman, Mississippi Medical and Surgical Association; Project
Director, Jackson-Hinds Health Center, Jackson, Mississippi

Victor Sidel, M.D.
President, American Public Health Association; Chairman,
Department of Social Medicine, Montefiore Medical Center, Albert
Einstein School of Medicine, New York, New York

Myron E. Wegman, M.D.
Dean Emeritus, University of Michigan School of Public Health;
Professor Emeritus of Pediatrics, University of Michigan Medical
School, Ann Arbor, Michigan

*

Local Physicians Participating in Field Investigations

Joseph Blanton, M.D.
Ferguson Clinic, Sykeston, Missouri

Beverly Boyd, M.D.
Director, Divison of Family Health Administration,
Montgomery, Alabama

Ramiro Casso, M.D.
Family Physician, McAllen, Texas

Katherine Christoffel, M.D.
Children's Memorial Hospital; Northwestern University
Medical School, Chicago, Illinois

William Dow, M.D.
Physician, Pittsboro, North Carolina

James Dykes, M.D.
Roanoke-Amaranth Community Health Group,
Jackson, North Carolina

Tony Earles, M.D.
Washington University Medical School, St. Louis, Missouri

Effie Ellis, M.D.
Consultant, Department of Human Services, Chicago, Illinois

Stanley Fisch, M.D.
Pediatrician, Harlingen, Texas

Carol Geil, M.D.
Medical Director, Young Children's Health Center, University of New Mexico School of Medicine, Albuquerque, New Mexico

Robert Greenberg, M.D.
Chairman, Department of Pediatrics, University of New Mexico School of Medicine, Albuquerque, New Mexico

Maxine Hayes, M.D.
Pediatrician, Jackson, Mississippi; Faculty, Harvard School of Public Health

Norton Kalishman, M.D.
Chief School Physician, Albuquerque Public Schools; University of New Mexico School of Medicine, Albuquerque, New Mexico

Samuel Katz, M.D.
Chairman, Department of Pediatrics, Duke University School of Medicine, Durham, North Carolina

George Kerr, M.D.
Associate Dean for Academic Affairs; Director, Human Nutrition Center, University of Texas School of Public Health, Houston, Texas

Naomi Kisten, M.D.
Cook County Hospital, Chicago, Illinois

Robert Korn, M.D.
Suburban Pediatrics, Creve Coeur, Missouri

Richard L Kozoll, M.D.
Director, Checkerboard Area Health System, Cuba, New Mexico

David Levy, M.D.
Child Development Clinic, University of Mississippi School of Medicine, Jackson, Mississippi

Howard Levy, M.D.
Chairman of Pediatrics, Mount Sinai Hospital, Chicago, Illinois; Former Chief of Pediatric Nephrology, Walter Reed Army Hospital, Washington, DC

Michael Nelson, M.D.
Chairman, New Mexico Pediatric Society, Albuquerque,
New Mexico

Max Pepper, M.D., M.P.H.
Professor and Chairman, Department of Community Medicine,
St. Louis University School of Medicine, St. Louis, Missouri

James Perrin, M.D.
Director, Division of Pediatrics, Vanderbilt University Medical
Center, Nashville, Tennessee

Jorge Prieto, M.D.
Chairman, Department of Family Practice, Cook County
Hospital, Chicago, Illinois; President-designate, Chicago Board of
Health

Donald Rager, M.D.
St. Francis Medical Center, Peoria, Illinois

Jose Rodriguez, M.D.
Clinica La Fe, El Paso, Texas

Irwin Rosenberg, M.D.
Director, Clinical Nutrition Research Center; Professor of
Medicine, University of Chicago; President, American Society for
Clinical Nutrition

David Satcher, M.D., Ph.D.
President, Meharry Medical College, Nashville, Tennessee

Evelyn Schmidt, M.D.
Lincoln Community Health Center, Durham, North Carolina

Myrtis Sullivan, M.D.
Cook County Hospital, Chicago, Illinois

J.C. Walker, M.D.
Jellico Indian Mountain Clinic, Jellico, Tennessee

Patricia Woodall, M.D.
Mountain People's Health Council, Huntsville, Tennessee

Thomas Yeager, M.D.
Fellow, General Pediatrics, Metropolitan Nashville General
Hospital, Nashville, Tennessee

Quentin Young, M.D.
University of Illinois Medical School; President, Health and
Medicine Policy Research Group, Chicago, Illinois

Paul Zee, M.D.
Chief of Nutrition, St. Jude's Children's Hospital,
Memphis, Tennessee

★

State Coordinators and Consultants

The Physician Task Force on Hunger in America wishes to
thank and acknowledge the many people throughout the nation who, with energy and dedication, worked with us to plan
and carry out our field investigations. The following is a partial list:

ALABAMA

Brenda Cummings
Bill Edwards
Jack Guillebeaux
Roberta Hampton
Wanda Jackson
Jennifer Johnston
Gaye Joyner

Rhoda Kelly
Roxie McAdams
Nita Morrison
Alice Parris
Al Rohling
Reverend James Tuohy

MISSISSIPPI

Rims Barber
Dr. Ann Brooks
Larry Haynes

Joie Kammer
Margaret Kibbe
David Winters

TENNESSEE

Karen Braswell
Callie Hutchison
Tilda Kemplin
Joseph McLaughlin
Reverend Mark Matheny
Bill Moynihan

Linda Moynihan
Bill Murrah
Dixie Petrey
Sundra Thompson
Janet Wolfe

NORTH CAROLINA

Thomas Bacon, M.D.
Scott Dedman
Al Deitch
Chuck Epinet
Reverend Dennis Gabriel
Connie Gates
Richard Harding, M.D.
Jennifer Henderson

Daniel Hudgins
Linda Johnston
Reverend Mac Legerton
John Niblock
Thomas Plaut, Ph.D.
Virginia Stevens
Carolyn Wallace
Reverend Gary West

NEW MEXICO

Pat Cleveland
Buddy Gallegos
Elmer Jackson
Sally McCabe
Reverend Daniel
    Martinez-Erdman

Mike McEuen
Glenn Remer-Themart
Velia Silva-Garcia
Charles White

TEXAS

Joe Anderson
Elaine Blatt
Ofelia de Los Santos
Pete Duarte
Nancy Epstein
Paula Gomez
Fay Gray
Reverend Lary Grimm
Bobbie Kidd
Rachel Lucas

Nancy McCall
Norma Plascencia-
    Almanza
Alicia Reyes
Robert Rivera
Jose Rodriguez
Rina Rosenberg
Susan Tibertsma
Jo Williams

ILLINOIS

John Arnold
Sandy Barnard
Sister Judy Birgen
John Colgan
Ronald Cooley

Jean Hughes
Marjorie LaFont
Luz Martinez
Sister Norma Reiplinger
Pat Terrell

Reverend Jack Cramer-
    Heurman
Erma M. Davis
Tom Fox

Yolanda Hall
Frank Tipton
Betty Williams
Marge Yuriostequi

MISSOURI

Sally Barwinski
Eddie-Mae Binion
Steve Campbell
Alex Cooper
Larry Driver
Beth Drennan
Marian Holtgrewe, Ph.D.
Herbert Herzog
C. B. Huber

Diane Huneke
Father Robert Johnston
Michael Klein
Erma Motton
Joan Peters
Nancy Williams
Otis Woodard
Leroy Zimmerman

*

Task Force Staff and Consultants

Deborah Allen, M.S.
Judith dePontbriand, M.A.
Deborah Frank, M.D.
Maria Creavin, B.S.
JoAnn Eccher, M.P.H.

John Kellogg, M.S.
Katherine Petrullo, M.A.
Francine Shapiro, B.S.
Glenn Wasek, M.A., M.S.

Foreword

Hunger in America is a national health epidemic.

It is our judgment that the problem of hunger in the United States is now more widespread and serious than at any time in the last ten to fifteen years.

We do not reach this conclusion lightly. Some of us have spent a significant portion of our professional careers trying to eliminate hunger and malnutrition in this nation. In 1967, we accompanied a team of United States Senators to look into hunger in regions of the nation. We stood by Senator George Murphy (R-California) as he expressed his despair at what he had seen in this nation: "I didn't know that we were going to be dealing with the situation of starving people and starving youngsters."

During that year we went into health centers and homes across this nation and examined children and the elderly. We saw children whose nutritional and medical condition was shocking even to a group of doctors whose work involved them daily with disease and suffering. In child after child we saw evidence of vitamin and mineral deficiencies, severe anemia, eye, ear and bone diseases associated with poor food intake. We found children who were listless, suffering from fatigue and exhaustion, children who got no milk to drink and who never ate fruits and vegetables. They lived on grits and bread.

Some of our medical colleagues reported our findings to the U.S. Senate: "We do not want to quibble over words, but 'malnutrition' is not quite what we found . . . They are suffering from hunger and disease and directly or indirectly they are dying from them—which is exactly what 'starvation' means."

Ten years later some of us were among the teams of doctors sent into these same regions of the nation to determine whether hunger was still a serious problem. During that decade our people, through their federal government, Republicans and

Democrats, responded to the problem of hunger. The food stamp progam was expanded so that poor families could purchase food. School lunch and breakfast programs were increased so children could have adquate nutrition while they learned. Elderly feeding programs were established to reach lonely older Americans isolated in their homes. And the supplemental food program for poor pregnant women and their babies was established to reach recipients when nutrition makes such a critical difference.

In 1977, we went back to Appalachia where we had seen severe malnutrition a decade before. We returned to the Mississippi Delta where we had found malnourished infants and listless elderly citizens living on the brink of starvation. We again visited Indian reservations and returned to the ghettos of some of our nation's major cities. What we found gave us great professional and civic pride.

America's nutrition programs had succeeded. While we still saw immense poverty, we no longer saw widespread hunger and malnutrition. Poor people reported that they had food to eat. Teachers no longer reported children coming to school hungry. And doctors and nurses found that malnutrition was not a severe problem among the poor. To be certain, things were not perfect, but they were greatly improved.

It is now 1985, and hunger has returned as a serious problem across this nation. To be sure, hunger is not yet as bad as two decades ago, but the situation has greatly deteriorated.

We believe that today hunger and malnutrition are serious problems in every region of the nation. We have, in fact, returned from no city and no state where we did not find extensive hunger.

Nine-year-old Lee, who resides in the rural "Boot-heel" region of Missouri, has the stature of a six-year-old because he doesn't get enough to eat. He and the other malnourished children we found there are little different from the children who dig for food in the dumpsters outside apartment buildings in St. Louis.

Little Regina, a listless five-year-old who sat before her empty plate at a North Carolina day care center, is experiencing growth failure because she gets little to eat outside the program. But she may be faring better than the numerous younger children we examined that day who had no milk to drink and whose refrigerators were bare.

A young father in Pasadena, Texas, broke into tears as he told us that he sometimes cannot feed his wife and three sons. But he is little different from the fathers in Montgomery, Alabama, Peoria, Illinois, and other cities who cried as they told us the same thing.

Ninety-two-year-old Laura McAfee, who subsists on white beans and potatoes in her Nashville home, is thin and anemic. But her health status is little different from that of Mr. Alvarez, seventeen years her junior, who collects cans in his home near Brownsville, Texas, so his wife can eat and his little granddaughter can have milk to drink. And neither of these elderly Americans differs greatly from the thousands whom local churches and agencies report remain in their homes, alone, hungry, often malnourished.

Perhaps never in the past half century has hunger in this nation spread so rapidly. It returned, we believe, because the programs which virtually ended hunger in the last decade have been weakened.

Hunger has returned to our nation primarily due to governmental failure.

Hunger is an example of much that can go wrong in Washington. Problems get looked at in terms of Washington, in terms of politics . . . and not in terms of people. Some political leaders deny the obvious fact that hunger exists because it does not fit their ideological framework. More sensitive leaders recognize that there is hunger, but avoid intellectual honesty about its seriousness, pointing with pride to the few, halting steps they have taken to address it.

Political "reality" and the niceties of consensus politics permit otherwise decent leaders to discuss limited responses to a growing crisis even as the crisis worsens. It is easier to gain acknowledgement of hunger in other nations than it is to do so at home where we are more directly responsible.

Admittedly, we are not politicians. But as a group of doctors and health care professionals, we believe it is time to stop avoiding the problem of hunger. Americans neither deserve to be hungry, nor do they deserve leaders who permit hunger to exist. We call upon the leaders of this nation to respond to the hunger crisis, America's latest health epidemic.

HUNGER IN AMERICA

1. TASK FORCE PURPOSES AND FINDINGS

"I for one do not cherish the idea of visiting the Mississippi Delta in 1994 and finding the same conditions of hunger and malnutrition."[1]

Dr. Aaron Shirley is a man with a lot of patience. But clearly his patience is growing short. Three times now this Mississippi doctor has joined national teams of prominent physicians to look into the problems of hunger and malnutrition in this nation. They have not always found the same conditions, and this perhaps is what prompted Dr. Shirley's remark following the most recent physician field investigations.

In 1977, this clinician was among the doctors from across the country who found that hunger had diminished since they had first traveled into regions of the nation in 1968. In 1977, they had reason to believe that the hunger problem had virtually been eliminated; they took professional pleasure in our nation's having eradicated this dreadful problem.

But hunger returned. Not only did it return to Mississippi, but it returned across the country. And its return demanded that Dr. Shirley and medical colleagues once again investigate this latest outbreak of a problem our nation should not have.

Creation and Purposes of the Task Force

During the autumn of 1982, the Harvard School of Public Health was approached for assistance by emergency food programs in the Boston area. Supported by religious and philanthropic organizations, these programs were concerned about the growing number of hungry people with little to eat. Harvard faculty and staff helped program administrators establish a monthly monitoring system to keep track of food distribution and of the number of individuals and families in need of emergency food assistance. The data from this system was startling. The number of people in need doubled from one year to the next, and monthly increases in people reporting that they were hungry were as high as 20%. Moreover, many of the 207 emergency feeding programs reported that they could not keep up with requests for food, and that people were going hungry as a result.

Research staff began to look into the reasons people were hungry. Interviews with emergency food providers as well as the hungry themselves revealed that many of the hungry were recently unemployed, or were people who had been terminated from food assistance programs such as food stamps and school lunch. The apparent relationship between economic and federal policy changes, on the one hand, and increased hunger, on the other, was intriguing.

In April, 1983, a two-day conference was convened at the Harvard School of Public Health to consider the meaning of available data, and the possible problems they reflect.[2] Conferees concluded that available evidence suggested that hunger was a growing problem, and that its potential health consequences posed a threat to vulnerable populations such as young children and the elderly. Moreover, the problem of hunger appeared to be associated with federal policy and economic changes.

Growing out of this conference, the Citizens' Commission on Hunger in New England was established in June, 1983. Composed of physicians and religious and academic leaders, the Commission was charged with documenting the problem of hunger in the region, determining what population groups are at greatest risk, ascertaining the health effects of hunger and why hunger exists, and making recommendations to remedy the problem.

In February, 1984, the Commission released the results of its inquiry in a report entitled *American Hunger Crisis: Poverty and Health in New England.*[3] This report was based on public hearings throughout the New England region, interviews with public officials (governors, mayors, and program administrators), independent research, and extensive field investigations carried out by a panel of twenty-eight physicians from major medical schools and teaching hospitals in every New England state.

Traveling by car and plane, they spent two days and nights at a time carrying out their work. They went to New Haven, Connecticut, the seventh poorest city in America. They traveled to Providence and Warwick, Rhode Island. They traveled the back roads in Southern Vermont, and the highways connecting old mill towns in rural Western Massachusetts. And they traveled to Maine, spreading out across a region between Portland, Bangor, and Augusta. They stopped in people's homes in South Paris, Casco, Naples, Lewiston, and Brunswick as the first January snow of 1984 fell on the region.

The doctors talked with hungry people and those who try to help the hungry. They looked at the evidence, first-hand, and they saw the human face of hunger.

The doctors and their colleagues reported in their study that hunger had recently grown to be a serious problem in the New England region, and that the number of hungry people was still growing. Moreover, the panel found that hunger was associated with ill-health, including malnutrition and growth failure among children, and malnutrition and chronic disease in the elderly. In short, they said, the problems were serious and, from available evidence, getting worse.

The report of the Commission received substantial national attention, particularly among members of the media, medical and health professions, and Members of Congress. It also aroused the concern of several national foundations which have been concerned with hunger in this nation for some time. Chief among these were the Field Foundation and the New World Foundation.

The interest of these foundations in poverty, hunger, and malnutrition in America was long-standing. It was the Field Foundation which had convened the national team of doctors who, along with United States Senators, reported on the hunger problem in the nation in 1968. And it was this same foundation that, ten years later, sent teams of doctors back into regions of the nation to determine what impact federal food programs were having on the problem of hunger.

Field Foundation executives found the 1984 report of the

Commission alarming. Not only had a prestigious panel of doctors and other professionals documented widespread hunger in an entire region of the nation, but the problem existed in a region somewhat more well-off than others in the nation. The New England economy is relatively strong; during the recent recession, for example, its most populous state, Massachusetts, had the lowest unemployment of the top ten industrialized states. And the health care system in that region provides greater access to care for the poor than in some other regions of the country.

If hunger and malnutrition were serious problems in New England, the foundations asked, what must it be like in other regions? With that concern in mind, these foundations, along with several others, asked a national panel of doctors to go into the other regions of the United States to report on the problems of hunger and malnutrition.

The Physician Task Force on Hunger in America was established in early 1984. Composed primarily of prominent physicians and health experts from around the nation, and joined by academic and religious leaders, the members reflect longstanding professional interest in hunger and malnutrition.

The Task Force was asked to go into the different regions of the nation to carry out the following tasks:

• Document to the extent possible the nature and scope of the problem of hunger, particularly how widespread hunger is and what groups of Americans are hungry;
• Analyze any regional variations in the problem of hunger, and identify any common threads in the picture of hunger across the regions of the nation;
• Assess the health effects of hunger, especially among high-risk groups such as children, pregnant women, and the elderly;
• Determine why hunger is a problem, and make recommendations to remedy the problem and, if possible, prevent it from recurring.

Operating independently, and entirely supported by private foundations, the Task Force spent nearly ten months carrying out its work. Care was taken to look into hunger in different regions of America, to the extent that financial resources permitted. Altogether, Task Force members and staff analyzed the Deep South, the Mid-Atlantic region, the Southwest, and the Midwest. Interviews were conducted with representatives of many sectors: political leaders (governors, mayors), administrative agency heads (commissioners and program directors), health care providers (doctors, nurses, nutritionists), educators (principals, teachers), emergency food providers (ministers and social service agencies), community organizations (unions, religious and health groups), and hungry people (families with children, elderly people).

Epidemiological data was analyzed, and federal program statistics were monitored and reviewed. The Task Force obtained information on the health status of population groups in each state, and on problems associated with poor nutrition such as low birth-weights, growth failure, and certain chronic diseases. Emergency food program records were reviewed to establish patterns over time such as numbers of people served, proportions of families, children, and the elderly, as well as total pounds of food distributed. Finally, the physicians went into hundreds and hundreds of homes in the regions of the country. They looked into the nutritional status of families, talking with them about what they had to eat on a daily basis. They did dietary recalls, and they determined how much money people had each month to spend on food. And they looked into pantries and refrigerators—a practice many of the doctors found as informative as all the statistical data analyzed.

The rich mix of statistical and descriptive data gathered by the Task Force in its work was obtained primarily through field investigations. On four separate occasions, from April through October, 1984, teams of up to sixteen doctors, Task Force members, and physicians from the states visited, spent a week at a time investigating hunger and malnutrition in a region of the country. Breaking up into smaller groups, the physicians worked from early morning into the night, going into government agencies and churches, making home visits, eating with the hungry in community programs, and discussing health trends with medical colleagues in hospitals and health centers.

The doctors talked with hungry people and with those who try to feed them. They talked with malnourished children and the doctors who treat them. They looked at all the evidence they could, and sometimes more than they needed.

What the Task Force found is the subject of this report.

Major Findings and Conclusions

Hunger is a problem of epidemic proportions across the nation.

Hunger in America is a serious and widespread problem. It is in fact so widespread and obvious that its existence has been documented by fifteen national studies, and even more state-level studies, during the past few years.

While no one knows the precise number of hungry Americans, available evidence indicates that up to 20,000,000 citizens may be hungry at least some period of time each month. In the 1960s, before the expansion of federal nutrition programs, hunger was a daily problem for millions of citizens. Today, evidence indicates that weaknesses in these same programs leave millions of citizens hungry several days each month, and often more.

Hunger in America is getting worse, not better.

Evidence from the states and regions of the nation indicates that hunger continues to grow. Reported improvements in the economy appear to be having little, if any, impact on the problem of hunger.

Almost without exception, emergency food programs across the nation report significant increases in the number of hungry people. Accordingly, the pounds of food provided to alleviate this growing problem are, themselves, increasing at a steady rate. It appears that most Americans who are "recovering" economically were never hungry, and those who are hungry are not recovering.

Malnutrition and ill-health are associated with hunger.
Hunger and poverty are frequently associated with malnutrition and other forms of ill-health. Today, compelling evidence indicates that members of vulnerable population groups, particularly children and the elderly, are at increased risk of adverse health outcomes due to hunger. Malnutrition is a problem which impacts somewhere in the vicinity of a half million American children. Growth failure, low birth-weights, and other outcomes associated with inadequate nutrition are serious among low-income pediatric populations, and health problems and chronic diseases associated with undernutrition are serious among the elderly poor.

Hunger is the result of federal government policies.
Hunger in America is the result of a series of governmental policies, some within the past few years and others of longer duration.

Hunger does not just happen in a nation with more than enough food to feed itself and a good part of the world. Hunger occurs because policies either produce it or fail to prevent it. Today our leaders have permitted poverty in this nation to reach record levels and then cut back on programs which help our citizens endure economic hardship. As a result, America has become a "soup kitchen society," a spectre unmatched since the bread lines of the Great Depression.

Present policies are not alleviating hunger in America.
Hunger is getting worse, and no evidence indicates that it will lessen as a problem.

Poverty in the country is at the highest rate in twenty years, and purchasing power for the poorest forty percent of the population is lower than it was in 1980. It is unlikely that economic changes helping the better-off will assist those who are hungry.

The bottom line is that policies which supposedly were to help the poor have not done so.

We believe that our political leaders must end their laissez-faire attitude toward hunger. Millions of Americans are hungry now, and political leadership—Republican and Democratic—is required to address their plight. Even if things do improve in the future, our job is to make sure that all of our citizens have the opportunity to reap the rewards of democracy today.

2. HUNGER AS A WELL-DOCUMENTED PHENOMENON

Erma Motton looked directly into the faces of the doctors sitting around the table of her community center in Caruthersville, Missouri. The sparsely furnished office contained folding chairs and piles of paper, some of which she placed before her visitors who had just arrived to investigate the extent of hunger in this rural community.

"What I'm giving you, gentlemen," Mrs. Motton explained, "is detailed information on hungry people right there in this community . . . a survey with names, addresses, children, income, illnesses, and what they have had to eat in the past month. As you can see, they don't eat much. They can't. They're poor and they're hungry and things are getting worse."

Only three months before, some of the same doctors had gathered around a different table to hear of hunger in another community. "Please tell Mr. Meese and the White House that there is hunger in America," pleaded Nashville Mayor Robert H. Fulton, as he addressed the physicians who had arrived for a first-hand look in his city.

The Mayor described the growing number of soup kitchens which have sprung up in that city to feed growing numbers of hungry families. Almost as an aside he noted that he seldom goes to the facilities distributing the food. Too many of the people waiting for something to eat are former schoolmates with whom he grew up. He is afraid his presence will embarrass them.

The mayor from Tennessee and the community worker from Missouri are two of thousands of officials and agency heads across the nation who are trying to respond to the epidemic of hunger in America. That hunger exists in their states is not remarkable, for it has returned as a serious problem in virtually every state in the nation. What is remarkable is that they felt compelled to establish it as a problem—to "prove" that hunger exists.

The proof they offered may be accepted simply as a measure of their sincerity and concern. That they felt the need to offer proof in light of substantial evidence of hunger throughout the nation is a measure of the intractability of the problem, and the desire of some political leaders to ignore rather than address it.

The Evidence That Hunger Is a National Problem

The reappearance of hunger in the United States crept up relatively unnoticed until it burst into the public consciousness in 1982. In the earlier stages of the problem, churches and agencies began to notice increasing numbers of citizens confiding that they did not have enough food for their families. Then, in that particular year, doctors in parts of the nation began to observe in their clinical practices that an increasing number of patients said they were hungry, and patients manifested more illness associated with hunger.

Later that same year appeared the first of a growing number of reports documenting the widespread existence and continuing growth of hunger in this nation. Altogether, fifteen studies were conducted on hunger between October, 1982, and November, 1984 (see Table 1).

The impact of these diverse studies is uniquely consistent: all available evidence leads to the conclusion that America has a serious hunger problem. In this chapter we will examine the data upon which this conclusion is based. We will first review each of the national studies cited above. In the next chapter we will present evidence we gathered in our own research and from field investigations in different regions of the nation.

The first official recognition of America's hunger crisis came in a report by the U.S. Conference of Mayors in October, 1982. The group of Republican and Democratic chief executives of the nation's cities and towns conducted a national survey which found hunger to represent "a most serious emergency."[1] This bipartisan alarm was disconcerting to the mayors themselves, and a number of them began to call for federal emergency re-

Table 1. *Recent Reports Documenting Hunger in America*

Report or survey	Date
United States Conference of Mayors Survey	October, 1982
United Church of Christ Report	January, 1983
U.S. Department of Agriculture "Case Studies of Emergency Food Programs"	May, 1983
Center on Budget and Policy Priorities, "Soup Lines and Food Baskets"	May, 1983
United States Conference of Mayors, "Hunger in American Cities"	June, 1983
Salvation Army of America Report	June, 1983
U.S. General Accounting Office, "Public and Private Efforts to Feed America's Poor"	June, 1983
National Council of Churches, Work Group on Domestic Hunger and Poverty	August, 1983
Bread for the World, Hunger Watch	September, 1983
United States Conference of Mayors, "Responses to Urban Hunger"	October, 1983
Food Research and Action Center, "Still Hungry"	November, 1983
Harvard School of Public Health, "American Hunger Crisis"	February, 1984
Save the Children/American Can Company, "Hard Choices"	September, 1984
United States Conference of Mayors, "The Urban Poor and the Economic Recovery"	September, 1984
Food Research and Action Center, "Bitter Harvest"	November, 1984

lief just as they do when their communities are hit by floods or tornadoes.

Mayor Ernest Morial of New Orleans requested an immediate federal response to stem the flood of hungry citizens.[2] A short time later Mayor Coleman Young of Detroit declared a state of emergency to help residents of that city "avoid starvation."[3]

In June, 1983, the Conference of Mayors followed up their initial survey with a national report, "Hunger in American Cities." In that document, the nation's mayors reported a dramatic increase in hunger—an increase of relatively recent origin. Most of the emergency food programs in their cities, they reported, "were established only in the last three years."[4]

Just a month prior to the mayors' report a study commissioned by the U.S. Department of Agriculture concluded that examination of emergency food needs in the regions of the nation pointed to a dramatic situation. The study found a sharp increase in the need for food to feed Americans on an emergency basis, and concluded that hunger "is increasing at a frenetic pace and the emergency food available for distribution is quickly depleted."[5]

During that same month a non-partisan and widely respected national research organization released its own study on hunger in the nation. The Center on Budget and Policy Priorities, whose director had previously run federal nutrition programs for the U.S. Department of Agriculture, conducted a random-sample survey of 181 emergency food programs in the United States. Assisted in its work by Second Harvest, the umbrella agency for a nationwide network of food banks, the Center reported the results of its findings:[6]

• More than eight of every ten programs reported an increase in hungry people served between February, 1982, and February, 1983.

• One-third of the agencies in the nation experienced an increase of 100% or more in the number of hungry people coming for help, while a significant portion of the agencies saw increases of over 200% in that one year alone.

Within a month of this study the General Accounting Office (GAO) released the results of its own study, based on an examination of some twenty-eight emergency food centers in the nation. The GAO reported that "in almost all cases the (centers) were serving more today than in the past. Many centers reported that food assistance needs were greater than ever . . ."[7] The study concluded that hungry Americans are made up of those who fail to receive government nutrition program assistance, as well as those for whom such assistance is inadequate.

Meanwhile, American church organizations, troubled by a phenomenon striking at members of their own congregations, began to analyze the hunger problem. In January, 1983, the United Church of Christ reported that the numbers of hungry people appearing at church-operated emergency food centers increased from 40% to as much as several hundred percent during the period surveyed.[8]

A few months later the national assistant director of the Salvation Army told the General Accounting Office that his organization was seeing dramatic increases in the need for food assistance across the country. In New England alone the number of families seeking food from the Salvation Army had tripled from 1981 to 1982. The Army was forced to launch new programs to respond to the growing crisis.[9]

Adding to the evidence from the national religious community was the Working Group on Hunger and Poverty of the national Council of Churches. Recognized as a bellwether of trends throughout the nation owing to its member denominations in communities throughout the country, the Council had asked its director to investigate the hunger problem. In August, 1983, he reported that: "The hunger problem nationally is three—in some places four times—worse than it was a year ago. Every group I talked to is up that high and that's 106 of them . . . from Maine to California."[10]

Corroborating this conclusion was the 42,000-member Christian organization Bread for the World, which released results of its own national survey. It reported that private agencies in the United States were seeing a "greatly increased demand" for emergency food, and that they were virtually unable to keep up with the need.[11]

Before the year ended yet another study was completed. In November, 1983, the Food Research and Action Center reported that it found hunger to be "a large and growing problem once again." Noting that the evidence of hunger is compelling, the Center found that the food stamp program no longer provides adequate assistance to the needy, and that it fails to reach many who are hungry.[12]

In a period of just over a year, some eleven national studies on hunger had been released. While their sponsorship varied from government agencies to religious organizations to independent policy groups, their results bore the same ominous message: hunger had reappeared as a serious national problem.

But just as the lines of hungry Americans would continue to grow outside the nation's soup kitchens, so too would the evidence of their existence. During the next year four additional studies citing increasing hunger in the nation appeared. In February, 1984, the Harvard School of Public Health released a regional study compiled by the Citizens' Commission on Hunger in New England, a blue-ribbon panel of physicians, clergy, and university officials.[13] Although the Commission analyzed available data from around the nation, its chief contribution was a comprehensive, in-depth examination of hunger in an entire region of the nation. The Commission conducted its own research on the extent and growth of hunger in the six New England states, analyzed the relationship of the economy and federal program changes to hunger, held public hearings in the region, and sent a panel of more than two dozen doctors from teaching hospitals and medical schools to investigate both hunger and malnutrition. The study concluded that hunger is widespread and increasing, and that it is associated with malnutrition and illness.

Later in the year William Woodside, chief executive officer of American Can Company, commissioned a profile of hungry Americans. Conducted by Save the Children, this study addressed the impact which hunger has on the nation's families. Enlightening in approach and tone, this document reflected growing recognition on the part of some of the country's industrial leaders of the existence and costs of hunger in the United States.

Toward the end of 1984, the U.S. Conference of Mayors conducted a follow-up survey of cities and towns across the nation, to determine whether and how the reported economic recovery was affecting the poor, including the problem of hunger.[15] The city officials reported that overall conditions for the poor had not improved. In fact, cities and towns in general experienced increases in need for emergency services throughout 1984, with hunger and the need for food assistance among the needs at the top of the list.

Nearly 75% of all cities and towns reported that the need for emergency food assistance had increased during 1984. Only 7% reported a decrease in need, with the remainder reporting no change in the numbers of hungry families seeking food throughout the year. During 1984 the number of facilities— soup kitchens and food pantries—increased by 15% according to the cities and towns reporting, and the total number of meals provided increased by more than 50% across the nation, while individual cities reported even greater increases: Dallas-100%, Chicago-182%, and Boston-200%.

Perhaps the most ominous data in the U.S. Conference of Mayors survey were the projections for 1985. More than half the chief executives of the nation's cities and towns expected hunger to increase, with most of the rest anticipating that although need might not increase, neither would it diminish. Fewer than 4% thought there would be a decrease in the number of hungry citizens.

In November, 1984, a larger survey was conducted by the independent Food Research and Action Center. Covering nearly 300 emergency food programs geographically distributed across the nation, this survey reported the following: [16]

• Nearly two-thirds (65%) of the facilities reported an increase in the number of hungry households seeking food in 1984 over 1983.

• The average number of households fed increased by more than 20% between 1983 and 1984.

• Some 71% of the soup kitchens and food pantries reported that private charity cannot meet the need for food assistance in the local communities.

• More than 60% of the respondents indicated that over half the hungry people they serve are families with children.

The Evidence of Hunger at the State Level

The evidence revealed in these fifteen national studies is clear and consistent: hunger in America is a serious problem once again. Yet as compelling as this evidence is, there is still more. During the period in which the national studies were conducted, a number of state studies were carried out in different parts of the nation. They, too, are remarkable in their consistency: each state report found hunger to be a serious and growing problem.

Examples of the available studies are enumerated:

Texas. The Senate Interim Committee on Hunger of the Texas Legislature, a bipartisan committee which held twelve hearings throughout the state, reported that hunger in the state, measured by requests for food, increased by 300% between 1983 and 1984. In Houston, the increase was 1,000%.[17]

Ohio. Desperate poverty and hunger have been identified in parts of the state by the Ohio Senate Task Force on Hunger, which described the problem as having an "Appalachian character." Serious hunger in rural areas parallels that found in some central cities where emergency feeding programs now report increasing numbers of hungry people, including families with children.[18]

Louisiana. New Orleans Mayor Ernest Morial established a Nutrition Task Force to address what he called "the lack of food and the hunger which affects so many in our community." The group's interim report concluded that hunger and inadequate nutrition are serious problems.[19]

Florida. Florida IMPACT, an interdenominational group including the Lutheran Church, the Presbyterian Church, the United Church of Christ, the Episcopal Church, and the United Presbyterian Churches, reported that "over a million people, most of them women, children and the elderly, are poor and often hungry in Florida."[20]

California. The Interfaith Hunger Coalition of Southern California reported that in metropolitan Los Angeles sixty-three of the ninety food pantries surveyed were not located in the city, "a fact which belies the myth that hunger exists only on skid row." Most of the pantries, according to survey findings, had an increase of at least 300% in the numbers of people served from 1982 to 1983, when the results were released. A number of pantries reported that they consistently run out of food.[21]

Oklahoma. In its report, *Hunger and Malnutrition in Oklahoma,* the Oklahoma Conference of Churches reported that hunger had returned as a major social and health problem in the state, and that 400,000 residents have incomes so low that they are incapable of living on an adequate diet.[22]

Michigan. The Michigan Nutrition Commission surveyed twenty counties and found that emergency food facilities reported an increase of over 100% in their caseload during the first two years of the decade.[23]

New York. Dr. Victor Sidel, chairman of the department of social medicine of Montefiore Medical Center, reported in 1983 that his research on a sample of 400 persons considered at risk of nutritional deprivation showed that 40% were eating less than they knew they should; one-quarter of respondents reported that there were times they are hungry and must go without anything to eat. Twenty percent of parents reported that their children sometimes go to bed hungry.[24]

Maryland. The Governor's Task Force on Food and Nutrition reported in November, 1984, that the number of hungry people has grown dramatically. Emergency food programs now number 250 in the city of Baltimore, and over 400 statewide, the latter number growing steadily. In addition, soup kitchens in Baltimore grew from 12 in 1982 to 27 in 1984. The Task Force reported that not only has the number of soup kitchens increased, but utilization of them has also gone up. The Franciscan Center, the oldest kitchen in the city, increased from nearly 21,000 people in 1979 to over 65,000 in 1983.[25]

Virginia. The Virginia Forum, a nonprofit, nonpartisan group analyzing public issues in the state, reported in late 1984 that in the past three years the number of soup kitchens and food pantries throughout the state has increased between 300–400%. In 1983, the state's four food banks distributed some 7,500,000 pounds of food through a number of local agencies, the latter reporting that they cannot keep up with the demand for food from the hungry.[26]

Wisconsin. The Wisconsin Nutrition Project reported that emergency food programs in the state had doubled in 1984 over the previous year. The Project reported that "most of the people coming to the food programs now are families," noting that "people who could barely exist a few years ago on food stamps can't make it any more."[27]

New Jersey. Rutgers University School of Social Work studied families whose welfare grants had been cut off and found that only 39% of the families received food stamps while off welfare, and 40% reported that since being off welfare there were times when the family went hungry.[28]

Illinois. The Legislative Advisory Committee on Public Aid reported to the state Senate in May, 1984, that hunger is a serious problem, citing Chicago where, it reported, there had been a nine-fold increase in the demand for emergency food between 1981 and 1983.[29]

Kentucky. Some 27,000 residents lost food stamp benefits, and 17,000 low-income children are no longer able to eat school meals owing to federal policy changes, according to the Kentucky Task Force on Hunger. Of the 350 emergency food programs operating in the state, half were organized in 1981, to respond to hunger caused by federal budget cuts. The programs report annual increases in the demand for food ranging from 75% in some areas to more than 400% in others, by mid-1984.[30]

Colorado. The Boulder County Department of Community Action Programs conducted a study to determine the impact of federal budget cuts on nutrition programs since 1981. Some 23.4% of county food stamp recipients lost food stamp benefits as a result of the changes, and other programs were impacted as well. Between 1981 and 1982, people being fed by emergency food programs increased 35.6%, "and current figures indicate that [this] trend is continuing."[31]

California. A recent survey of emergency food recipients, conducted in the counties of San Francisco, Alameda, and Santa Cruz by the Northern California Anti-Hunger Coalition, found the following: 60% of parents go without food so children can eat, yet 22% of respondents report that their children sometimes go to bed hungry. Nearly half the respondents surveyed spent under $10 on food purchases the previous week.[32]

Arizona. The Hunger Action Center, located in Tucson, conducted a survey of local emergency food assistance programs. Since 1982, the need for emergency food among low-income residents increased substantially, with the Community Food Bank providing 60% more food in 1983. Food assistance was provided some 94,000 times each day in the area in 1983, up from an estimated 75,000 times the previous year.[33]

Fig. 1. *Food Distribution by Massachusetts Food Banks, 1982–1984*

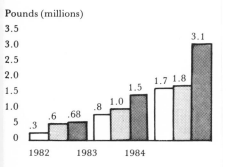

Pounds (millions)

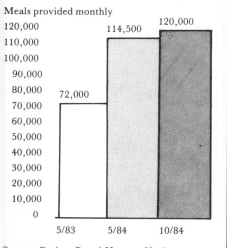

☐ W. Mass.
▨ Worcester
▨ Boston

Source: Individual food bank records.

Fig. 2. *Boston Soup Kitchens, 1980–1985*

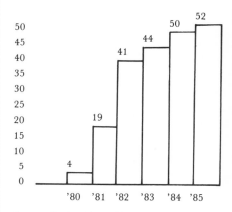

Source: Project Bread Hunger Hotline, Paulist Center, Boston.

Fig. 3. *People Fed by Boston Area Soup Kitchens, 1983–1984*

Meals provided monthly

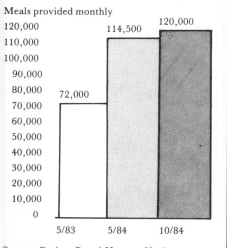

5/83   5/84   10/84

Source: Project Bread Hunger Hotline, Paulist Center, Boston.

Fig. 4. *People Fed by Boston Area Food Pantries, 1982–1984*

No. of people monthly

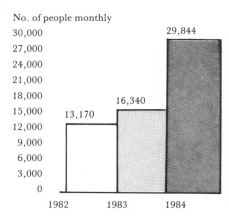

1982   1983   1984

Source: Project Bread Hunger Hotline, Paulist Center, Boston.

Delaware. A survey of community and religious organizations assisting the poor, conducted in 1984 by Food Conservers, Inc., found that increasing numbers of families are being faced with a "heat or eat" dilemma, and that requests for emergency food are rising as a result. Programs see a continuing increase in the number of hungry people, as demand outstrips supply "no matter how much food a community organization or church group has."[34]

Following the 1984 study of hunger in the Northeast, conducted by Harvard School of Public Health and the Citizens' Commission on Hunger in New England, individual states in New England continued to report sharp increases in the numbers of people coming for food to emergency programs throughout the region.

In Massachusetts emergency food programs are serviced by three food banks located in the eastern, central, and western portions of the state. The one in Boston serves not only the metropolitan area, but also parts of Maine, while the food bank in western Massachusetts serves parts of Vermont. Each of the three banks had reported a sharp increase in food distributed from 1982 to 1983, a trend which continued throughout 1984 (see Figure 1).

In Greater Boston, need escalated significantly in 1984, according to the Project Bread Hunger Hotline, an umbrella organization operating out of the Paulist Center which monitors monthly trends in emergency food needs. As shown in Figure 2, the number of soup kitchens in Boston, which rose from four to nineteen between 1980 and 1982, continued to increase during each of the last three years, to a total of fifty-two. Moreover, the number of individuals fed by the soup kitchens (see Figure 3) rose as well, to some 120,000 in 1984.[35]

Meanwhile, area food pantries, which provide bags of groceries to hungry families, increased their distribution significantly, reaching almost 30,000 people monthly at the end of 1984 (see Figure 4). Notably, the increase during 1984 was greater than the increases of the preceding years.[36]

Two other New England states are served by statebased food banks, both of which reported increases in food distribution

Fig. 5. *Rhode Island Food Bank, 1982–1984*

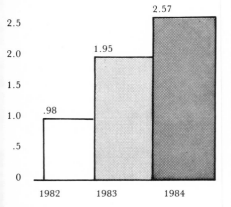

Pounds of food (millions)

Source: Food Bank records.

Fig. 6. *Connecticut Food Bank, 1982–1984*

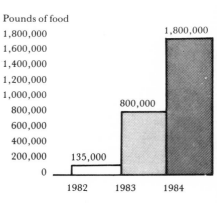

Pounds of food

Source: Food Bank records.

Fig. 7. *Second Harvest National Food Bank Network, 1979–1984*

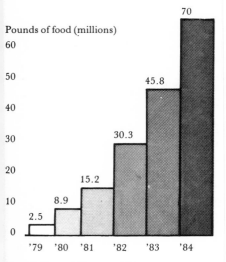

Pounds of food (millions)

Source: Second Harvest, Chicago.

during 1984, as their member agencies experienced more people coming to them who were without food.

The Rhode Island Food Bank distributed just under 1 million pounds of food in 1982, and nearly 2 million in 1983 (see Figure 5). During 1984, the distribution level went up to 2,570,655 pounds of food.[37] Meanwhile, the number of food baskets (boxes of groceries) provided by agencies in communities served by the food bank increased from 3,303 in 1983 to 7,017 in 1984—an increase of 112%.[38]

The Connecticut Food Bank, located in New Haven, distributed 800,000 pounds of food in 1983, and had projected distribution of 1,200,000 pounds in 1984. Instead, demand for food was up so significantly among churches and social service agencies feeding the hungry that the food bank actually distributed 1,800,000 pounds of food in 1984, as Figure 6 indicates.

The pattern of increasing hunger reported in state and national studies, and reflected in the distribution of food by the New England-based food banks, is paralleled nationally by Second Harvest, the umbrella organization for some seventy food banks across the nation. Each year for the past six, according to Second Harvest records, the amount of food distributed by state food banks to local programs feeding the hungry has increased steadily. At the beginning of the decade less than 10,000,000 pounds of food was distributed nationally through member food banks. By this past year that number had risen 700%, to an all-time high of 70,000,000 pounds (see Figure 7).

From his Chicago headquarters, Second Harvest director Jack Ramsey explained the significance of this trend:[39]

Our numbers don't accurately reflect hunger; they reflect industry availability (of food). In no way have we begun to saturate the market of need . . . we could distribute three times what we do now and still not eliminate hunger.

In no way are we and our member food banks the answer. You can't feed the people of this country properly with hand-outs.

3. THE INCREASE OF HUNGER
IN AMERICA

The studies and survey data establish beyond doubt that hunger has become a serious problem again in America. The varied nature of the evidence makes it all the more compelling. Documentation comes from agencies of the federal government as well as state and city government agencies, and state legislative committees; it is provided by universities, religious organizations, and a number of independent policy bodies at the federal, state, and local levels.

But the variety of sources documenting the problem of hunger is not what is most impressive. The most compelling factor, we believe, is the overwhelming preponderance of the evidence. There have been 15 national studies on hunger in the past three years; at least that many more state and local studies on hunger have been carried out during the same period of time. What is clear is the *uniformity* of their conclusions: Hunger has returned to this nation, and all evidence indicates that it is continuing to grow as a problem. Seldom do the public and our policy-makers have the luxury of studies and surveys about a major national problem which all reach the same general conclusion.

Most of the studies cited have limited themselves to documenting the existence of hunger, or the fact that it is increasing. Few have sought to address the question of why hunger returned to this nation, or why it is increasing during the reported economic recovery. More important, perhaps, few of the studies were designed to assess the impact of hunger on its victims, including the problems of illness and malnutrition. To assess these and related problems, the Physician Task Force on Hunger in America set out to conduct field investigations into hunger and malnutrition in the regions of the nation.

Several of us had participated only a year before in the New England study based at the Harvard School of Public Health.

Others of us had traveled to regions of the nation looking into the same problems in 1968 and again in 1977. We found these previous experiences invaluable, since they provide physicians and academicians who usually look at individual patients, or sets of data, a first-hand look at a problem in its regional context.

Altogether, we went into eight states in four different regions of the nation to try to better understand the prevalence and impact of hunger.

Hunger in the Deep South—Mississippi and Alabama

Everything is so clear in the Mississippi Delta. One drives down the long roads of rich farmland stretching to the left and right, land which has supported productive soybean and cotton crops for 200 years. Suddenly the panorama is broken by a stand of trees with a big house and several little houses trailing away from it, homes for the poor black tenants whose families have lived in the unheated shacks for decades.

Signs proudly proclaim the name of each plantation. No attempt is made to hide, excuse, or change the enormous disparity between rich and poor, black and white, in this region of the nation. So long have many of the residents lived in this environment that they defend it without shame. "There's no hunger here," one local doctor reported, generalizing from his wealthy white patients, no doubt, to the poor blacks he never treats. "Every specimen I see on the street is fat and shiny."

But there is substantial hunger in this rich agricultural region. It is simple to find and easy to see. But so are all the other problems which accompany hunger here. People don't just get to be hungry in the Delta without having other things that are not right in their lives: dilapidated housing, no jobs, lack of health care. We easily found a substantial number of people crippled by the experience of poverty and racism, lives that cannot easily be repaired by a particular program. But the people are also hungry, and that is a problem quite easy to remedy.

In fact hunger in this region was substantially alleviated by the federal nutrition programs during the last decade. Some of the physicians in our group had seen the progress first-hand, having lived in Mississippi all their lives. Others had actually traveled to the Delta with the United States Senators in 1967, and had returned in 1977 to find dramatic improvement insofar as decreased hunger and malnutrition.

The four doctors were visibly shaken by what they saw. Inside the remnants of a house, alongside a dirt road in Greenwood, lived a family of thirteen people. Graciously welcomed by the mother and father, the doctors entered another world—a dwelling with no heat, no electricity, no windows, home for two parents, their children, and several nieces and nephews. Clothes were piled in the corner, the substitute location for closets which were missing; the two beds in the three-room house had no sheets, the torn mattresses covered by the bodies of three children who lay side by side. In the kitchen a small gas stove was the only appliance.

No food was in the house. The babies had no milk; two were crying as several of the older children tried to console them. "These people are starving," the local guide told the doctors. Twice a week she collected food from churches to bring to the family. It had been this way for two months while the family waited for the local food stamp office to determine whether they were eligible for food stamps. Only the flies which crawled on the face of the smallest child seemed to be well fed. The parents were not; they had not eaten for two days. The children had eaten some dried beans the previous evening.

A few houses away two other doctors spoke to a hungry, pregnant woman whose infant son recently died. She had been cut off welfare benefits after a dispute over eligibility, leaving her $60 monthly food stamp allotment as the only income each month for herself, the unborn child, and her five-year-old Her refrigerator had three sticks of butter and some powdered milk.

One of the doctors quietly shook his head: "What you're looking at are the faces that become infant mortality statistics."

"My overall impression is quite sad," reported Harvard psychiatrist William Beardslee, a southerner who had accompanied doctors to this region a decade before. "Clearly there is not the widespread hunger or malnutrition found in 1967, and for people still served by food programs there is some benefit as we saw in 1977. But the improvement has crested. The overall picture is one of increasing difficulty. Hunger is again obvious, the malnutrition apparent, not yet as bad as 1967, but bad. In a curious way things are much worse than 1967, however, because then these people had hope. Now they despair, they are tenuously hanging on as things are getting worse again."

So stark is hunger in the Delta today that it shocked even the local doctors who accompanied our field investigation teams. "I was here as a medical student back in 1969," reported Dr. Maxine Hayes of Jackson, Mississippi, "and things were so bad that the local health center was actually prescribing food. I know hunger and poverty in this area, but I must admit that the degree of hunger we find today is overwhelming, even for me!"

Ample reason exists to find Mississippi overwhelming. Nearly one-quarter of the state's population, over 580,000 people, lives below the federal poverty level. A third of the state's population is so poor that it is eligible for food stamp assistance, yet only 19% of the people receive the benefits of this program. Some 300,000 needy people fall through the cracks, standing at high risk of hunger and its attendant health problems.[1] Evidence presented by state officials, doctors and nurses, teachers and ministers as well as the people trying to feed the hungry, reveals much about which to be concerned.

The Governor told us that Mississippi has a serious problem, and that his staff had cooperated with President Reagan's Task Force on Food Assistance "to accurately expose the extent of hunger, malnutrition and attendant health problems in this state." The Governor felt that their efforts had been to no avail: "After the release of their alleged findings we were dismayed, indeed angry, that the lives of so many of our people were lost or forgotten on the way to the White House."

The lives about which the Governor worries are disproportionately at the ends of the age spectrum—the young and the old. During the past decade, for example, the proportion of elderly in the state increased to nearly 16%, nearly one-third of whom live below poverty.[2]

Yet the hungry elderly citizens of Mississippi are hidden, tucked away in the privacy of their homes and not easily seen. When one visits Mississippi the image indelibly etched in the mind is one of children, young children and many of them. They are frequently hungry, observed Alice Emmanuel, director of the Jackson County Welfare Department: "Many children still go to sleep hungry with certain knowledge that there will be little or no nourishment the following morning."

How easy it is to find hungry children is reflected in the visit of a Congressional subcommittee to Mississippi in June, 1984. One Congressman left his colleagus to talk to two young girls staring at the visitors. "Hi, girls," called the Congressman, who received a "hello" in unison from the two as he approached. "Are you happy that school is out?" he asked, anticipating the affirmative response one would normally elicit at the start of summer vacation. One child shook her head, while the other articulated their feeling: "No, sir." Taken aback, the Congressman asked why they felt unhappy to be out of school. "Because," one child explained, "when we is in school we gets to eat lunch, but in the summer we only gets supper."[3]

These girls appear to represent the face of hunger in Mississippi today. Clearly they are not starving, but they are hungry and they are easy to find. "You will not find people starving on every corner," notes Rims Barber, a twenty-year resident of the state and staff member of the Children's Defense Fund. "But within blocks of here you will find people hungry. Hungry people are common again in Mississippi."

All available evidence confirms Barber's observations, as churches, clinics, and social service agencies across the state report more hunger. In towns and rural areas of the Delta hunger is obvious. The St. Francis Center, a Catholic social service agency in Greenwood, has seen a continuing rise in the number of hungry people. Seventy-five-year-old Joie Kammer, a Center worker, described the community response to the announcement that our doctors would hold a hearing in their community: "It was a sad time to see the large hall crowded with 200–300 people literally crying out that they are hungry. Only some people could testify, but there were enough present who wanted to that the hearing could have gone on indefinitely. Also there were telephone calls from the elderly asking that the doctors come to visit their homes."

In the same community Captain Schneider of the Salvation Army told us that hunger is now worse, as requests for food have gone up "tremendously" during the past few years.

Teachers for the Headstart program in Greenwood and neighboring Sidon serve 647 children in their program. The program, they reported, is the main source of food for half their children, who often get only one and at most two meals a day. This causes them to worry about the 200 children on the waiting list to get into their program. Eloise Sample, one of the teachers, said that about 20% of the children ask for two breakfasts on Monday mornings, indicating that they have little to eat over the weekend when school is out.

In nearby Marks, Mississippi, a recent screening of over 90 children for the Headstart program found that over half were anemic. Home health aide Odell Williams reported that some families simply have nothing to eat.[4]

Staff at the health clinic in Tutwiler reported seeing hunger and malnutrition fairly regularly. Dr. Anne Brooks has practiced in the area only about a year but sees signs of hunger and malnutrition, describing a year-and-a-half-old child who weighs only sixteen pounds to underscore her point.

Hunger and ill-health are not unique to the Delta towns, however. Testifying before the President's Task Force on Food Assistance, Dr. Aaron Shirley, a resident and practicing pediatrician in Jackson, and president of the board of the Mississippi Medical and Surgical Association, offered clinical evidence of the problems he encounters: "In our clinic 70% of 5,000 children . . . have dietary histories deficient in vitamins A and C. Another 45% are deficient in iron and 30% deficient in protein. In these children ages 3–5, 15% are deficient in calcium."

Emergency food providers in Jackson established a food bank in response to increased need for emergency food. Warren Yodes, director of that city's Operation Shoestring, reported that

Fig. 8. *Mississippi Food Network, Jackson, 1984*

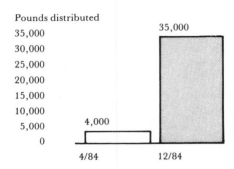

Source: Food Network records.

demand has increased 300% since 1981. In written testimony provided to our doctors, Robert Thomas of the Jackson-Hinds Clients Council reported an influx of requests to his agency for food from newly unemployed people. "More than twice as many people need our help now as did only two years ago." Lamar Branton, president of the Mississippi Association of Community Services Agencies, reported the experience of member organizations: "More requests for food subsistence have been received now than ever before."

But Jackson and the Delta communities are not the only areas seeing an increased amount of hunger. Reverend Bruno Schroeder of the United Church of Christ Back Bay Mission on the Mississippi coast drove three hours to report "my conviction about the gravity of the need" in his community. "I go into homes where they don't have refrigerators. They don't even have food to cook." Not far away the Gulf Coast Community Action Agency in Gulfport reports more requests for food assistance "than ever before." They opened a soup kitchen in response to the need.

Elsewhere other churches and agencies report that hunger is growing. Rev. Sammie Rush of the United Baptist Church in

Cleveland, Mississippi, reported that he sees "Masses of people existing with little or no food." Elsewhere his counterparts in the religious community find conditions quite similar: Rev. Carl Brown of the Valley Queen Baptist Church in Marks, and W. Lee Robinson, pastor of the Baptist Church in Belden, the latter reporting that "poor black and white are suffering together for one of the most basic needs, and that is food."

The Pearl River Valley Opportunity Program in Columbia has noted an increase in hungry families in the past two years. Many of them have never requested assistance before.

But whether new to hunger or long-time victims, those affected are predominantly the young and the old. The Southern Mississippi Area Agency on Aging, for example, reported that in a survey of 15 counties it found many elderly citizens not getting adequate food to eat. Nearly a quarter of the elderly ate two or fewer meals each day. The Agency estimated that it was able to reach just over a third of the hungry elderly through the elderly meals program.[5]

We found elderly citizens berated by physicians for not complying with diets they couldn't possibly afford. Laura Jane Allen, a 76-year-old hypersensitive, had lived on peas, beans, and bread for five days before we visited her. "They tell me what I should eat," she commented. "I'm supposed to have fresh vegetables and fish and stay away from that pork, salt and cheese—but I just can't buy the right food with the money I have." A Tutwiler, Mississippi, social worker reported that of every 100 hospital in-patients she sees each month, about one-third are malnourished elderly people. Most, she said, have nutrition-related diseases: hypertension, stroke, diabetes. She told us that they experience recurrent hospitalizations because they lack resources for proper food.[6] A Greenwood nurse echoed this impression, "It's a vicious cycle. Before you know it they're in the hospital because their blood sugar dropped too low or they had an insulin reaction from not being able to eat. And this goes on all the time. We have patients eating the wrong things because it's the only things they can get and they wind up in the hospital with strokes.[7]"

"Most of my clients," reported home health nurse Joyce

Stancil, "have been a maid or yard boy or worked on a plantation, mostly for white people, and a lot of them never had social security payments. The 'man' worked them for 40–50 years and never paid a dime for them. It's horrible to see what our old people have to go through."

As if by some cruel egalitarian act of nature, the hungry people who lined up outside the Delta food stamp office at 8:00 in the morning were evenly divided among young, old, and middle-aged. As the late spring sun began to bear down, doctors mingled with food stamp recipients, trying to learn about the common threads in their lives which caused them to be there. Several of the people had been seen previously by the doctors as they had fanned out among the small Delta towns to go into homes and to look into refrigerators. Home after home had little or no food; it was the last of the month and food stamps had long since been exhausted. Today, many of the people who had not eaten for several days lined up early hoping to be among the first to get their stamps so they could go to the grocery.

Over and over the doctors heard that these people had been without food for several days. Some of the babies had had no milk for three, four, five days. Two elderly women, neighbors, shared their food until it ran out "maybe three or four days ago, it's kinda hard to remember I been so dizzy lately," one explained.

So shaken was one of the doctors by the line of hungry people at the brightly colored food stamp office that he was reminded of the hunger and malnutrition in his native South Africa.[8] Another doctor observed that he was glad a crew from NBC Evening News had come along, against his initial objections. "At least," he noted, "I will be less likely to dismiss this experience as a bad dream."

Given the kind of hunger we had previously observed in the New England states, it is difficult to say that hunger is all we observed in Mississippi. We really saw people as close to the brink of survival as one is likely to find in this nation. Local Mississippi psychiatrist Kinlock Gil put it aptly perhaps:

"When you're talking about poverty around here, you're really talking poverty. We have to do a lot of things people would not call mental health because we're dealing with people's *survival*. Every month our caseload goes up. The incidence of retardation is very high due to the risk factors of poverty and hunger. Things were getting better in the 1960s and 1970s; now they are getting worse again."

Alabama Governor George Corley Wallace shifted in his wheelchair and pulled himself closer to the desk. "Yankee doctors," he said with a slight smile on his face as he glanced at the physicians gathered around him in the historic State Capitol of Montgomery. "You know, I been up North before. But why are you coming down here to see us?"

The menacingly good-natured comment of the Governor led to discussion of the situation among people in his own state. Yes, he told us, there is a hunger problem in Alabama, "especially since the federal government cut the food stamp program right while the economy was going bad." Offering our group the key to the state and making our chairman an Honorary Lieutenant Colonel in the Alabama State Militia, the Governor displayed a mixture of Southern hospitality along with official concern that he has a growing problem on his hands. If we found some way to feed his people, he asked us, please tell him how. Things were very difficult these days, he explained, with "the federal government turning its back on human suffering."

Alabama is a more industrialized state than Mississippi, with its own unique history and economy. Toward the center of the state, south to north, lie the major cities of Montgomery, Birmingham, Decatur, and Huntsville, the sources of industrial output and jobs for workers in steel and other industries. But outside these cities lie some of the most impoverished counties in the nation—Lowndes and Butler outside Montgomery, and the western counties of Choctown, Greene, Pickins, and Sumpter on the Mississippi border.

In order to actually see first-hand the problems presented in such a diversified economy—rural and urban, poor and wealthy— we divided our doctors into teams, some driving through the rural counties to meet with local doctors, health center staff, ministers, teachers, and county officials, as well as visiting the homes of scores of families to learn what they have to eat and why they are hungry. Other members went by plane directly to Montgomery and the larger cities, dividing their time in these urban areas as well as the rural ones which surround them.

Despite its industrial areas, Alabama is poor, with 20% of its population, some 720,000 people, living below the poverty level. More than a quarter of its residents are so poor that they qualify for food stamps, although only 15% actually receive them.[9]

Alabama's unemployment rate has run about third highest in the nation during the past months.[10] That fact, along with the low payments for families receiving AFDC welfare ($148 monthly for a family of four), makes it virtually impossible not to find hunger in this state. Even with food stamps, for example, a mother and three children are forced to live on a combined income, welfare and stamps, of $4,800 a year. Exacerbating this is the state sales tax of up to 6.7% on all goods, including food, which means that impoverished families pay the equilivant of two and a half weeks of groceries in food taxes annually.[11]

Available evidence indicates that poverty and hunger may be taking a toll on Alabama citizens. In 1982 Alabama's infant mortality rate increased from 12.9 per thousand live births to 13.8. The increase for black infants was even sharper—from 18 to 20.1 deaths per 1,000 live births.[12] Yet these overall data mask statistics from the more impoverished counties we visited. Hale County, for example, had an infant mortality rate of 31, almost three times the national rate, and as high as many Third World countries. More than 10% of the babies born here have low birth-weights, a major risk factor for mortality that is linked with maternal nutrition.[13]

The general environment in which poor babies and their families live in Alabama is grim, "wretched beyond acceptability," according to the associate dean of the University of Alabama School of Public health.[14] On the day we arrived the environment was particularly wretched as a series of tornadoes struck the area killing several people and bringing darkness and torrential rains across the state. With the radio in

Bessemer announcing tornado warnings and encouraging people to remain in their homes, we ate in a local soup kitchen with over 100 men, women, and children forced to brave the obvious peril by pangs of hunger. The Episcopal priest who runs the kitchen told us that attendance is even higher on good days.

Others of us sat through lunch with hungry people miles to the south in Montgomery as tornadoes struck around that city. The captain who runs the Salvation Army Soup kitchen, we learned, had taken sandwiches the previous day to outlying counties hit by the tornadoes, thinking that the people would not otherwise eat. To his astonishment he found that many had not eaten the previous day either, not because of the storms but because they had nothing in their refrigerators.

During the past three years the Salvation Army has seen a steady increase in people having to resort to soup kitchen meals. Captain Price provided his records for that time (see Figure 9). At the end of each month the Salvation Army sees more families and elderly people, who replace the more transient male population the Salvation Army once served. The fluctuation in attendance reflects the distribution of food stamps at the start of each month. Families begin to run out by the third week and are desperate by month's end, thereby increasing demand at all local soup kitchens.

Hunger in Montgomery is higher than any time in the past five years, according to the Captain. The city's soup kitchens serve some 11,000 individuals each year, out of a total population of 177,000. He estimates that at least 25% of the hungry people they serve are able to get only one meal a day.

Dorothy Banbridge, director of St. Jude's Social Services in Montgomery, concurs with the Salvation Army's report. They are seeing more families with children coming to them for assistance, especially toward the end of the month when food stamps run out. It is not unusual, she reported, to see families who have not eaten for 24 hours or more, and that, she emphasized, includes children. The nearby Catholic Social Services is seeing a similar phenomenon. That agency served nearly 1,000 people in the first three months of 1984, a population described as increasingly hungry. It sees many families with children among its clientele.

Fig. 9. *Salvation Army Soup Kitchen, Montgomery, Alabama, 1982–1984*

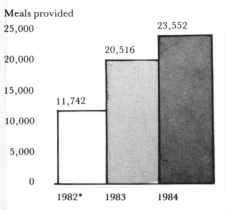

Meals provided

25,000 — 23,552
20,000 — 20,516
11,742

1982*   1983   1984

*Ten months only.
Source: Salvation Army records.

Fig. 10. *Birmingham Community Kitchens, 1980–1984*

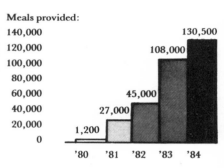

Meals provided:

140,000 — 130,500
120,000 — 108,000
100,000
80,000
60,000 — 45,000
40,000 — 27,000
20,000 — 1,200

'80   '81   '82   '83   '84

Source: Birmingham Community Kitchens records.

Fig. 11. *Trinity Episcopal Soup Kitchen, Bessemer, Alabama, 1983–1984*

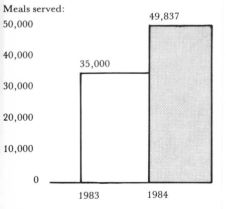

Meals served:

50,000 — 49,837
40,000 — 35,000
30,000
20,000
10,000
0

1983   1984

*member, Birmingham Community Kitchens
Source: Trinity Kitchen records.

Some of the hungry in soup kitchens have families, but they eat alone each day, represented, perhaps, by the 27-year-old father with whom we ate in Montgomery's Salvation Army facility. The father of four children, ages 9, 5, 4, and 7 months, he had left his family in Birmingham five months ago to look for work. He explained that Alabama provides no AFDC assistance to unemployed families if the father is in the home. Laid off from his steel mill job, he was forced to leave home once his unemployment checks stopped, in order to make his wife and children eligible for aid. As he wistfully eyed seconds which the soup kitchen cannot provide, he answered the questions asked of him:

Q: I have children too. I imagine you must miss yours, having to be away so far.

A: I misses them mister . . . I misses them a lot (tears trickling down his cheek as he stared into his empty plate).

Q: I suppose any father would cry. It hurts, huh?

A: I cried too many times to have many more tears.

Q: Do you ever get to talk to your children and wife?

A: No, they got no phone, but I writes letters to them so they'll know I'm thinking about them . . .

Q: Where do you sleep?

A: Wherever I can.

Q: How about last night?

A: By the river until it rained. Then I stood on a lady's porch 'til she got scared and ran me away.

Later in Birmingham we learned of the seriousness of hunger in this father's hometown. Al Rohlig, director of the Birmingham Housing Authority, announced that the city's United Way provides more than 2 million pounds of food a year to social service agencies trying to feed the hungry. One of the larger programs, the Birmingham Community Kitchens, is experiencing an onslaught of hungry citizens comparable to that reported in Montgomery (see Figure 10). Episcopal minister Rev. James Tuohy pointed out that after five years the coalition of churches and agencies in the Community Kitchens realizes that not only is hunger in Birmingham increasing, but "our efforts are all insignificant compared to the need."

In the same city the Jimmy Hale Mission served 1,200 meals

a month in 1981. By 1983 the number served each month increased to 9,700—well over 100,000 meals a year. The staff reported to us that the number was up in 1984, and it looks as if "there is no end to the increase" in sight.

Wherever we went in Alabama we found evidence of hunger as a serious problem. We found it not only in Montgomery and Birmingham, but among the hardhats who sat at the soup kitchen in Bessemer, in the rural homes outside Tuscaloosa, and among the parents of children in Lowndes County. We were told of hunger by staff at the West Alabama Health Services in Gainesville and the Wonderland Day Care Center in Greenville. And Nita Morrison, a Tuscaloosa community worker, told us that local churches are finding more of their members who are hungry.

Increasing hunger is reported even by the officials responsible for feeding the hungry. Food Stamp Supervisor Sarah Lunn knows that more of her clients are hungry. Poverty in the county she serves has increased, but the number of people getting food stamps has gone down owing to federal policy changes: "They (the federal government) made us stop our outreach effort to locate people who need food. It no longer exists. Instead we have to do more paperwork. The name of the game now is saving money, but I can tell you for a fact that they're not even doing that. With all the extra paperwork Washington requires they're making us spend more . . . and not to feed people either."

"In Alabama everything that helps people is federal dollars," observed Dr. Beverly Boyd, director of family health for the state's Department of Public Health. Joining our team for its visit to the state, Dr. Boyd pointed out that with cutbacks in federal nutrition programs and more cumbersome administrative procedures required by Washington, the poor in her state have suffered. One manifestation of that suffering is hunger.

As if to underscore her point, when this physician accompanied us to the Jones Day Care Center the director told us that the children eat voraciously on Monday mornings after having been home over the weekend. Sitting quietly nearby was a three-year-old who looked to be the size of a child of 18 months. Upon examination the little girl was quite thin and exhibited much less motor activity than most of the children. She had difficulty maintaining her balance as the doctor holding her on his lap supported her back. No, the director told us, most of the children are not this way, but most of them are hungry when they are not in her program. She told us it is this way "all around here, you can go and see for yourselves."

We took her suggestion, walking right across the street and randomly knocking on the doors of nearby residents. The first woman stated that they were unemployed and received no food stamps. One child was ill and, yes, they did have problems getting enough to eat. A visit to her pantry revealed cupboards and a refrigerator largely bare. Another mother acknowledged that the doctor at the clinic she attends recently told her that her four-year-old son and her daughter, age one, are both anemic. She had milk in the refrigerator, only milk. No food. But, she professed: "We're doing okay, really, just got no food."

The empty refrigerators we observed in this neighborhood could have been in any city. We saw them over and over wherever we went. In Montgomery, the refrigerator of Ms. Pat Jones wasn't exactly bare, but it was close. Doctors visiting her and her three-year-old son found it to contain three eggs, one slice of cheese, and a container of water. The boy had had no milk to drink for three weeks. He had finished the last of the cereal that morning, having eaten it with water as he did each day previously.

In Birmingham, Betty Childs, the mother of three youngsters, summarized what a group of Headstart parents there had been telling us. Each had described a personal struggle for food, some making an almost full-time job of hunting for sales, shopping with children in tow, no car, or walking from the soup kitchen back home each day. Most of the parents reported that they sometimes fail to feed their children and go hungry toward the end of the month. Said Ms. Childs: "A lot of people here are hungry. When you see people on T.V. saying there are no problems in this land of plenty, you get angry because they are lying."

Seventy-three-year-old Phoebe Ellington was but one of the scores of elderly residents of Alabama whom we visited in their homes. Living alone in the Windy Hill section of a housing project in Gainesville, this woman receives $52 monthly in food stamps to supplement her $177 check from her husband's pension. She had eaten corn bread and ketchup for three days prior to our arrival, a practice she follows toward the end of each month as she awaits her next check. The empty refrigerator starkly underscored the monthly drama which takes place in her home.

In Montgomery, 83-year-old Rosa Smith, blind in one eye, sat on her soiled sofa. She was hungry; her food stamps had been cut off. Why were they cut off, one of the doctors asked. "I don't know," she replied, "they never told me, they just cut me off."

Governor Wallace had been right: there are many hungry people in Alabama. From the teachers, to the doctors, to the Lee County bus driver who told us some children on her bus each morning cry with nausea because they have had nothing to eat, the evidence in Alabama is one of children suffering from hunger. From those who serve the elderly, like Doris Ingram of the Montgomery Council on Aging, who described hunger and poverty as a "sleeping giant" that awaits the elderly, the evidence is clear that many old people are hungry in this state.

From Beth Williams, supervisor of the state's Department of Pensions and Security, who reported increases in premature births in the state, associated with inadequate diet, to her boss, Commissioner Leon Frazier, who said that cutbacks in federal programs have led to a resurfacing of hunger and malnutrition, it is clear there is a problem in this state. From Virginia Durr, the patrician white woman who years ago bailed Rosa Parks out of jail for not sitting at the back of the bus, to Larry Gardella, a young attorney working among the poor of Alabama, we learned that hunger is serious again in the state.

As poverty increased in Alabama, the number of people receiving food stamps actually declined. Private agencies moved in to help those who were being neglected. The bigger ones such as the Salvation Army increased their statewide volume significantly, providing food and other emergency assistance to 1,354,216 families in 1983, in contrast to 789,144 in 1981.

But the smaller ones which serve fewer people, we learned, themselves increased their volume proportionately, if not more.

One of our doctors described the evidence of hunger observed in Alabama and Mississippi during our week-long investigation as tragic. Tragic is a strong word, but one commonly used to describe hunger in this part of the country. Nita Morrison, outreach worker for a community service agency in Tuscaloosa-Bibbs counties, used the same word as she described the "tragedy I see across my desk every day." She captured the problem with the example of a young man who had recently stopped by her office on the way home from his hospital dialysis treatment:

> I don't have one bite in my refrigerator for my three children when I go home tonight. My wife has been with me in the hospital and the children stayed with an older aunt that's on a very close income. They haven't eaten the way they should with her.
>
> I am dying and I know it. While I am dying it's a heartache to see my children going hungry and I can't do anything about it.

The young man, we were told, had come to our public hearing at the county court to talk to our team of doctors about his situation. But sitting and listening to the tragic stories of others who are hungry, he left the meeting early without speaking. He found it unbearable.

Hunger in the Mid-Atlantic Region—Tennessee and North Carolina

North Carolina physician Arden Miller is chairman of the Department of Maternal and Child Health at the University of North Carolina School of Public health in Chapel Hill. Joining medical colleagues from other states for a field investigation into hunger in his own, Dr. Miller dispassionately reported on what he learned in the Appalachian county of Buncombe:

> Voluntary agencies are attempting to cope with hunger problems in Buncombe County. December, 1983, and January and February, 1984, were the busiest months they had ever experienced. They had more clients than ever before . . . greatly increased demand for meals, most

of them for entire families. . . . Representatives from the Seventh Day Adventists reported that in spite of the fact the recession seems to be easing, the hunger problems are getting worse, especially among families with small children and among the elderly who live alone. The Buncombe County Health Department since 1981 has had a steady increase in enrollment in the primary care clinics. . . . The physician in charge reports but cannot document that he is seeing more seriously ill people. Dr. Murray reports that he has seen an increase of infants with failure-to-thrive. Also he believes he has begun to identify a syndrome he calls failure-to-thrive among the elderly.

Green and lush Buncombe County lies nestled in the Smoky Mountains of Appalachia. Nearly midway between Memphis, Tennessee, to the west and the Atlantic coast towns of North Carolina to the east, the area provides a stark reminder of the contrasting terrain along this thousand-mile stretch of the United States. It also aptly stands as a reminder of the hunger seen throughout this region of the nation, itself standing in hidden contrast to the pockets of wealth which dot the states.

For a period of one week, 15 doctors, frequently dividing into five separate teams, went throughout this region covering every major city, many rural counties, and mountain areas, looking into hunger and malnutrition. Some, like Dr. Miller, were residents of one of the two states covered; others were from as far away as Louisiana, Michigan, and Massachusetts. But like Dr. Miller, each of us found hunger throughout this region. And each of us found the problems in Buncombe County to be little different from other areas visited—hunger, malnutrition, illness.

Our field investigation began in Nashville where Mayor Robert Fulton asked us to "please tell Mr. Meese and the White House that there is hunger in America." Upon direct inspection, we did find hunger in Tennessee: the mountain family with eight children that had three biscuits, butter, and neck bones in their refrigerator, the wife and quadraplegic husband on a special diet who recently cut down from two meals a day to one, and the woman who responded with tears when a local organization brought her food: "I'm glad you came; my husband was going to find a gun to rob a store."

While robbing a store may be an extreme solution, her words

reflect a frustration faced by the numerous people who Virginia Carter told us collect cans to feed their families. It's the frustration of the mother with an infant who told us that "a mother hurts when she can't feed her baby." It's the frustration of 93-year-old Laura McAfee, who lives on white beans and potatoes in Nashville.

Unfortunately, these people are not mere anecdotes. They are real, and they are representative of many others. Nutritionist Denise Griffith at Nashville General Hospital reported that a survey of its patients found 34% run out of food every month. Day care teachers reported that they see little food in the homes of children they visit, and they now provide extra food on Friday, hoping the children can cope over the weekend. Headstart teachers report that children are hungry on Monday mornings, and slowly "pick up their weight after being away during the summer." A state representative told us that some children say they do not want Christmas to arrive because they will not get their school meals. But, he said, it is not only children: "At the foot of Lookout Mountain recently I saw a young man with a sign that read 'I'm out of work. I'm hungry.' His family was with him and he had his tools ready to work wherever he could."[15]

The trends reported by mayors, welfare directors, teachers, and doctors in Tennessee are supported by the data from soup kitchens and food pantries trying to feed the hungry in the three regions of the state.

The Second Harvest Emergency Food Box Program in Nashville has seen a steady increase in hungry families during the past several years. In 1981 the program provided 7,333 boxes (a three-day supply of food) to families in the area. Two years later demand had gone up nearly 200% (see Figure 12). Anne Ruggiero, director of Nashville Metropolitan Social Services, provided data on the hungry who obtain food from her program, which serves the elderly (see Figure 13). Older people in her community, she pointed out, have a choice between food, medicine, and heat. Most poor seniors choose not to eat in order to obtain the other things they need. The growth of more than 100% in meals served to elderly recipients, she added, does not reflect better services by her agency; it represents in-

Fig. 12. *Nashville Emergency Food Boxes, 1981–1984*

No. boxes provided
(thousands)

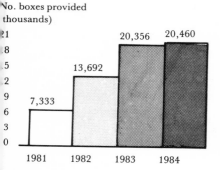

7,333   13,692   20,356   20,460

1981   1982   1983   1984

Source: Second Harvest, January, 1985.

Fig. 13. *Nashville Metropolitan Social Services, Meals Served to the Elderly, 1982–1984*

Number meals
(thousands)

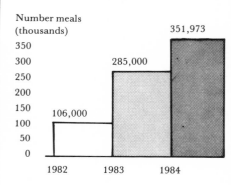

351,973

285,000

106,000

1982   1983   1984

Source: Social Services records.

Fig. 14. *Memphis Food Bank, 1983–1984*

Food distributed
(pounds)

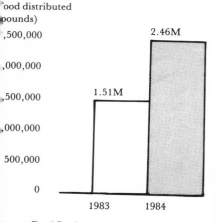

2.46M

1.51M

1983   1984

Source: Food Bank records.

Fig. 15. *Southern Appalachian Food Bank, Knoxville, Tennessee, 1983–1984*

Pounds of food

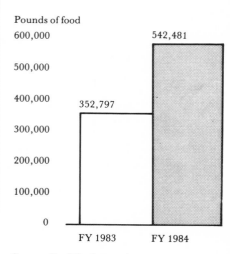

542,481

352,797

FY 1983   FY 1984

Source: Food Bank records.

creasing need. Hunger is a problem which is getting worse, she told us.

The increase is reflected in other programs, both smaller and larger than the elderly feeding program. MANNA provides food boxes for families, and noted a rise in demand from 1983, when they assisted 2,452 people, to 1984, when the number increased to 2,833. On a larger scale, the Nashville Food Bank has distributed a total of more than 1.7 million pounds of food during the past year to some 75 agencies trying to respond to the increasing number of families and individuals who come to ask for food.

In western Tennessee emergency food programs are seeking, unsuccessfully they report, to keep up with the increasing hunger they observe. The Rossville Health Clinic in Haywood County sees symptoms of the hunger problem. More than 50% of the Clinic's patients are anemic. "Iron deficiency anemia is the rule, not the exception," reported the medical director.[16] In nearby Jackson the local food bank was started by the Salvation Army and Hope Church to serve the increasing number of people unable to obtain the food required for themselves and their children. Serving more than 25 food pantries in the area, the staff estimates that at least 15% of the population in the area lacks sufficient food.[17]

The Memphis Food Bank, established to address the same problem in that large city, has seen a constant increase in hunger. Director Virginia Dunaway sees a continuing "erosion of the status of those in need" in her area, leading to a greater and greater effort by the food bank to respond to the need. In March, 1983, the bank distributed 90,000 pounds of food to agencies serving the hungry, a number which went up to 180,000 for the same month in 1984. This increase is mirrored in the annual food distribution by the bank over the past two years (see Figure 14).

While the food distribution data for Memphis reflect one part of the picture of hunger in that area, its fuller dimensions are manifested in malnutrition and ill-health. Major Arrowood of the Memphis Salvation Army described for us the relationship between hunger and illness in his community, reflected by the greater numbers of people requiring medical attention.[18] Many of the people, including families, who eat some of the more than 200,000 meals provided by the Salvation Army each year suffer illnesses related to their inadequate diet. Between 8% and 18% of preschoolers surveyed by local physicians, for example, were deficient in vitamins A, B_1, B_2, C, serum iron, transferrin saturation, and hemoglobin, a situation described by Paul Zee, Chief of Nutrition and Metabolism at St. Jude's Hospital, as "epidemic levels of marginal undernutrition."[19]

The South Memphis Clinic staff told us that they are seeing fewer patients who qualify for health insurance but more who require medical attention. Many, they reported, have serious nutrition-related illnesses.

At the other end of the state the mountainous scenery provides a very different backdrop from Memphis and Nashville, but the picture of hunger and malnutrition is much the same. Some of the evidence is medical: at the Clear Fork Clinic in the rural area north of Knoxville, we learned that 22% of children seen are below the tenth percentile in height—evidence of chronic malnutrition. White Oak Mountain Care Center director Tilda Kemplin reported seeing "children not up to snuff; after they're here a few weeks and get enough food into them, they perk up a lot." She worries, however, about the children in the mountains whom she knows are there but are not getting the help which they and their families need.

In the City of Knoxville, largest in eastern Tennessee, as well as in Knox, Claiborn, Hancock, and Jefferson counties, agencies involved with health care and food distribution for the poor report significant—and increasing—problems. The increased need for food has been particularly sharp.

The Wesley House in Knoxville has seen a nearly 100% increase in need between 1981 and 1983, and a nearby agency reported a 113% increase from January, 1983, to January, 1984.[20] Rev. Robert Walker, a local Presbyterian minister, noted that the need continues to increase: in the first three months of 1984, Emergency Food Helpers served 163% more people than the same period in 1981. During that latter time period, some 23,317 people in this area had to rely on the food provided through local donation.

In Murfreesboro, the Rutherford County Food Bank (known as St. Rose's) has experienced a similar increase. Director Jo McCall noted that when they began, they served 455 families. They now feed ten times that number of families (see Table 2).

The Knoxville-based Southern Appalachian Food Bank shows increased demand similar to that of its sister agency in Murfreesboro. Sponsored by the organization SHARE, the bank helped to feed 59,000 people in 1983, a number which increased to nearly 152,000 in 1984. To the surprise of workers, the number of pounds of food distributed has risen each year since the bank opened in 1982, recording a 54% increase in pounds of food distributed in 1984 over the previous year (see Figure 15).

In Knoxville, the FISH agency served 2,622 families in 1982, and 4,173 in 1983. During 1984 FISH saw a continuing rise in requests for help, 487 during the month of February, and 667 in March, 1984. During this latter month the program fed 1,104 adults, and 1,019 children—evidence one worker noted "that shows we are almost starving our children in this rich nation."

The Emergency Food Helpers program operates in that same city, an operation which encompasses the FISH program. The director provided us with data indicating the situation faced by member agencies (see Table 3).

Without question hunger is a serious problem in Tennessee, and available evidence indicates that it is one which is getting worse. Emergency food providers—food banks, soup kitchens, and food pantries—report that the need for food among hun-

Table 2. *Number of Families Fed by Rutherford County Food Bank, Murfreesboro, Tennessee, 1982–1983*

Year	Families fed	Adults fed	Children fed
1982	5,734	9,133	6,049
1983	3,290	5,436	5,700

SOURCE: Food Bank records.

Table 3. *Number of Families Fed by Emergency Food Helpers, Knoxville, Tennessee, 1981–1984*

Agency	Families fed				Percent increase '81–'84
	Q₁ '81	Q₁ '82	Q₁ '83	Q₁ '84	
Baptist Goodwill	175	200	312	277	58%
FISH	573	675	773	1,793	213%
Ladies of Charity	476	534	699	1,014	113%
Salvation Army	125	138	358	468	274%
TOTAL	1,349	1,547	2,142	3,552	163%

SOURCE: Food Helpers records.

gry families is increasing. Clinics and hospitals serving the poor report patients unable to obtain the food they need. Moreover they are seeing increased ill-health, much of which they attribute to that lack of food. And demographically, state income trends show that the situation is becoming more difficult, as poverty rose from some 16.5% of Tennessee residents in 1980 to an estimated 20% of all residents today.[21]

These facts support the inescapable conclusion that hunger is severe in this region of the nation. And they lend credence to the concern expressed by the director of a Tennessee day care center: "We previously had to worry about our children on weekends. Now I have to worry if they'll get any food at night."[22]

The state border between Tennessee and North Carolina runs along the Great Smoky Mountains. Just as the scenic beauty of the land does not stop at the border dividing one state from the other, neither does the hunger which afflicts the residents.

North Carolina is a state known for its universities and high technology industry, epitomized by the well-known "Research Triangle," encompassing Raleigh, Durham, and Chapel Hill. Internationally recognized, these centers of productivity and learning mask another North Carolina, that of carpenters and mechanics who lived and worked all their lives in this state and now find themselves poor and hungry for the first time, and that of the more "traditional poor," frequently people who have lived on the land for decades eking out a living now imperiled by changes in the economy and in government policies.

Eighteen percent of the population in the state lives in poverty, somewhat over the national average of 15.3%. This proportion includes 415,000 children. Poverty continues to worsen, in some areas more so than others.[23] The Director of Social Services for Durham County, for example, announced that from 1981 to 1983 poverty increased 42%.[24]

But poverty is not the only thing increasing in North Carolina. In 1983, the state experienced the first increase in its infant mortality rate in several years.[25] And other health outcomes are not encouraging. In Madison County 20% of the babies in the WIC supplemental feeding program are anemic;[26] in Durham over a third of pregnant women and 60% of WIC children are anemic.[27] And evidence suggests that nutrition-related problems are not limited to the young. In Durham, for example, home health nurse Alice Walker has detected nutritional deficiencies in three-quarters of her 400 elderly patients.

But neither are adverse health outcomes the only thing increasing in this state. During the past year or more, governmental and private agencies which serve the impoverished have detected a serious increase in the number of hungry people, particularly families, in North Carolina. Hunger in the state, they report, is widespread.

We saw hunger in the homes we inspected across the state. We saw it in the house of a 17-year-old boy whose father was hospitalized and who had stayed home from school to try to find some food for his younger sister to eat. We saw hunger in the face of Regina, a listless child we examined in a day care center. We saw hunger in Hollister in the home of a young mother of four whose husband had lost his job. Her infant lay on the bed holding an empty bottle, ignoring the flies swarming around his face. When we asked to look inside her refrigerator, we found the remains of an omelette, some government commodity cheese, and nothing else. There was no milk and there had been no milk in the house for eight days.

We saw hunger in Roanoke Rapids, in the home of an elderly woman whose blind son and two others lived in a corrugated metal shack. The residents had no indoor toilet and no water. They had only a little food. The old lady was in mourning because another son had recently died, a man, our local guide explained, who used to beg for food on the corner at a nearby intersection. And we saw hunger in Robeson County, where Doctors Kenneth Locklear and Herman Chavis reported that many residents don't get enough to eat and that the prevalence of anemia among children in their area is about 25%.

Throughout the state, in urban areas which include the Research Triangle as well as in the rural counties to the south and the Alantic-coast counties to the east, we found hungry people, families with young children as well as the elderly living alone. To visit the homes is to understand the private agony and suffering these people face. To talk with doctors and nurses who treat them is to understand the interaction between their hunger and the illnesses which beset them. Yet, to talk to the ministers and social service workers trying to feed them provides yet another dimension, representing the cumulative impact of hunger—what one person referred to as "hunger by sheer volume."

Volume is the business of the Raleigh Food Bank, large volumes of food distributed to agencies which feed the hungry. In 1982, the food bank provided over half a million pounds of food, an amount that went up the next year by a third, and again in 1984 to a level double that of 1982 (see Figure 16).

Not surprisingly, the agencies supplied by the food bank are serving more hungry residents. The Raleigh Urban Ministry was started three years ago by more than 30 churches in the area which were experiencing increased demand for food. The program serves many families with young children, most of whom receive food stamps which run out routinely before the end of the month. Nearly half the people aided each month are new, never having come previously to request food assistance. Sister Helen, the nun who supervises the program, reported that the number of families in need keeps increasing.

The Catholic Parish Outreach, another program in the same

Fig. 16. *Raleigh Food Bank, 1982–1984*

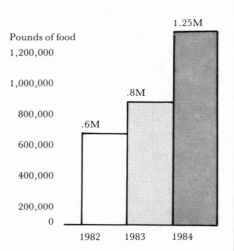

Source: Food Bank records.

Fig. 17. *Cape Fear Community Food Bank, Fayetteville, North Carolina, 1983–1984*

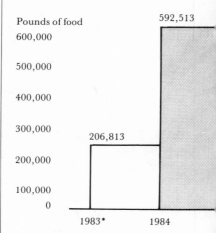

*Pro-rated based on three quarters.
Source: Food Bank records.

city, serves more than 1,000 people a month. Having begun the program, the agency volunteers were surprised to note that the number of people requesting assistance increased rather than diminished. Because the demand increased so rapidly, Catholic Parish Outreach had to cut back on its food assistance in order to avoid depleting its own financial resources altogether. "Sometimes," noted supervisor Frank Van den Eyden, "you wish the government would do its job."

In nearby Durham the First Presbyterian Church now has more than 600 families a month asking for food. They are capable of helping only half that number, having to turn away the rest. Associate minister Nancy Rosenbaugh described the problem like this: "We are not able to do the task we are called upon to do. We have been overwhelmed by the increase in need in the past three years." Other church leaders testified to a similar rise in the number of hungry people they are called upon to serve.

Local government augments the voluntary church effort to feed the hungry in Durham. Dan Hudgins, welfare director for Durham County, is seeing local resources stretching beyond capacity. The number of families given emergency food in 1982 was 611; the following year the number increased by 100%, to 1240. While the number of requests for emergency food assistance in 1984 are not yet reported, they have increased once again.

Elsewhere in the central and eastern parts of North Carolina, agencies report that hunger is increasing. At the Union Mission in Roanoke Rapids, Rev. Jones had to increase the number of people he feeds each day from 60 to 80. This is in addition to the families for whom he prepares food boxes (bags of groceries) daily. Need, he says, is increasing, especially among the elderly and families with young children. He commented: "Things have gotten much worse in the past several years. . . . It's even harder now to get commodity food for the hungry. The government's tightened everything down."

In Halifax County food providers report an increasing number of calls for food; the director of an elderly center estimates that half the people she serves in her program obtain their only meal of the day there. Hunger in Halifax County is apparent not only to emergency food providers, but to doctors in the area who observe it from their own perspective. Dr. James Dykes, a family practitioner who traveled with our members as we investigated the problem in North Carolina, went into homes in the county he serves. Along the highway stand a number of shacks, dwellings for families cramped several to a room. Dr. Dykes was startled to see patients of his: "I ran into a family whose child I had admitted twice to the hospital, once for failure-to-thrive, and once for pneumonia. It seemed their living conditions and extent of their poverty helped explain what had previously been only clinical diagnoses."

At the westernmost end of the state, Asheville agencies show a clear upward trend in the number of people requiring food assistance. Virginia Eldreth's job is to feed the hungry; she's the food stamp administrator for the county. But instead of serving more people as poverty increased over the past three years, the number she assists through the program has actually declined. She attributes the decline to policies enacted by the federal government which make it less likely that the hungry will qualify for food stamps, a problem reported by her food stamp administrator colleagues elsewhere in the country. But Ms. Eldreth, like them, knows that more people are going hungry. She sees some of them in her office and learns about them from her workers and other professionals.

Rev. Scott Rogers is one person who tells her about them. Director of the Christian Ministry in the city, an agency which serves all Buncombe County, the minister noted a 68% increase in food requests in one year. The month we arrived he had distributed government commodity cheese in the community under a plan which strictly controls eligibility for recipients. To his astonishment, 6,000 people stood in line, each seeking a block of cheese.

During 1984, the Christian Ministry served a total of 16,000 people in Buncombe County who were in need of food. That is 16,000 out of a total low-income population of 19,000. Altogether, 84 tons of food were distributed last year by the Ministry.

Lest he give us the impression that food providers in the area are preventing hunger by their admirable efforts, Rev. Rogers told us that they themselves consider their efforts "stop-gap at best." Visits to homes in the area demonstrated why this is so. In Black Mountain we visited a husband and wife and their two pre-school children. Only recently did the man agree to apply for food stamps, the $253 monthly allotment representing the total income for this family of four. He had heard that it was not "manly" to rely on assistance, so resisted doing so until his children began to suffer. For nearly three months the family had very little to eat, at most one meal a day even while the woman carried their second child toward the end of her pregnancy. The child was born prematurely, weighing only 49 ounces. During his first year he "stopped growing for a while and that was when we applied for food stamps," reported the mother. The child gained weight after that, but at the age of

Fig. 18. *Northwest North Carolina Food Bank, Winston-Salem, 1983–1984*

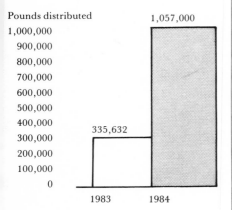

Source: Food Bank records.

Fig. 19. *Albemarle Food Bank, Elizabeth City, North Carolina, 1983–1984*

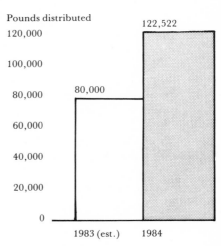

Source: Food Bank records.

Fig. 20. *Metroliner Food Bank, Charlotte, North Carolina, 1983–1984*

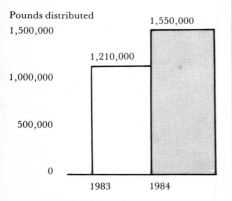

Source: Food Bank records.

three does not talk in sentences. His sister, one year older, has rotten teeth.

To visit this family and the several dozen others who allowed us into their homes as we tried to understand their situations, provides a descriptive backdrop against which Rev. Rogers' statistics may be evaluated. But the families in this part of North Carolina are not a great deal different from those we had visited elsewhere in our travels across that state:

• The 68-year-old woman with crippling arthritis and hypertension who lives on a $250 monthly pension. She pays $85 a month for heat, and takes medicine which costs one dollar a capsule. On the day we visited her she had been out on the truck to pick blueberries, but had to return because her arthritic hands pained her too much. When asked what she had eaten, she reported that she had had some grits the previous day.

• The young family of two adults and three children, ages 7, 1½, and 3 months, who live in a mobile home with no electricity. The father works full-time at a low-paying job and most of the income is taken up by the rent and medicines. The baby is constantly out of formula, and the other children seldom get fruit or vegetables.

• The old woman who finally was convinced to apply for food stamps because she was hungry most of the time. While filling out the application her hands began to tremble uncontrollably, prompting the worker to ask if anything was wrong. The old woman had noted the signs on the office wall saying food stamp fraud would result in prosecution, and she was afraid she would make an error and be sent to jail.

From the west to the east—across North Carolina—there is hunger. It is obvious to those who care to look. It is apparent to the ministers and priests and nuns who serve the poor. It is obvious to doctors and nurses and teachers who administer unto them. It is in the records of clinics and hospitals and soup kitchens and food pantries. It is in the faces of the hungry themselves.

Ironically, with its wealth and industrial base, North Carolina is a state that need not have hunger. But it does. Perhaps this fact is what the director of an elderly Meals-on-Wheels program had in mind when he told us that when people are hungry "it is justice, not charity, that is needed."[28]

Hunger in the Southwest—New Mexico and Texas

As the airplane descended in preparation for landing at the Albuquerque International Airport, the doctors peered out of the small windows to see the earth tones of a city enveloped by vast spaces, interspersed with red cliffs rising directly from the dry soil. The approach was to prove an omen for the unique face of hunger in yet another region of the nation, proving that the varied beauty of this vast land frequently veils more unpleasant man-made problems.

The weather was hot and dry as the doctors embarked by car on the three-hour journey to Crownpoint, a small town on the Navajo Reservation near the border of Arizona. Leaving their colleagues to spend their time in Albuquerque, the travelers were off to meet with a home health aide, their guide on the expansive reservation, prior to an afternoon meeting with Peterson Zah, chairman of the Navajo Nation.

Miles and miles of land stretched on either side, an impressive vastness broken by hills and rises, mesas and buttes, but with no inhabitants for the most part. Here water determines the use of the land, most of it used for grazing or nothing at all. The physicians were briefed on the area by a local doctor joining them for the field visit. Conversation ranged from Navajo culture to vitamin deficiencies to the colors of the land, extraordinary hues—reds, tans, browns, interspersed by the dark green mesquite and piñon trees and, in contrast, the lighter colors of the wildflowers.

The 93-year-old woman squatted on the dirt floor of her hogan, an octagonal structure with a stove pipe running up the middle through the mud roof. Many times the nutritionist who brought us had spent the hour and a half at breakneck speed in her carryall van over the back roads of the reservation, making visits to the old woman and her family.

A diabetic with two other chronic diseases, the woman had moved out of the hogan of her epileptic son. In Navajo culture someone with seizures is a witch. The old woman and her relatives ate squash, corn, and potatoes. There was no refrigeration and no milk, no fresh fruits and no other vegetables.

Afterwards the doctors found the experience hard to describe: the visual richness of the hogan set among hills, the heat of the day, the fire going to make it even hotter, the house with the epileptic boy nearby, the old woman, her daughter, and the nutritionist speaking Navajo, a language of lilting rhythm, dark skins, dark beautiful eyes, friendliness, and yet a world beyond comprehension.

More than a hundred miles away Dr. Fitzhugh Mullen, director of health services for the New Mexico Department of Health and the Environment, was briefing the doctors who had remained in Albuquerque. "Based on death records alone," he began, "six residents of this state died last year of malnutrition . . . that's just what we know about and, as you know, it was probably far more than that." Despite his dispassionate presentation, Mullen's face betrayed a bit of anger. This physician who once headed the National Health Service Corps, a federal program placing doctors in high-risk, under-served areas, knew that the federal government had dismantled health data systems in the past two years. It was now even harder to pinpoint the causes of illnesses and deaths.

Mullen did know about his own state. Last year, owing to federal budget restrictions, he had been able to reach only 28% of the infants and children eligible for the WIC supplemental feeding program. Of those served, 24% of the infants were underweight, as were 23% of the children. Some 36% of the children were below the fifth percentile for growth, a sign of chronic malnutrition.

Ona Porter, a staff member of the Albuquerque Indian Health Board, knew things unknown even to Dr. Mullen. Her job is to visit the rural communities on the Navajo Reservation, and to take steps to improve the health of its residents. She told what she saw and what she, along with medical officer Dr. Helen Oden, knows to be the situation for many of these American citizens: "Every year a few old people starve to death in these Indian communities. Most of the elderly are malnourished. At least one-third of the children have iron deficiencies. Nearly all the pregnant woman are anemic and suffer vitamin deficiencies."

Even as Ona Porter's words were spoken, the other team of doctors on the reservation had driven on to Window Rock, Arizona, where they saw the conditions about which she was speaking. One of the members, veteran physician Aaron Shirley, who had traveled with the Senators who looked into hunger in his native Mississippi in 1967 and had accompanied doctors across the nation again in 1977, recalled what they learned this particular day. Seventeen people had died of starvation (marasmus) in the past year, some of them children, according to the local nutritionist. Yet the deaths by starvation seemed not to strike Dr. Shirley so deeply as the total unnecessity of it all:

"Many schools on the reservation are unable to provide much-needed school lunch and breakfast because they cannot afford the equipment required by the U.S. Agriculture Department. It is tragic; the benefits of the programs are being denied these children because of an insensitive bureaucracy. Somewhere stacked away on military installations is enough surplus kitchen equipment to bring every one of those schools up to standard for the school meals programs."

Tribal officials confirmed the problems they face with the federal nutrition programs. Roger Wilson, aide to Navajo Chairman Peterson Zah, described the impact of cutbacks in federal programs, already underfunded, which make it even less possible to reach the hungry and starving people on the reservation. The WIC program for pregnant women and babies serves only a handful of those in need. Nutrition education has been cut significantly, and restrictive regulations increased, making the work of Ona Porter and her colleagues all the more difficult. School lunch cannot be served in many schools on the reservation because of bureaucratic requirements such as those noted by Dr. Shirley. Even elderly meals were denied at congregate sites because the facilities do not pass sanitary inspection.

"Hunger," the Albuquerque Health Center nutritionist told us the next day, "is *the* primary problem among our infants and children."

"It's not just children," retorted the nurse practitioner. "Our elderly patients suffer a lot, too; many of them are malnourished." "That's true," agreed the nutritionist, adding: "And we get babies sent to us right from the hospital. Parents have no food at home. They just send the entire family right here to us!"

The medical director at the clinic, Dr. Leman, confirmed what his staff was reporting. His facility simply cannot keep up with the increasing number of Albuquerque residents coming for help, mostly food these days. Eighty percent of his patients live in poverty, many of them also being undocumented aliens. Their financial status, American citizen and alien alike, deteriorates along with their health. Calls come into the clinic saying, "I can't feed my baby, can I get some food?"

Public health nurse Teresa Lazaria visits homes of the patients. She reports a lot of children hospitalized within a year of birth because no food is in the home. Sometimes families will receive assistance from a government program for the one or two children in the family who are born in the United States. Obviously, she pointed out, they share it with the other children. But it doesn't last.

As she spoke she found it easy to provide examples from the families which she sees daily:

• The young Mexican-American mother who is "basically starving" while her baby receives some help from the WIC program.
• The 57-year-old woman who is down to 89 pounds and oftentimes eats nothing during a 24-hour period.

So quickly did these families and individuals come to the nurse's mind that one became convinced they are not merely "anecdotes," but American citizens whose suffering reveals something deeply wrong.

Across town at the Young Children's Health Center, Dr. Carol Geil gathered her clinical staff to inform us about what they face. Hunger is definitely on the rise. Every day clinic nutritionists see more people in need of food. She underscored the absurdity of the phenomenon: health clinics in America having to feed people much like scenes in some Third World nation. There is more hunger at the end of the month, when food stamps or other benefits run short. Sometimes mothers haven't enough money to purchase badly needed jello for babies suffering from diarrhea. Health is impaired as a result of poor nutrition. Dr. Geil is seeing more pregnant women who are anemic.

Dr. Pressman, the Albuquerque health officer who attended the clinic session, reported that hematocrits (blood counts) are low in low-income clinics in the area she supervises. Is this because of hunger, we inquired?

From the available evidence, it is. Dr. Geil, in preparation for our site visit, pulled a random number of patient records from her files and conducted a survey of 14 families. When asked if their children ever went hungry because of lack of food, four said yes. Another said they often ran out of milk, and yet another said that toward the end of the month meals were incomplete. When asked whether the parents themselves ever went hungry so the children could eat, 11 of the 14 said yes.

School nurse Maureen Nash, at the Harrison Middle School in the city, conducted a similar survey of families to better understand what she perceived to be a growing problem. Five of ten families reported that they sometimes go without food so their children can eat. This 1984 survey paralleled what we were told by other school officials in Albuquerque. The nurse at the Ernie Pyle Middle School surveyed 50 families to ask about the importance of the school lunch program. Numerous parents reported that on weekends their children ate only one meal a day. Some parents cried as they explained that they lacked resources to feed the children on weekends and in the summer.

Recently things have become even more difficult for families living on the edge. Elaine Adkins, director of school food services for the Albuquerque school system, reported that many children had to drop out of the school lunch program when the federal government changed eligibility. Participation for the entire school system, she revealed, dropped from 42,149 students in 1980 to 38,343 in 1983. It decreased again for the 1984–85 school year, even though overall school enrollment had not changed much. Particularly distressing to Adkins is the fact that some 2,122 children were dropped from the free meals category, one which Washington politicians promised not to harm when they cut the school nutrition budget.[29]

Elementary school principal Ms. Coffey reported that children clean their plates thoroughly at lunch. Some remain hungry, a fairly common problem reflected by the example given by another principal: "Today two little boys came to see me after lunch to say they were still hungry. It's against federal regulations to give a child more than one meal. But I looked down at their 22-inch waists and told them to get in line again." Another school staff member, Vida Aceveda, told us that many Albuquerque teachers have begun preparing sacks of food on Fridays for some of the children because they know the parents have little to give them at home. Their efforts seem to help some, as they note fewer belly aches on Monday mornings when the children return.

The Albuquerque teachers and clinic staff are not the only ones trying to feed the hungry in the Southwest. The area is not without its own network of emergency food providers. But like their counterparts elsewhere in the nation, the programs have a problem: the number of hungry people keeps increasing.

Buddy Gallegos is director of the Roadrunner Food Bank, which supplies many of the New Mexico churches and social service agencies with food. In 1983, the food bank served 6,456 families, a number which rose the next year to 15,316. The number of individuals served went from 23,973 in 1983 to 48,100 in 1984. Pounds of food distributed went up substantially also (see Figure 21).

Albuquerque has ten emergency feeding programs, most of which are supplied by the food bank. Half the programs started within the past two years to respond to increasing need, serving well over a thousand meals every day.

We arrived at the Good Shepherd Refuge at 6:30 a.m. as the line of approximately 150 people began to enter for breakfast. A religious organization started some years ago, the refuge has increased by 400% the number of people it served in the past two years (see Figure 22). It now provides more than 400 meals

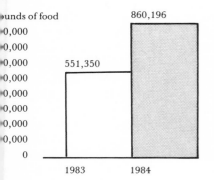

g. 21. *Roadrunner Food Bank, lbuquerque, New Mexico, 1983–984*

unds of food
0,000
0,000
0,000   551,350
0,000
0,000
0,000
0,000
0,000
0
     1983   1984

urce: Food Bank records.

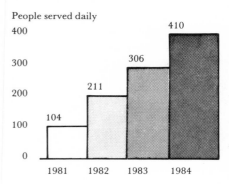

Fig. 22. *Good Shepherd Refuge, Albuquerque, New Mexico, 1981–1984*

People served daily
400   410
300   306
200   211
100   104
0
   1981   1982   1983   1984

Source: Refuge records.

a day, 10% of its clientele being families. This latter figure is up from only one percent five years ago.

Thirty-year-old Robert sat quietly eating his breakfast, somewhat bemused by the group of doctors who had entered to eat with the people who had been standing in line. An unemployed school teacher from Slat Lake City, Robert came to Albuquerque looking for work, possibly substitute teaching. He wasn't certain, however, about jobs in the teaching field. Trying to provide some encouragement, one doctor asked if he had heard that the President wants the first civilian in space to be a teacher. Robert looked up from his bowl of oatmeal solemnly: "I don't want to go to the moon. I just want to go to work."

At the First Baptist Church, Mike McEuen started a meals program for the hungry. The first day he expected about 50 people. More than 300 were on his doorstep when he opened.

"Our valley is a hungry valley," a worker at Casa Armijo told us on our last site visit in the area. This four-year-old agency, located in Albuquerque's impoverished South Valley, sees many clients who are hungry, frequently because they have been cut off the food stamp program. "I don't understand," the worker continued, "if we know there's so much poverty and hunger, why do we make it so difficult for them?"

According to local food stamp administrator Virginia Baca, present at the meeting, that is exactly what has happened. As poverty and hunger have increased, more people have been cut from the food stamp program. Ms. Baca sought to answer a question none of us raised, but which she had obviously heard before: "The problem is not that people getting food stamps don't know how to handle their money; they've been doing it since they were married. The problem is that now they don't have enough. It just doesn't last anymore."

State Secretary of Human Services Juan Vigil summarizd much of what we had been told about the impact of federal program cuts on hunger. Poverty has increased dramatically in New Mexico in the past several years. It is over 17% state-wide, and 33%, he reported, in the Third Congressional District. Yet as poverty went up, the federal government made it harder to serve the poor. Consequently food stamps were actually cut, as was AFDC assistance for families with children. Among changes implemented, one was particularly harsh in this part of the nation where land means so much in the culture: in order to qualify for assistance programs, many people are required to give up their land, most of which has been in the family for generations. The assessed value of the land may make it look attractive; the market value may be substantially different. Its actual value is in grazing and for passing on from father to son, as is done in the culture. Yet, Secretary Vigil pointed out, federal policies force hungry people to give up their land in order to eat.

We found the hunger and malnutrition we came to investigate in New Mexico. More of it than we anticipated. Little did we guess, however, that hunger would somehow be tied directly to the beautiful land we encountered as we arrived.

"These aren't Harvard graduates," the speaker explained to his audience. "I'm absolutely convinced we're using red tape to turn away literally thousands of people who are in dire need of emergency food."[30]

For two years Texas State Senator Hugh Parmer has led the bipartisan Senate Interim Committee on Hunger to some twelve regions of Texas to determine the extent, impact, and causes of hunger in that state. In its recent report the Committee presented the following conclusions:

• Emergency food assistance has increased 300% statewide in Texas since 1980.
• Houston has seen an increase of 100% in emergency programs to feed the hungry in the same period of time.
• Growing numbers of Texas residents go to bed hungry at night, including young children and the elderly.[31]

Outside the Armco Steel Plant in Houston stands a large billboard which proclaims that "Houston Works." Inside a nearby hall sat a group of burly steelworkers who don't. They are among a group of 3,100 workers and 2,000 managers who lost their jobs when the Armco plant closed. Men and women who have worked for 28 or 30 years are suddenly out of work, and over 70% of them have exhausted their unemployment benefits.[32] "We're running out of options," reported Bart, a strapping worker. "For some of us the middle of the river is the next stop."

Bart's dilemma was real. Laid off two years ago, he has lived on beans, rice, and corn meal with his family, which includes five children, ages 3 through 14. Bart has gained 50 pounds in the two years, eating filling meals, mostly potatoes, so the children can have more nutritious foods.

The Armco Steel union president, a man who identified himself as "Early," provided a litany of family suffering, much of which we heard directly from the people surrounding us. Hunger is a daily problem. For some, suicide is an option which they no longer ignore, be it the worker who thinks about jumping into the river, or the man who told us that he sometimes wishes "I could just go to sleep and never wake up."

Across the state, the city of El Paso lies on the Rio Grande River, which separates the United States from Mexico. In a tiny office on a side street our physicians met with another group of American workers—farmworkers who pick the crops of this nation. Some twenty people with tanned faces and dark eyes sat quietly and spoke respectfully, with a certain reserve which seemed to reflect a reluctance to share their problems with a group of visitors who would not be staying long.

What they did share was a pattern of exploitation where workers hoping to pick crops the next day must be on the streets by midnight as field bosses drive their buses through the crowds selecting people who will ride and work for them. The process may go on for three hours, the buses finally departing for the fields where picking begins just before sunrise. Each six-gallon barrel of produce brings a red chip to be converted into cash at the end of the day. Many bosses do not provide water, but instead sell beer to the workers to increase their own income.

Hunger is but part of a larger problem for these Americans. It is subsumed under their general poverty and exploitation. One of them made a startling statement when we talked about a balanced diet. "There is nothing we have to balance," he said. The evidence we found in El Paso indicates that this is in fact true for many of the residents.

The Archdiocese in the border town of Brownsville, lying at the southernmost tip of Texas, reported that hunger in that area is widespread, worse than it has been in fifteen years. In the "colonias," unincorporated areas frequently without any water or sewer services, live communities of people, each with a shack on a small plot of land. In many ways the colonias are a wild parody of the suburbia in which their more affluent fellow-citizens live. But to visit in the homes eliminates any incipient amusement.

Seventy-eight-year-old Mr. Alviso and his wife live with their five-year-old granddaughter. They once received food stamps for the child, but the benefits had been terminated for reasons unknown to the family. Each day the old man sets out to collect bottles and cans, which he will redeem at the local store to buy food for his wife and grandchild. The little girl gets no milk at home, and the family never eats meat. They could not remember when they last had fresh vegetables. Their daily diet is rice, beans, and potatoes.

Urbano Cortez lived in a colonia near Harlingen, Texas, with his wife, a daughter, and a grandchild 12 years of age. They ate the same thing every day as the Alvisos—rice, beans, and potatoes. The doctor told Mr. Cortez he must eat fresh fruit, advice he found amusing since they often ran out of food altogether. He worried especially about the little girl, who got no fruits and vegetables at home and none at all when school was out for the summer.

Mr. Cortez reported that things were "three times" better now than they ever had been. He began working when he was eight, and did so for 55 years before his health required him to stop. He began earning forty cents a day and ended over five decades later earning $60 a week. Things, he said, had improved greatly. Mr Cortez died shortly after our visit. His doctor said his death couldn't be attributed to any one factor. Not hunger, although he knew the family was often hungry. Not malnutrition, although he did say that Mr. Cortez had had many nutritional deficiencies.

We had asked Mr. Cortez what he thought needed to be done to end the hunger that his family and neighbors face. "Jobs," he said. "Jobs is the way to end hunger. More selfless leaders and more jobs."

These three regions of this huge state are unique in their own ways. But they all have a common problem. And the problem they have in common was found by senate committee in its investigation in 12 regions of the state. People are hungry, and they are hungry in increasing numbers.

"Hunger," observed El Paso physician Jose Rodriguez, who traveled with the national group of doctors touring the state, "is a discrete epidemic which is spreading." The clinical evidence provided by clinicians around the state, as well as the data presented by churches and other emergency food providers, indicates that Dr. Rodriguez' observation is correct. In his own community, the largest soup kitchen in El Paso, the Rescue Mission, has seen demand increase significantly, and has tried to respond by providing more meals. In 1982, some 2,500 meals a month were provided. By 1984, that number had risen to more than 4,000 monthly. Across the state other emergency food facilities report the same trend, although most of them serve much larger numbers of people and, for many, the need is increasing at a faster rate.

The Houston Food Bank distributed just over a half million pounds of food in 1982. In the two-year period ending in December, 1984, the bank's annual food distribution had risen by over 600% (see Figure 23). Even this increase has left many of the pantries and soup kitchens which prepare and distribute the food to hungry families without adequate resources to meet the demand.

In a meeting with emergency food providers in the city, organizations ranging from the Salvation Army to the South Main Emergency Area Coalition reported that the demand they face has not only increased steadily, but that requests for food in August, 1984, were the highest in more than a year and a half. Not all the programs have records which extend back that far, but all records available show the constant increase which the agency directors reported (see Figure 24).

Rosemary Hornsby, director of Northwest Assistance Ministries, told how the number of families requesting help had increased since they opened some 14 months earlier. Initially serving about 50 families, the number rose to more than 80 within several months.

The Saint Stephen Presbyterian Church in South Houston, in the midst of a middle-class suburb, served 38 people its first year, 121 the next year, and then saw a jump in demand its third year to 814 people. According to church records, only five persons were repeaters. "The problem is growing, at least in this particular community," announced Pastor Pat Abrams.

Houston Metropolitan Ministries, an interdenominational federation of groups established to serve the poor, runs fifteen separate programs. The Metropolitan Ministries found that among home-bound elderly persons served in the Meals-on-Wheels programs, some 76% reported that the one meal delivered each weekday is the only food they eat. They have no other resources. Moreover, they have a significant number of such people on a waiting list for food, because their program budget is limited. Officials of the Metropolitan Ministries, in testimony before the Texas Senate Interim Committee on Hunger, said that they have seen a 1,500% increase in the number of calls each month asking for assistance.

Donald Johnson, executive director of the Star of Hope Mis-

Fig. 23. *Houston Food Bank, 1982–1984*

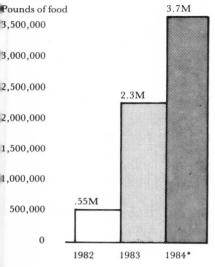

Pounds of food

*Includes 0.7 million pounds in USDA commodities.
Source: Food Bank records.

Fig. 24. *South Main Emergency Coalition, Houston, 1983–1984*

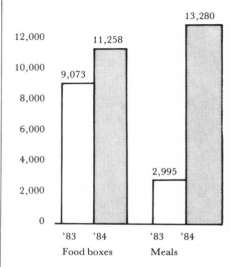

Source: Coalition records.

Fig. 25. *St. Vincent de Paul Society, Houston, 1982–1984*

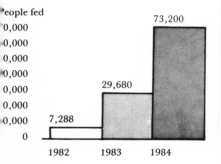

People fed

Source: Society records.

Fig. 26. *Star of Hope Mission, Houston, 1982–1984*

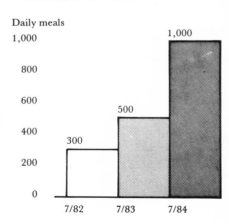

Daily meals

Source: Mission records.
(rounded as reported)

sion in Houston, reported that "we are currently experiencing a dramatic increase in the number of people that come to us daily for meals." Data maintained and presented by the Mission make that point self-evident (see Figure 26). Other programs presented similar evidence. The Christian Community Service Center, composed of fourteen churches in the southwest Houston area, experienced a 500% increase in requests for food and was forced, as a result, to place restrictions on eligibility for help. Director Dean Robinson estimates that some 10,000 home-delivered meals are needed to serve the city's poor elderly. Yet for the past three years fewer than 1,000 have been served annually.

The Woodforest Presbyterian Church operates a food pantry. The food, according to elder Jane Strange, sometimes runs low. The only food pantry in the North Channel area, it feed between 40 and 200 people in a month, depending on how long church resources last. She described the trauma faced by the families forced to rely on others to feed their children, recalling particular circumstances as she made her point: "Another example is a family of two parents and small children, and in this case a grandmother who could not work. The husband was a professional construction worker, out of work for a year. The mother was suicidal at this point because her children had potatoes and ketchup, and that was all."

Statistical data from the 190 emergency food providers in the Houston area provide a picture of increasing need. But in interviews with the people operating the soup kitchens and food pantries, one begins to develop a broader understanding of the problem. Agency after agency pointed to the fact they now serve families, many of which have never before been poor and hungry. And a significant portion of these programs admitted, often with great sadness, that they simply cannot keep up with the need. The Fair Haven United Methodist Church is one program unable to respond to the growing need it faces. After finding that the number of requests skyrocketed from approximately 3,800 a month in late 1983 to some 7,000 a month in early 1984, the church was forced to set zip code limits for the families it could help. Even with these restrictions there is a fairly constant demand, especially from families (see Table 4).

Table 4. *Number of Families Fed by*
Fair Haven United Methodist Church,
Houston, Texas, March–August, 1984

Month	Families fed	Adults fed
March	620	3,110
April	603	3,004
May	586	2,930
June	682	3,410
July	723	3,580
August	712	3,204

SOURCE: Church records.

Many other programs are seeing a dramatic increase in the number of intact families requesting assistance. The Salvation Army runs a program in suburban Pasadena which serves 1,000 people every week, mostly families. It runs another program which feeds people on the site, some 700 lining up in this bedroom community each evening to be fed.

Describing the phenomenon of "new poor" and hungry families, one food pantry director recalled a man driving up in a late model Lincoln Continental. "My staff asked why I gave him food," she said. "I told them it was because that car was *all* he has. He lost his job; lost his home. Finally he lost his wife. He lives in the car."[33]

Minister Steve Cartwright told of his surprise when his church decided to open a food pantry to respond to the hunger in his Houston neighborhood. "The people who are hungry were not those we anticipated. They came in cars, they dressed well. They looked just like us!"

This phenomenon is not limited to Houston, according to Senator Parmer. He and his colleagues found that it runs pretty much throughout the state—newly poor families, joining the people who have been poor for a long time, in bread lines. With a slight touch of irony, the Senator told how a hunger study commissioned in his more well-to-do district of Fort Worth found that 5% of the residents go to bed hungry on occasion.[34]

But the phenomenon of the "new poor," while recent, is but

one aspect of the hunger story in Texas. Other population groups, are hungry, some for a much longer period of time. Dr. Tony Zavaleta regularly observes this other face of hunger in Texas Valley town of Brownsville, Harlingen, and Raymondville. He reported that hunger and malnutrition for the people of this predominantly rural area "is a clear and present danger, an example . . . of starvation in the shadow of plenty."

Agencies feeding the hungry in this region describe conditions and needs which reinforce Dr. Zavaleta's analysis. The Hidalgo Community Action Program notes a dramatic increase in hunger in the area, much of it among people who have always been on the economic margins (see Figure 27).

St. John the Baptist Parish in San Juan is trying to administer to the hungry parishioners it sees. Father Warren Brown reported that "people come in and cry. . . ." For a fifty-seven-day period the parish obtained surplus food to distribute. The priest reports that they served 90,691 plates to people who came to eat, averaging for a time over 2,000 meals a day seven days a week.[35]

In Brownsville itself, a health survey conducted among low- and moderate-income residents found that 40% of those surveyed could not obtain enough food for their families.[36] Brownsville teachers, as well as their counterparts located in school systems adjacent to the city, found this to reflect a problem they had long ago detected among their students.

A Brownsville school principal, himself a teacher for eighteen years, reported to us that 90% of his student body comes to school hungry each day and cannot perform well academically because of its hunger. He added: "In my ten years in the Brownville system I find the problem worse now. Most of it is due to poor nutrition. Our children are seeds for the future. The problem is that we're not watering them."[37]

The descriptive images raised by the principal's strong conviction were matched by professional counterparts in the health field here and across the state.

The Houston Health Department reported that infant mortality in that city increased from 1982 to 1983, rising from 12.11 deaths per thousand live births to a rate of 13.61. In some parts of the city the rate is much higher. In the area served by the

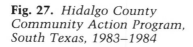

Fig. 27. *Hidalgo County Community Action Program, South Texas, 1983–1984*

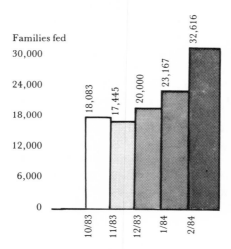

Source: Community Action records.

Riverside Health Center the infant mortality rate was 23.54—more than twice the national rate and as high as the rate in some Third World nations.

Reported Health Department official Barbara Jacobs, "We are seeing the results of hunger and malnutrition in our health clinics." A department study revealed an anemia rate of 54% among children 0–18 months of age in one city neighborhood. In another neighborhood survey among children 1–5 years old, 70% get too little milk, 90% consume too few fruits and vegetables, and over half get too little vitamins A and C.[38]

Nutritionist M. T. Di Ferrante of the Houston Health Department told us that the trends observed in clinics of the city are disquieting. "The ill-health we see in Houston is often directly related to hunger," she acknowledged.

Our physicians found that another type of hunger affects health in Texas—the hunger for adequate and safe drinking water. The lack of clean water in the colonias around El Paso, for example, directly impacts on both food preparation and health.

We saw an unusually high number of children with skin rashes of unknown etiology. Local physicians suggested that the rashes may be related to the water which residents purchase from truckers in 50-gallon drums which were formerly used to transport chemicals. On one such truck we observed a drum label which read "Potassium Cyanide—Poison."

Lack of water affects health in other ways as well. One way is in food preparation. The purchase and preparation of green leafy vegetables is unlikely to take place because of the amount of water required for cleaning. Moreover, families openly admit to purchasing large quantities of soda for their children to drink as a water substitute because they know the soda is "safe." Water also affects sanitation, which in turn impacts on the health of the residents. Sanitary sewage disposal is non-existent in many of the homes. In the colonia of Sparks we observed each of these problems in the homes we visited.

The water problem in the El Paso area acts in conjunction with the problem of hunger to impair health. One local physician reported that anemia and low-birth-weight babies are quite common in his practice, outcomes which he attributes to poor nutrition and inadequate food intake.[39] Another El Paso physician serving low-income patients said it is common for parents to give infants soft drinks in their bottles because they run out of the more expensive formula, a practice to which he attributes some of the health problems he sees among his impoverished patients.[40]

Another Texas physician, joining his medical colleagues in El Paso, pointed out that while he has practiced in Texas for some 15 years and has witnessed the impact of poverty on health, "things are actually much worse than I expected and, as we gleaned from our interviews and direct observations, are deteriorating even further."[41]

Deterioration of health was reported by doctors, nurses, and nutritionists in the Rio Grande Valley as well. Local physician Stanley Fisch, a longtime resident with a private practice in that area, described the hunger, poverty, and illness among the residents, many of whom are farmworkers: "One-third of

the children in this county are born at home. These are not typical American homes; they are buildings with a washboard basin on a dilapidated porch. Kids' shoes are stored in a plastic milk container with the top cut off. The refrigerators contain lard and rice. Oftentimes they contain nothing."
Many of the residents routinely go without adequate food. Some go without health care, epitomized by the young boy we examined with a healed but unset arm. He had been refused help at the local clinic because the family did not have the $9 required for a visit, let alone the $250 deposit required at the local hospital. "How is it possible to have these problems in America?" asked a local grocery store owner who described for us the conditions faced by her customers who reside in the area.

The same question was asked by nutritionist Gwen Olson at Su Clinica, an extraordinary health care center located in the Harlingen area. A registered dietitian who has worked in the area for five years, Ms. Olson previously provided health care in South America. "Most of the people I see here are undernourished, just like the people I saw in the Third World," she reported. She told us that clinic patients frequently run out of food altogether; others live for a week or two on starches until they are able to obtain something more nutritious. Many of the people going without proper nutrition are children and pregnant women.

In testimony before the Texas Senate Interim Committee on Hunger, she described conditions of hunger and ill-health:

Q: You've seen an increase (in hunger)?
A: Yes, it's an increase, a definite increase . . . I swear to that. And I also keep food records on all my patients. I have diet histories . . . and I have had doctors show me marasmus cases.
Q: What's a marasmus case?
A: Marasmus is protein calorie malnutrition. In kwashiorkor the child would be getting adequate calories but not enough protein. . . . I'm not a doctor, but they (children) are puffy, their hair has started falling out. It's gotten really thin. It changes from dark to reddish or pale and yellow.
Q: Your testimony is that you are finding the same kind of cases in the Rio Grande Valley that you found in South America?

A: Not the same number, definitely no. The same type . . . definitely. Almost everyone I see is undernourished.

Ms. Olson's observations about hunger and ill-health were corroborated by local officials and physicians. McAllen City Commissioner Armando Garcia said that he sees the hunger firsthand: "All you have to do is to go out there and watch the people shoving and pushing in line, trying to get something to eat." The problem, he noted, is not so much hunger as trying to get influential people to admit that there is a problem.

One person who acknowledges the problem is Dr. Brahmin, medical director of another health center. This physician minced no words:[52]

The majority of my patients wander all over America working the crops. They have no education and poor conditions. They are hungry. Our people have become human garbage. They are damned.

I am told that elephants don't die of disease; they die of starvation when their teeth fall out. That is the same thing that happens to my patients.

One in five patients at the clinic has malaria, parasites, or infectious hepatitis. A quarter of the patients are subclinically anemic. Kids are fed first when the family has food, then the husband eats. The woman eats whatever is left. As a result there is much obesity among the women, especially during pregnancy, as they seek to fill their stomachs with carbohydrates, which are less expensive than fruits and vegetables.

The nurse midwife in nearby Raymondville sees a high rate of anemia among her pregnant patients, and a great deal of weight loss during pregnancy as well, pointing out that patients are either obese or underweight. She admonished one patient who had lost five pounds in two weeks during her pregnancy. The woman explained: "But sister, I'm watering down the milk for my kids now. I can't drink it myself."

Hunger in the Midwest—Illinois and Missouri

One cannot help but appreciate the special irony of hunger in America's breadbasket. The prolific crops which spring from the fertile land produce hundreds of thousands of tons of grains and other food products, so much that each year millions of excess tons are stored in underground caves. Yet American citizens living within a short distance of this productive system are hungry.

The huge, overwhelming complex of buildings known as Cook County Hospital is located right in the middle of Chicago, the nation's third-largest city. It is an unlikely place to find kwashiorkor and marasmus, the Third World diseases of advanced malnutrition and starvation, which were reported to us in south Texas. As our team of doctors listened, joined by the Administrator of the hospital and the Chief of Internal Medicine, Dr. Stephen Nightingale, we learned that these conditions do exist in urban America: "They say we don't see kwashiorkor and marasmus in this country, but we do. I see 15–20 cases every year in my hospital."

The person speaking was Dr. Katherine K. Christoffel, Chair of the Committee on Nutrition of the Illinois Chapter of the American Academy of Pediatrics. The hospital about which she spoke is Children's Memorial Hospital, where she is Attending Pediatrician in the Division of Ambulatory Services.

Despite her impressive credentials, members of the visiting team of physicians remained skeptical until her report was corroborated by yet another Chicago doctor with his own impressive credentials and experience.

Dr. Howard B. Levy is Chairman of Pediatrics at Mount Sinai Hospital, and previously was Chief of Pediatric Nephrology at the Walter Reed Army Medical Center in Washington, D.C. A member of the American Academy of Pediatrics and the American Medical Association, Dr. Levy joined us to express concern about what he is seeing: "We too are seeing kwashiorkor and marasmus, problems which I have not seen since I was overseas. Malnutrition has clearly gone up in the last few years. We have more low-birth-weight babies. We are seeing so much TB that my house staff is no longer excited by it; it excites me that they are not excited by this trend."

Dr. Levy underscored the significance of what he was reporting: "clear, measurable, methodological phenomena" which demonstrate that the health of the patients is getting worse. More and more patients, Dr. Levy observed, have inadequate money to purchase food necessary to prevent growth failure and other nutrition-related problems among the pediatric population.

Well-known Chicago pediatrician Effie Ellis concurred with this observation: "We have a problem here of serious proportions. Social service agencies are having to provide medicines, and hospitals and clinics are having to give out food."

Cook County Hospital gives out food itself and is asked regularly for more by hungry patients. Dr. Nightingale, the Internal Medicine Chief, said that he admits 20 people a day whose problems stem from inadequate nutrition. Pediatric social worker Brenda Chandler has patients come to her saying, "Do you have anything I could eat?" Dietitian Mary Jo Davis sees hunger among "patients" who are not really admitted to the hospital. "Almost every day we have people looking around trying to find out where the hospital leaves its garbage," she reported. Elaborating, she added: "Our hospital patients can't worry about special diets; they do well just to have food in their homes. Sometimes we do dietary recalls over the past three to four days for patients and find that the pages are entirely blank!"

The Chicago Department of Human Services reported that applicants for emergency food have increased 900% in the last two years, a phenomenon seen by social service and religious organizations in the city. The Salvation Army presented statistics showing hunger up significantly for 1984 over 1983, and other agencies, such as the Association House, state that hunger is their number one problem.

Betty Williams of Chicago United Charities placed the mounting hunger problem in a unique perspective:"Our agency is over 100 years old, and this period is as bad as many of us can recall." According to Joel Carp, Chairman of the Mayor's Task Force on Hunger, at least 600,000 Chicago residents are hungry or likely to be hungry every month. These are people of all ages living well below the federal poverty line: people, he said, "like the old folks on the North Side whom we found living on dog food."

Later that day, some of our team of doctors would confirm

this report during their visit to the Marillac House, a large Catholic settlement house in the city. In discussions with the director and her staff, as well as home visits conducted in a housing project, we learned that it is not uncommon for elderly people, living alone in apartments with no cooking facilities, to consume an evening meal of a tin of cat food and a raw egg.

The mayor's office reported that at least 224,000 residents seek emergency food assistance each month, and that the actual number may be twice as high. To respond to the increasing demand, the number of soup kitchens in the city jumped over 80% in the last two years, and now serve 11,500 meals a week. The number of church-related food pantries increased 45% in the same period of time.[43]

Data from 40 food pantries, surveyed on an ongoing basis, reflect the increased food distribution during the past several years (see Figure 28).

The Chicago Health Systems Agency presented survey data to the mayor's office showing food distribution in the city tween 1981 and 1983, as part of the city's Emergency Food Program. Approved requests for food assistance rose from 19,312 the first year to 223,500 the last year.

Another barometer of food assistance to the hungry is the Greater Chicago Food Depository, which distributes 400% more food today then it did two years ago (see Figure 29). Increasing need is one variable at which we looked. Another is the profile of the hungry and the impact of hunger on their lives. In southwest Chicago our inquiry into the situation faced by laid-off steelworkers at the Wisconsin Plant could have taken place at the Armco Plant in Houston. Frustrated and angry, unemployed workers and their families stand in lines for 5-pound block of cheese and a loaf of bread. Frank Lumkin, president of the Save Our Jobs Committee, explained the dimensions of the problem. "It's having 100 bags of food to give to the families and finding 500 people show up, already in line, at 7:00 a.m."

The hungry are also the elderly. There are 8,000 poor elderly in need of food who are not being served, according to

Fig. 28. *Chicago Food Pantry Survey, 1981–1984*

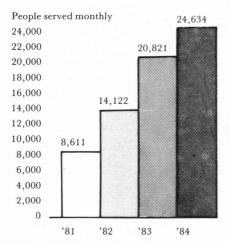

People served monthly

Source: Chicago Hunger Coalition survey records.

Fig. 29. *Greater Chicago Food Depository, 1982–1984*

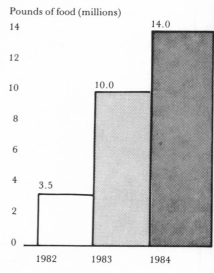

Pounds of food (millions)

Source: Food Depository records.

Fig. 30. *Central Illinois Food Bank, Springfield, 1983–1984*

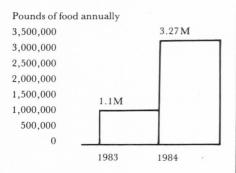

Pounds of food annually

Source: Food Bank records.

Chicago Office for Senior Citizens.[44] Director Robert Ahrens points out that it is believed that this figure is considerably under the number who are in need of food.

The hungry in Chicago are the families seen by the Visiting Nurse Association, whose district offices have been forced to open food pantries to respond to the lack of food among their patients. "These babies are hungry," implored executive director Margaret Ahern. But, according to her, not only babies. She cited many instances of parents and the elderly also going hungry, some whose caloric intake is as low as 550 calories and 24 grams of protein. "In the prison camps of Germany," she noted, "the daily ration was 800 calories and 40 grams of protein."

The hungry are the patients at the South Lawndale Health Center. The medical director, Dr. Alvarez, and the clinic staff report that health problems related to poor nutrition are not uncommon. Some 10% of their pediatric patients have iron-deficiency anemia, and pulmonary tuberculosis is seen in young people they serve, itself often a result of compromised nutrition. Health workers note that, when they do home visits, they find families unable to purchase adequate food. Children often consume only coffee and an egg for a meal.

The hungry, according to other Chicago agencies, are the undocumented workers whose fear of being deported prevents their even standing in line for cheese. Hector Hernandez sees the realities faced by these families, who come through the Immigrant Services branch of the Traveler's Aid office. Hernandez says that the families often have very little to eat and receive no help as a general rule. Many of them, he explained, have children born in the United States. Yet, if parents seek help such as emergency food assistance, they stand the risk of being reported to Immigration. Immigration may well attempt to deport the parents of the children who are U.S. citizens, thereby breaking apart the family. In this fundamental sense, he explained, the ability of some American children to eat brings with it the likelihood that they will lose their parents.

Hunger in Chicago is the faces, young and old, black and

white, of people living on the margins, and many who live beyond the margins of a full stomach:

- The 81-year-old man and his wife who come for a meal at
the Uptown Ministries, who live on $293 monthly in social
security benefits and $24 in food stamps. They eat mostly grits
and oatmeal, sometimes rice and beans.
- The 30-year-old woman whose acknowledged racism was
turned around when she saw more people suffering who are
white, as she is, than blacks and Spanish. "I used to go without food just so my kids could eat, but now they often go
without also."
- The patient in a hospital who, along with her three children, stuffed food into their mouths by hand. They had had
nothing to eat for three days.
- The mothers whom doctors find diluting their infant's
formula in order to make it last the month.[45]

These American citizens are hungry. They are the "anecdotes" which together reflect and comprise a large problem in
this city—people without adequate food to eat. They are the
individuals behind the numbers which Dr. Howard Levy and
his medical colleagues in the city tabulate: increasing low-birth-
weight rates, 50% anemia rates, and the high proportion of
children failing to grow, which other doctors noted in a recent
study.[46]

"These people are human beings," Charles Betcher reminded us when we visited the soup kitchen at the Uptown
Baptist Church. "You can't live long on two pieces of bread a
day." Both the center at which Betcher works and this church
are among the many agencies in the area trying to feed the
hungry, a task that is getting bigger, not smaller.

It is perhaps what Jack Ramsey, director of Second Harvest,
umbrella organization for food banks around the nation, had
in mind when he observed: "When you see government agencies making referrals to small food pantries that are running
out of resources, that's an American tragedy."

Ramsey was not the only person to see the extent of hunger
in this major city as a tragedy. Psychiatrist Gordon Harper, a
physician who has examined hunger in other regions of the

nation, visited a soup kitchen run by the Missionaries of Charity, the order started by Mother Teresa in Calcutta. Reported Dr. Harper: "We observed the spectacle and the tragedy of Missionaries of Charity coming from Calcutta to the West Side of Chicago to provide food for the hungry in America."

It's only a short distance from the Peoria airport to the George Washington Carver Center, a social service and health center which provides food assistance to many families in this city, right in the heart of America's breadbasket. Within minutes of landing we confronted registered dietitian Marjorie LaFont of the Cooperative Extension Service: "When I started in 1972, we had to hunt to find hungry families. Today we are overwhelmed. Taxpayers who supported feeding programs are now in line for help. Emergency food programs used to see a let up in the summer. This summer it did not let up."

"Are there hundred children in Peoria?" Ms. LaFont asked rhetorically. "Just go to any school and ask." She added that she sees much malnutrition that goes undiagnosed because many of her young patients and their families are too poor to seek medical care.

Ron Cooley, director of the Friendship House in Peoria, says that hunger is getting worse as unemployed families have exhausted all benefits and supports. They are now destitute and hungry. Linda Cranston, who runs an emergency food program in the city, reports that their rolls have risen 300% in the past three years.[47] The Peoria Food Bank opened in 1984, in response to growing hunger in the city, as witnessed by local agencies. During that year it provided more than 600,000 pounds of food to some 87 organizations. Jack Cramer-Heuerman, pastor of the Forest Hill Methodist Church in Peoria and president of the food bank, estimates that they feed "between 150,000 and 200,000 people a year, about 10,000 being families from Peoria."

The Central Illinois Food Bank, of which the Peoria bank is a satellite, serves 67 counties, distributing over 300,000 pounds of food a month. Director Bob Hunt reports that its food distribution has tripled in the past two years and is up 1,000% since 1982 (see Figure 30). Moreover, the number of churches and agencies giving out food is up substantially, and much more could be given out if they had it to give.

Throughout the breadbasket region of southern Illinois, agencies feeding the hungry report increasing need. In June, 1984, the Salvation Army conducted a telephone survey of ten food pantries located in various counties in downstate Illinois (see Table 5). Selected randomly to present a representative picture of pantry experience, the agencies were asked to compare caseloads (however they maintained their records) this year and last. Only one pantry, the Salvation Army in West Frankfort, reported a slight decline in need, a factor attributed to a union and other churches in the town opening food facilities. All the rest report increasing hunger.

The Salvation Army survey reflects the data reported by others whose records we examined. The Friendship House in Peoria, which went from feeding 400 families in 1982 to 2,400 in 1984, perhaps depicts the dimensions of the problem in that city, where hunger is of unusual proportions. Zack Monroe, Peoria welfare director for some 32 years, sat before statistical tables piled on his desk as he analyzed trends over recent years: "Things are getting worse, not better. Even in the Depression there weren't as many people in need of help as now."

"I grew up in the Depression," reported a woman at an elderly feeding site. "I never thought I'd see this again." But there is evidence of Depression-like hunger and suffering in this area. At the Labor Temple in Peoria, we met with unemployed workers and their families. "Thank you for coming," the business manager said as he welcomed our group of doctors, "and for trying to understand the pain and suffering in our lives."

A 30-year-old woman, neatly dressed and self-confident, spoke first. Employed until her factory closed, she and her son now live on AFDC and food stamps, a total income of $368 monthly. "I don't like coming here to reveal my personal life in front of everyone," she admitted, 'but I got to because of my son. I'm willing to work, I always have. Just try me."

Among numerous others speaking was a 53-year-old Army veteran, a painter out of work for two years. A tanned, lined face and light hair reflected the features of many in this re-

Table 5. *Caseloads of Downstate Illinois Food Pantries,*
1983 vs. 1984

Food pantry	Period of year	1983 figure	1984 figure	Percent increase '83–'84
St. John's, Decatur	May	58 referrals	113 referrals	95%
Concern Office, Peoria	May	427 families	541 families	27%
Salvation Army, Mattoon	Jan.–May	500 people	1,000 people	100%
Jacksonville Pantry, Jacksonville	Jan.–May	481 families	662 families	38%
We Care, Vandalia	"Double and increasing"			100+ %
Salvation Army, Kawanee	Jan.–May	76 families	498 families	555%
First Methodist, Dixon	Jan.–May	1,018 people	2,029 people	99%
Salvation Army, Kankakee	Jan.–May	$1,003 spent	$4,770 spent	n.a.
Opportunity Council, DuQuoin	whole year	237 people	331 (projected)	40%

SOURCE: Salvation Army, June, 1984.

gion of the nation. Now with no income, no car insurance, and his children studying by candlelight since his electricity was shut off, he and his family frequently go hungry. "I was reluctant to apply for food stamps," he says. "The politicians keep saying there aren't enough to go around, so you think someone else needs them more than you. You keep hoping the phone will ring."

Another worker, sitting silently until prodded by his wife, who reported that her husband is a good man and tries hard to provide for his family, told his plight. He can't find work, and his family cannot live on what income he does receive. "You keep thinking you'll progress to middle-class, but instead you get poorer. My mother got us through the last Depression, and now I somehow got to get us through this one."

Peoria, Illinois, the all-American city. Southern Illinois, heart of American agricultural production. We found substantial hunger in this region of the nation, suffering reminiscent, as so many of the residents reminded us, of the Depression some 50 years ago.

In the 1930s, American farms produced more inconsistently. Today, they produce enough, some say, to feed the world. Yet many people who used to work those farms, and the workers who once built the machinery by which others farm, are now hungry.

Eighty-six-year-old Effie Alsop is hungry, but only sometimes. As the doctors talked to her in the living room of her modest home in the southern Missouri town of Caruthersville, Mrs. Alsop was a picture of emaciation:

Q: What did you eat today?
A: Nothing.
Q: You've had nothing all day?
A: No.
Q: You must get hungry.
A: I get hungry when food is in the house, but when I don't have any I'm not hungry. Isn't that funny, doctor?

The wrinkled, white face of Mrs. Alsop contrasted sharply with the younger black face of Mrs. Spain, mother of five children whose husband is desperately looking for work. In her refrigerator we found eight hot dogs, four peppers, a carton of milk, and some eggs. Are you ever out of milk, she was asked. "All the time." What would she do, we asked, if it got to the point that the children had nothing to eat. "I'd march them to the grocery, sit them on the floor, and give them food. . . . At least they couldn't arrest me for stealing." Her quick response betrayed the fact that this was a possibility she had already considered.

As the afternoon sun beat down on faces which were black and white, old and young, people stood in the commodity cheese line outside the town building, graphic evidence that hunger in this region respects neither age nor color. Whether the 79-year-old on social security or the 39-year-old unemployed mother of three, we learned that people simply don't have enough to eat. "Do you think we'd stand in line all day if we weren't really hungry?" asked one man of his inquirers. The "Boot-heel" region of Missouri, so named by the shape of this protruding section of the state that dips down into Arkansas, is part of a rich, fertile plain where cotton was once the main crop, now replaced by soybeans. The area is also one in which some of the worst poverty in the nation is found. Caruthersville, the largest town in the area, is only 9,000 in population, two-thirds of which is white. Visiting black and white areas of the community, we learned that old traditions do not disappear easily. As we entered homes in the black community a limousine circled nearby; the white owner of the shacks in which the black families lived had come to see what the "strangers" were doing in town.

Staff at the Missouri Delta Ecumenical Ministries briefed us on the hunger situation in the area, which they described as serious. Food stamps do not last and help from private agencies is limited. Erma "Tiny" Motton provided us with a survey of households in the area, graphic evidence of the food problems being found in the descriptions of meal contents. Further evidence was found in visits to local agencies.

Mrs. Mehrle directs the Headstart program which serves 120 low-income children in Caruthersville. All live below poverty. She reported that it is a common thing to go into the children's homes and find little or nothing to eat. Teacher Dolores Jones added that "You can't help but notice that they [children] come back in the fall having lost weight. There's a lot of hunger in the homes." "Yes," Mrs. Mehrle continued, "kids come to this program not knowing milk. The parents aren't bad, they just don't have the money to buy it."

We asked our local guides to stop at a low-income community we passed on the way to a health center. Standing on the sidewalk was 9-year-old Lee, a child who looked to be 6. One of the pediatricians in the group examined him later, as his mother described their situation. Yes, she acknowledged, the doctor at the local clinic had diagnosed Lee as being anemic, suggesting the types of food he needed to eat. She admitted trying, but not being able, to buy them frequently: "I do the best I can." In other homes we found more young children clearly in trouble nutritionally, along with several older people.

Health center staff in nearby Hayti informed us that undernutrition is not uncommon among residents of the area. In fact, they have opened an emergency food program which serves families and a lot of elderly. Why, they were asked, is a health center in the business of feeding people. The question drew a quick response: "Because they're hungry and nobody else is doing it."[48]

Washington County to the north lies in the midst of Missouri's mining districts. Settled by French farmers in the eighteenth century, the area soon turned to lead and barite mining. Today, the county is one of the poorest in the nation, with the mines mostly shut down.

Our doctors conducted home visits with the priests and lay workers of St. Joachim's parish, talking with elderly people who lived up dirt roads beyond streams that had to be crossed, families on farms, and individuals living alone in rusty trailers. Scrawny dogs and cats wandered around, as children carried water in old lard cans. Every household was not hungry, although nearly every one reported adequate food to be a paramount problem.

Typical of what the doctors observed was the Eckhoff family, the father of the household a disabled man who lives with his wife and seven children in a trailer home. Thanks to food stamps, the family members are able to purchase some food, although the main items eaten are hash and milk. Other families are not so fortunate, including a single parent raising several children. During the past two weeks they had eaten no meat; on occasion they have cereal. The usual staples for their meals are biscuits and fatty bacon, a diet which the mother reported to be all that she could provide her children. The children, she admitted, frequently go to school hungry.

Catholic workers in the parish report that hunger is common. They are trying to help as many families as they can because, as in Hayti, no one else is doing it.

It is not entirely correct to say that other efforts are not being made. Perhaps they are not adequate, but the effort is there.

The Central Missouri Food Bank, located almost exactly in the middle of the state in Columbia, began operation in late 1982. Since that time its efforts have grown immensely (see Figure 31).

Executive Director Diane Huneke reports that there is no sign that hunger in the counties served by her agency is diminishing. A survey of emergency food programs, in fact, showed an average increase of 21% in food provided for 1984 over 1983.[49] Some of the increases, depending on the geographical area, are much greater than this average. In Flat River, for example, located in the mineral mining area of the state northwest of Cape Girardeau, hunger is increasing steadily. The East Missouri Action Agency reports an increase of 328% in demand for emergency food services between 1983 and 1984.

"Look for a man with a dashiki, beads, and bangles," we were told as we departed early on a Friday morning for the warehouse of the Food Crisis Network, located in a St. Louis slum. The man we were to meet there is Otis Woodard, a Lutheran Family Outreach worker, who reported that in his neighborhood people are so hungry that it is not uncommon to see home burglaries where the only item missing is food.

During the day some of the doctors would encounter the "food theft" problem during their rounds in homes and neighborhood agencies. Fifty-seven-year old Lenore Phillips and her teenage son had their apartment burglarized two weeks before, while he was at school and she was at a job interview. Food was stolen from the freezer: cheese, green beans, stewed tomatoes, franks, hamburger, and leg bones. "They spent most of their time on the food, almost nothing else," remarked Ms. Phillips. Clearly, from the description of what was taken she and her son are not hungry, but Mr. Woodard's report of hungry citizens stealing food in order to eat took on a different meaning.

Otis Woodard's statement also would be echoed later that day by Evelyn Irving, an administrator at the Darst-Webbe Housing Project, who said that they have had to secure their garbage bins to keep mothers and children from eating from them. The food pantry operated by the project serves up to 1,000 people every month, most of them families. Nearby, the

Fig. 31. *Central Missouri Food Bank, Columbia, 1982–1984*

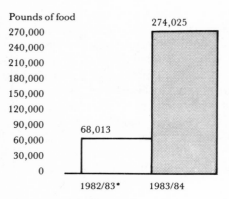

*Nine months only.
Source: Food Bank records.

Fig. 32. *Feed My People Program, St. Louis, 1983–1984*

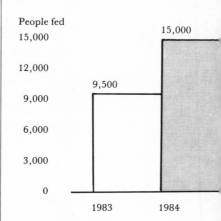

Source: Program records.

Guardian Angel Center, which used to give out bread, gave up the practice because the crowds became too large.

While some residents of St. Louis lose their food to hungry thieves, others lose their children because of their own hunger. At the Salvation Army Children's Center, formerly a Booth Home, staff reported that feeding problems are prominent among the children, about half of whom are in the lowest-fifth percentile of growth for their ages. But health and medical problems reported by the staff were not its only concern. Some families have their children taken away because they haven't adequate food for them.

One Salvation Army worker who had placement experience with St. Louis County, estimated that one-third of the foster and group care placements are made because parents had no food. She and other child care workers reported that hundreds of children are removed from their parents each year solely because they are hungry.

Hunger is not subtle in St. Louis. On occasion hungry people come into the emergency room of the city hospital; a few collapse on the floor, said Monsignor Shockley of the archdiocese, who knows of the cases from local doctors who see people forced to go without food for days at a time. Added Protestant minister Larry Rice: "You've heard that people here eat out of trash cans. What you need to know is how they fight to do it . . . how they fight over control of the dumpsters."

Rev. Rice reported that mothers and children come in to get food from his church, which, on occasion, has frozen foods donated by local merchants. "We give out frozen food and watch people eat it right on the sidewalk."

Ann Steinberg is the hotline operator for Operation Food Search, a local program to feed the hungry. She testified that she has lived in St. Louis all her life and often could not believe what she heard on the phone: "Kids come in here with their parents not even knowing some basic vegetables. Some families hear of us and walk eight miles to get food. We recently had a lady and her 11-year-old son who had lived on tea and bread for three weeks."

A sense of the dimensions of the hunger problem in St. Louis is provided by the local community agencies trying to feed the hungry. Hosea House, for example, operates an impressive program which includes nutritional education and food distribution. In January, the relatively small agency served 2,732 people, nearly half of whom were children. Nearly 100 new families come for help each month, according to the director, Steve Campbell.

Similar increases are being observed at the Northside Ministry and the Someone Cares Mission, where doctors observed what one termed the "special irony of the private sector donating rotted food for which some business will receive a 50¢-on-the-dollar tax deduction." Fortunately staff saw that such food was discarded, but the irony behind the motive for industry contribution to these small agencies did not go unnoticed.

The priest at the Notre Dame Parish had to reactivate the local St. Vincent de Paul Society program because of the tremendous amount of hunger he observed in his neighborhood. Staff worker Beulah Cambell, a Cherokee woman, said they served 140–170 people monthly, a 100% increase over the previous year.

Lutheran Family and Children's Services reports a 100% increase in requests for emergency assistance, from 3,500 a year in 1980 to 7,000 in 1984. The staff points out that this is 7,000 families, not just individuals, and it has been able to serve fewer than half of those who come for help.[50]

In South St. Louis the Feed My People program (see Figure 32) serves an essentially middle-class community of 350,000. Financial problems in the community are serious; some 10,000 homes in the area had heat shut off last year for nonpayment of bills. Hunger is also a problem, as food program records indicate.

Food bank and distribution operations try to service the agencies which distribute food to the hungry in the city. During a one-week distribution audit in 1984, Operation Food Search reported that 324 community agencies in St. Louis fed 26,000 people. Of this number, 44% were children between the ages of 0 and 17 years.

The large food bank, Food Crisis Network, has seen demand for food increase rapidly, an increase with which it has not been able to keep up. During 1983, the operation distributed just over 1 million pounds of food, a number which went up during 1984, even though it operated only ten months owing to relocation and reorganization.

Evidence of serious and increasing hunger may be deduced from the evidence presented by scores of churches and social service agencies. But to visit the agencies and to eat with the individuals and families provide deeper insight into the causes of hunger and the impact it has on citizens in the middle of America.

As two doctors talked with a man, his wife, and his 4-year-old daughter, who come to a local church to eat because their income isn't enough to meet their food requirements, Mrs. Love sat alone in a corner of the church basement having a doughnut and coffee. Now 51 years old, she is the mother of five children, two of whom are in the military service. She worked much of her life as a maid at a large St. Louis hotel until a bus ran over and crushed her foot five years ago. She never received any money from the bus company and was denied disability from the government despite a doctor's letter she displayed saying she is disabled. Her total monthly income is $146, half of which is food stamps, not enough to eat and pay her rent of $115 monthly. She lives in an apartment without heat and eats little.

Q: How long since you've eaten?
A: Just yesterday.
Q: And today . . . what have you had?
A: Coffee, four doughnuts, and two salads. When I can I eat potatoes and peanut butter.
Q: When you can? Do you ever go without food?
A: I been days without food. I get headaches but they go away if I get something to eat.
Q: And when you don't?
A: Know what I do? I get me some water and I put sugar in it and drink it. That helps.
Q: How much weight have you lost?
A: Since I been most hungry?
Q: Yes.
A: About 100 pounds.

The nun who works with unemployed men and their families in the St. Patrick's Center noted that they used to see mainly single men. Some of them are transient, like the father who recently appeared with an infant son in tow looking for work, or the young mother whose baby had no shoes. "Our people are not lazy," she said adamantly. "They're here early in the morning hoping to get into the labor pool. Otherwise they wait here all day hoping for something."[51]

One such man was 60-year-old Mr. Griffith, with two master's degrees from Tulane University. For 22 years he worked as an engineer, his education and training reflected in his speech. For nearly 18 years he managed a chain of convenience stores. Then the chain went out of business. He has no income; his wife and daughter died several years ago in an accident. A remaining daughter, with a husband and a child, lives in another state unaware of his situation because of his pride.

Mr. Griffith sleeps in Forest Park and hopes. But his hopes are not great ones: "Yes . . . I'm suffering a bit from depression. It doesn't seem like there's a lot of reason to hope. I wanted to wait until I was 65 and retire, but I didn't make it. There's not a lot for a man like me even though I feel like I have a lot still to contribute."

The People's Clinic serves some 20,000 St. Louis residents annually, many of whom are unemployed and destitute like Mr. Griffith and the men with whom we spoke. Nearly three-quarters of the clinic's patients live below poverty. On an average day, according to the clinical staff, it refers several patients to local food pantries.

Hunger is a chronic problem among clinic patients, and evidence of malnutrition is not uncommon. The doctor told us he frequently sees women who have blisters around their mouths from living on oatmeal. About the third week of each month patients come to the facility asking for work to do. Their food stamps have run out and they are hungry. The preschool program in the clinic found out that children were not getting breakfast when parents would ask quietly if it might give the children milk or something to eat before the day started. Nevertheless, clinic staff see children experiencing growth failure.

Across the state, Kansas City Mayor Richard Berkley commissioned a task force to look into hunger in that city. At the time the task force report was issued more than a year ago, area soup kitchens were serving 1,500–2,000 meals daily, and the demand for help outstripped the supply. In addition, some 3,000–5,000 households each month asked agencies for groceries, and the demand for help was increasing at the time of the report.[52]

The Metropolitan Lutheran Ministry reported that requests for food assistance more than doubled, to a figure of 900 families monthly. St. Mark's Church of Kansas City responded to the need it saw by opening a soup kitchen three days a week. Within a short period of time the church was forced to open every weekday. Nearby, the director of the Truman Medical Center Department of Social Services, Suzanne Meyer, reported that "the impact of poor nutrition can be seen most clearly in our pediatric unit and our maternity unit."

These reports were made in 1984. Since that time poverty

has increased, and emergency food programs in the city, as in the rest of the state, report that hunger also has increased. Just outside Kansas City is the small city of Warrensburg, home of Central Missouri State University. Professor Raymond Spatti recently conducted a research project on hunger in the area. His study, while a contribution to greater understanding of the problem, is perhaps not so important as his commentary:[53]

"As we sit above the caves filled with government stored food, and as we shudder at the nuclear warheads implanted in our fields, we are faced with the travesty that even in the Breadbasket of America there are empty baskets still waiting for food."

4. MALNUTRITION, ILL-HEALTH, AND HUNGER

The central issue that arises out of the Physician Task Force investigation, is whether hunger is adversely affecting the health of the poor. What we need, in order to answer the question, is an epidemiology of hunger. Epidemiology is the study of the prevalence and distribution of disease. It provides evidence to answer questions about who gets sick and about why they get sick. Epidemiologists look at the characteristics of affected individuals, trying to learn what distinguishes them from those who do not experience the illness. They seek to identify "exposures," the causal factors that characterize those affected.

The disease or outcome condition that we are worried about is malnutrition. The exposures with which we are concerned are hunger and poverty. We want to understand if poverty and hunger are linked to malnutrition and illness.

The persuasiveness of our finding will depend on several variables. A large study population and a strong and clearcut outcome contribute to the force of an epidemiological conclusion. Also important is the general biological context into which the finding fits: the relationship between exposure and outcome has to make sense biologically to be convincing. It must be consistent with related findings from other studies. We need to find ways of assessing the relationship between poverty and nutrition-related disease that meet these criteria.

In Ethiopia and other parts of the world in which hunger has advanced to epidemic starvation, the epidemiology of hunger is easily accomplished. Massive numbers of impoverished people are exposed to extremes of hunger with clearcut outcomes. The deprivation is so severe that it is frequently fatal. In a tragic sense epidemiology in Ethiopia is largely a matter of counting the dead.

In the United States, malnutrition is not so obvious. Deprivation is less extreme and we would not expect to find malnutrition so severe. The epidemiological effort required in this country is more subtle. Instead of a single clearcut outcome—starvation leading to death—we have to look for the multiplicity of outcomes that may result from mild or moderate malnutrition.

This job would be simplified if the United States had a nutrition surveillance system designed to provide information on the health of groups at high nutritional risk within our population.[1] Such a system would collect data on the income, diet, and health of a carefully chosen sample of Americans. It would make possible timely reporting of findings on Americans of all ages from across the country. Nutritionists, physicians, and others concerned with the health of the poor have proposed such a system, arguing that the information it generated would provide a firm scientific basis for health and nutrition policies. But no system so comprehensive or targeted now exists.

In the absence of a national nutrition surveillance system, the task of analyzing the impact of hunger on the health of the poor is difficult. It requires that we dig deep for information, take advantage of small studies from disparate sources, and analyze carefully the implications of what we learn. It is a hard job technically and analytically. But it is a crucial component in the development of a fuller understanding of hunger in America.

We divide the issue of the relationship between hunger and health into three parts. We consider first the impact of food and the lack of food on human health, growth, and well-being. We then look at the nutritional resources available to the poor, evaluating intake in comparison to national dietary standards. Finally and most important, we look at the information available on the health of the poor in America today.

The Impact of Nutrition on Health

Food is used by the body in several ways: it provides energy to fuel all activities, it provides the raw materials for growth and development, and it provides substances used by the body to promote health and prevent disease. When a person is malnourished, when food is chronically inadequate in either quantity or quality, any of these functions may be compromised.

The precise impact of malnutrition depends on the age and sex of the individual. It also depends on prior health and biological status: certain diseases and certain physiological conditions create particular nutritional needs which influence the impact of malnutrition. Human beings are particularly sensitive to the impact of malnutrition at certain stages of life. Pregnant women, infants, and children on the one hand, elderly people on the other, are likely to suffer greatest harm when food is inadequate. At any age, malnutrition can cause lethargy and weakness. It can involve impaired immune function, leading to greater susceptibility to infectious disease. Lack of specific nutrients may cause a range of deficiency diseases affecting all organ systems of the body. Malnutrition that is prolonged and severe may lead, directly or indirectly, to death.

The quality and quantity of food available to a pregnant woman are critical factors in the healthy development and birth of her child. The growing fetus requires a rich diet of protein, vitamins, and minerals as its tissues and organs develop. When nutrition is inadequate during pregnancy, a number of dangers arise.

First, the mother's health is compromised. When food is inadequate, stores of maternal nutrients may be depleted to provide for the baby. Maternal anemia reflects the absence of adequate iron to meet the increased needs of pregnancy. Toxemia, a complex of symptoms involving rapid increase in blood pressure and swelling of tissues due to excessive retention of fluid, is a common and serious hazard of pregnancy. Research suggests it may reflect inadequate nutrition, especially inadequate protein, during pregnancy. Toxemia, if uncontrolled, may be fatal to both mother and child.[2]

The infant's health may also be compromised by poor maternal nutrition. Risks include prematurity, defined as birth at or before 37 weeks' gestation, and low birth-weight, defined as weight under 2,500 grams (about 5½ pounds). The premature low-birth-weight baby is not able to adapt to the extrauterine environment with the ease of a fully developed new-born. Risks of prematurity include respiratory distress syndrome and weak immune response.[3] Even a full-term under-weight baby is at risk of health problems, including hypoglycemia, hypocalcemia, and polycythemia, as well as long-term growth and development problems.[4]

This range of hazards facing the frail newborn increases its risk of dying in infancy. In the United States, complex and costly technology is available to increase the high-risk infant's chance of survival. Even so, the low-birth-weight baby faces 30 times the normal likelihood of dying before the age of one. Low birth-weight accounts for more than half of infant deaths in the United States, and 75% of deaths to babies under a month. Low birth-weight is the eighth-leading cause of death in the United States.[5]

A wealth of scientific research helps us understand the effects of inadequate nutrition on the young. (Several studies are summarized in Table 6.) One major body of research goes back to World War II, when several European countries, historically well fed, were cut off from food supplies. As one study from the Food and Nutrition Service (United States Depart-

Table 6. *Deficits Associated with Premature and Small (for Gestational Age) Births*

Investigators	Group studied	Findings
Davie, Butler, Goldstein (1972)[a]	Infants born small at any gestational age	100% more physical and emotional handicaps
Rubin, Rosenblatt, Barlow (1973)[b]	Infants born small but full term	70% more school problems
	Infants born small and premature	40% more school problems
Vohr and Oh (1983)[c]	Infants born small and premature	25% more major neurologic problems; 117% more minor neurologic problems

[a] Davie, R., Butler, N. R. and Goldstein, H. From Birth to Seven. *The Second Report of the National Development Survey*, Longman, London 1972.
[b] Rubin, R. A., Rosenblatt, C. and Barlow, B., "Psychological and Educational Sequelae of Prematurity," *J. Pediatr.* 52:352, 1973.
[c] Vohr, B. E. and Oh, W. "Growth and Development in Pre-Term Infants Small for Gestational Age," *J. Pediatr.* 103:941, 1983.

ment of Agriculture) reports:[6] "During the siege of Leningrad by Germany, birth-weights declined significantly. . . . As birth-weights declined, there was a concurrent increase in infant mortality. Similar results were reported during the famine in Holland in 1944–45."

By contrast, England, subject to similar wartime suffering, developed a program to provide rationed food preferentially to pregnant women. Infant mortality actually declined in England during the war as a result.

A group of more recent studies demonstrates the positive impact of nutritional supplementation for pregnant women. The United States established the Women, Infants, and Children Special Supplemental Feeding Program (WIC) in 1972 in response to evidence of poor birth outcomes related to maternal deprivation. To date, at least seven studies have evaluated the impact of WIC on birth outcome.

Although these studies look at the program in different ways, their findings (summarized in Table 7) are universally positive. A prominent researcher explained results of two studies to a Congressional committee. Of the first, he said:[7] "WIC participation is associated with improved pregnancy outcomes; in particular, a 21% decrease in low-birth-weight infants, a major decrease in neonatal mortality, and a 45% reduction in the number of women with inadequate or no prenatal care. The benefits of WIC participation are strongest in women who participate in WIC for more than six months or two trimesters of their pregnancy."

The second study compared pregnancy outcomes for women in WIC to previous outcomes for the same women before they received supplementation:[8] "Participation in WIC is associated with a statistically significant reduction in the poorer outcomes of pregnancy; in particular, with 23% fewer low-birth-weight and very-low-birth-weight infants, fewer small-for-gestational-age infants, fewer premature infants, and fewer infant deaths."

Any young child, regardless of initial birth-weight and maternal nutrition, is at risk from postnatal nutritional deprivation. The human brain grows most rapidly during the earliest years of life. After the pre-school years, brain growth slows until

Table 7. *Women, Infants, and Children Special Supplemental Feeding Program: Summary of Findings of Seven Studies, 1976–1983*

Study	Mean WIC effect on birth weight
University of North Carolina, 1976	+43 grams (+136 grams in women on WIC for greater than six months)
Harvard University, 1978–1979	+122 grams
Massachusetts Department of Public Health Study, 1980	+23 grams (+110 grams in women on WIC for greater than six months)
Massachusetts Department of Public Health Follow-Up Study, 1982	+23.5 grams (+110 grams in women on WIC for greater than six months)
NTS Corporation, 1982	+96 to +116 grams
University of Oklahoma, 1982	+91 grams (+200 to 300 grams in "high risk" women)
Missouri Health Department, 1983	+ effect on birth weight

SOURCE: Developed by Dr. Eileen Kennedy from Kotelchuk, Milton. Testimony on the Special Supplemental Food Program for Women, Infants, and Children, Subcommittee on Nutrition, U.S. Senate, April 6, 1983.

maturity, when it stops.[9] Brain function is vulnerable to nutritional insult after this point, but size and structure are essentially established. The child deprived of adequate nutrition during the critical years of brain growth is at risk of cognitive and other developmental deficits.[10]

Other childhood risks from inadequate nutrition include delayed growth, or stunting, defined as height below the fifth percentile for a given sex and age; wasting, defined as weight below the fifth percentile for age or height;[11] and increased vulnerability to environmental toxins, including lead, which can affect the brain and compound the direct effects of malnutrition on intellectual development.[12] As at all ages, malnutrition in childhood can weaken resistance to infection. Poorly nourished youngsters are at risk of more frequent colds, ear infections, and other infectious diseases.[13] Thus the developmental hazards entailed in poor nutrition may be further compounded by absence from school and even curtailment of some childhood activities.

In fact, recent research suggests that functional impairment may result from poor childhood nutrition even in the absence of overt physical harm. Studies suggest that before easily measured changes in growth occur, and before the appearance of nutrition-related disease, a child's body may adapt to inadequate food by curtailing energy use. The implication is that a child who is poorly nourished may show no overt signs of impairment and yet be deprived of social and cognitive experiences which advance development. One expert suggests that in order to fully grasp the impact of poor nutrition on children, "we should be looking toward 'functional' measures as outcome variables."[14]

Loss of function also characterizes the effect of mild malnutrition on young and middle-aged adults. Reduced productivity at work and impaired social function are both potential outcomes. And of course adults of all ages are vulnerable to infection and deficiency diseases associated with malnutrition. In old age, the risks of malnutrition are heightened once again. In this period the impact of food on health maintenance and disease prevention is particularly crucial. Several factors determine the particular needs of elderly people. Among these are:

• Chronic conditions—the majority of elderly Americans (85% of those over 65) suffer at least one chronic condition that influences nutritional needs. Some ailments which are common among the elderly, such as hypertension, do not call for specific dietary treatment but rather for a generally high-nutrient, low-salt, low-calorie regimen. Other common ailments, such as diabetes, require more precise control over diet.[15]

• Deficiency diseases, which are common among old people, increase requirements for certain nutrients; calcium intake must be high to prevent osteoporosis, for example.[16]

• Some conditions of old age may impair digestion or absorption of nutrients, making the choice of nutrient-dense foods critical.[17]

• Old people, like the very young, are particularly susceptible to the effects of infection.[18]

Each of these factors makes it important that the elderly have access to high-quality diets. But old age entails a number of obstacles to acquisition of adequate food: difficulties in shopping and cooking, difficulty in chewing some foods, and lack of appetite due to social isolation and resultant depression can all interfere with nutritional health in old age. Furthermore, older people need fewer calories to fuel body function; since obesity entails risks, the old person must carefully plan and prepare his or her food intake. Finding food that meets all of these requirements may result in increased food costs. For the low-income elderly person, obtaining adequate nutrition may be problematic. As one expert on elderly nutrition wrote, "Poverty appears to be the main environmental determinant of inadequate nutrition among the elderly."[19]

The risks are serious for the old person unable to eat appropriately. An individual who is diabetic, for example, may suffer disability and shortened life as a result of malnutrition. But even without overt nutrition-related disease, the opportunity for any old person to experience and enjoy the prolonged life span possible in the United States today depends in part on adequate diet.

Nutritional Resources Available to the Poor

The definition of adequate diet is, of course, subject to significant debate in our society, involving both nutrition professionals and the general public. For purposes of simplicity, we will define an adequate diet in terms of the Recommended Dietary Allowances (RDA's) developed by the National Academy of Sciences.[20] In the discussion that follows, RDA's serve as the general standards against which the diets of the poor are evaluated.

The most comprehensive information on the diets available to poor Americans comes from three government surveys: the Ten-State Nutrition Survey, the National Health and Nutrition Examination Survey (NHANES), and the Nationwide Food Consumption Survey (NFCS). Unfortunately, none of these was conducted recently enough to provide data on what the poor eat now—given prevailing economic conditions and government policy. Because this is precisely the question with which we are concerned, our approach to the issue will be to look at what these surveys tell us, and then update that information based on available evidence about recent economic and policy changes.

The Ten-State Nutrition Survey was conducted by the United States Public Health Service between 1968 and 1970. The study population included more than 40,000 low-income individuals in ten geographically and economically diverse states. Among the information collected on each subject were levels of intake and body stores for several nutrients. The biochemical and dietary data gathered by the survey revealed, according to its director, that significant numbers of children, pregnant women, and elderly people had inadequate intake and depleted body stores of vitamins A and C, riboflavin, calcium, and other nutrients.[21]

The National Health and Nutrition Examination Survey is conducted periodically by the National Center for Health Statistics. A wide range of health and nutrition data is collected from a selected sample of Americans aged 6 to 74. So far three NHANES cycles have occurred: the first from 1971 to 1974; the second from 1976 to 1980; and the third, limited to the Hispanic population, from 1982 to 1984.

The first NHANES revealed a relationship between low income and inadequate intake of several nutrients. Greater percentages of poor individuals consumed inadequate calories, vitamin C, and iron.[22] NHANES II, from 1976 to 1980, produced similar findings.[23]

The Nationwide Food Consumption Survey (NFCS) is conducted periodically by the Department of Agiculture (USDA) to assess the eating habits of the American people. It produces data useful to the food industry; nutrition information is available as a byproduct of the process. The most recent NFCS, administered between 1977 and 1978, involved interviews with heads of 15,000 households, representing some 34,000 individuals of all ages in the 48 contiguous states. Questions covered not only dietary habits, but also household income, employment status of household head, race, and food expenditure levels.[24]

The study revealed two points of interest. First, it showed that diets of the poor had improved markedly between 1965–66, when the previous NFCS was conducted, and 1977–78. The U.S. Senate Select Committee on Hunger found that nutrition assistance programs, in place for ten years, were responsible for the difference.[25] Second, the study found that the poor still fared worse than the rest of the U.S. population, as the nutritional quality of diet varies directly with income. Those living at incomes below the poverty level consumed less, on the average, than the RDA's for food energy (calories), calcium, and iron. In fact, the study found that only 12% of households spending the money allotted by the food stamp program were able to meet RDA's.[26]

It is not entirely self-evident from these findings that the poor are deprived of adequate nutrition by inadequate resources. An alternative theory is that the poor lack the knowledge (and/or self-discipline) needed to make the best of limited but otherwise adequate funds. This analysis of the problem underlies the recent announcement by the USDA that a cookbook targeted to food stamp recipients, presenting nutritious meal plans, will help alleviate hunger in the United States.[27] Actually, however, the NFCS itself provided evidence to the contrary. It revealed that the poor actually purchase more nutrition per food dollar than other segments of the population.[28]

This, then, was the state of our understanding as of 1978. Government studies showed that poor diet and poor health were concentrated among poor people in the United States despite some gains from a decade of food assistance programs. We must now ask whether the situation has changed since the studies were completed.

It is an economic fact that it has gotten harder for the poor to purchase food since the end of the 70s. Food stamps are allotted to families based on a theoretical meal plan devised by the USDA, called the "thrifty food plan." When a family applies for food stamps, information about income and expenses is reviewed. If the family is determined eligible, stamps are allotted so as to bring their resources up to the thrifty-food-plan level for a family of their size. This process, which on paper seems a perfectly straightforward approach to meeting nutritional needs, does not, in reality, achieve that end. The basic problem is that the thrifty food plan was never intended to meet family nutrition requirements.

Since the initial development of the plan, a number of changes in the food stamp program have widened the gap between recipient resources and need: several categories of recipients have been ruled ineligible; restrictions have been placed on family expenses that can be deducted from income in setting benefit levels; increases in food stamp benefits are delayed when family income is diminished. Given these changes, a family with stable or even increased need may now have to purchase food with less than they had at the start of the decade. Furthermore, disproportionate inflation of certain nonfood expenses, particularly housing, energy, and medical care, has strained whatever discretionary funds poor families might once have used for food purchases.[29] Finally, a decreased proportion of those who are eligible for and in need of food stamps are presently receiving them.

The impact of decreased resources available to the poor is reflected in the rapid expansion of demand for emergency food over the past four years. The emergency food network—including food banks and the soup kitchens and food pantries they supply—has expanded in response to increased demand. While emergency food has been a critical stopgap, it is not a source of adequate, on-going nutrition for poor people.

During Task Force field investigations across the country, the physicians observed food preparation and ate meals in all kinds of emergency food agencies. They noted that the food tends to be overprocessed, that fresh fruits and vegetables and unrefined carbohydrates were rare, and that salt and fat were frequently excessive. Even where excellent meals were available, there were generally restrictions on how often an individual or family could turn to any one emergency site.

Two observations struck Task Force physicians. First, even food supplied by the government through its commodity distribution program is often nutritionally undesirable. The butter and cheese most widely distributed are high in sodium and fat content. These foods are potentially hazardous to individuals with hypertension, heart disease, and diabetes, all prevalent among poor Americans. Pediatricians were disturbed to find that honey, which can carry a strain of botulism that is dangerous (even potentially fatal) to infants under the age of one, was distributed by the USDA without even a label to warn parents of the hazard.

Second, the doctors frequently visited homes of old people suffering serious chronic illnesses, who were unable to afford diets appropriate to their needs. Medical instructions to "stay away from fried foods" or "restrict salt intake" were not and could not be complied with by people dependent on neighborhood charity, a daily home-delivered meal, or government commodities for their sustenance.

The evidence, therefore, indicates that things have worsened nutritionally for the poor since 1978. The poor have fewer resources for food purchase and often must rely on emergency food programs that are not able to provide adequate long-term nourishment.

Does Malnutrition Have an Impact on the Health of the Poor?

This brings us to the central question of this chapter: are there actually measurable impairments in the health of poor people in the United States as a result of hunger? To consider this question we will look at information of four kinds. First, we will examine what is known about birth outcomes among poor women. Statistics on infant mortality and birth-weight are widely used indicators of the general health of a society. They allow us to compare the well-being of the poor to that of other groups in this country. We will look next at information on the growth achieved by different groups of children. A high proportion of children who are too short or too thin, stunted or wasted in the technical terminology, indicates malnutrition. We will examine measures of "function": how individuals accomplish their daily activities, which experts increasingly feel is an important indicator of subtle nutrition effects. Finally, we will look at available data on morbidity and mortality. Information on a range of nutrition-related illnesses and on the causes of death after infancy among different social groups will be discussed.

The Infant Mortality Rate (IMR) is the number of children per thousand live births who die before the age of one in a given population. In the United States the IMR is determined annually by the federal government, based on compilation of records from all states. IMR is used internationally as an indicator of the general health of a population, particularly its children. Because it is calculated similarly all over the world, it provides a useful basis for international comparisons.

IMR does not reflect nutritional status exclusively or even primarily. Rather, it reflects a complex of health variables, including nutrition but also general standard of living, sanitation, maternal health habits, and access to preventive and curative medical care.[30]

Compared to other industrialized nations, the United States does not do well in guaranteeing the health of its newborns. Our national IMR, 10.9 per thousand live births in 1983, is behind that of comparably wealthy nations. In 1982, the last year for which many international figures are available, the U.S. rate of 11.2 ranked seventeenth in the world, behind most of western Europe, Japan, Australia, Singapore, and Hong Kong.[31]

We have no precise way of relating birth outcomes to poor women specifically. Birth and death certificates, from which infant mortality rates are determined, do not contain information about income. They do, however, contain information about race and place of residence. Since non-whites are more likely to be poor in the United States and residence is, in many cases, correlated with income, these two items serve as proxies for income when the birth outcomes of those with different resources are at issue.[32]

Race-specific IMR's for the United States tell us that black infants are about twice as likely as whites to die within the first year of life.[33] The black infant mortality rate of 19.6 per thousand is comparable to those in Cuba and Costa Rica, countries lacking many of the resources that we have to insure the health of American infants.[34]

Revealing infant mortality data is also drawn from small

geographic areas, for which relatively precise economic and social characterization is possible. In New York City, for example, the range of infant mortality rates among the city's 30 health districts is striking: from 5.8 per thousand live births in the Sunset Park section of Brooklyn, and 7.5 per thousand in Manhattan's "Silk Stocking" district (rates among the lowest in the world), to 25.6 per thousand in Central Harlem, and 25.3 in Brownsville, both predominantly black, impoverished communities.[35]

When the Physician Task Force visited Houston, it was provided with similar community statistics by local health officials. Infant mortality rates in 1982 ranged from 23.54 in the Riverside Health Center area to less than 10.0 per thousand in the Sunnyside area.[36]

Within a given community, variations in IMR over time may reflect changes in the economic circumstances of residents. From 1981 to 1982, IMR's increased in eleven states; for nonwhite rates went up in 13 states. While some fluctuation in state rates is to be expected for an outcome as complex as infant mortality, these increases occurred in the face of a stated national goal of improving birth outcomes for all Americans and reducing discrepancies between social groups.[37]

Some data is available which reveal changes in IMR from year to year in particular communities. In several poor neighborhoods of Boston, infant mortality rose 46% from 1981 to 1982.[38] In Pittsburgh, which has the highest black infant mortality rate of any city, the 1982 rate was 29.7 per thousand, up from 22.8 in 1981. In the same year white infant mortality in that city was under 10.[39]

These local figures, while extreme, do not seem to be isolated statistical aberrations. The U.S. IMR, like international rates, has shown a steady downward trend over the past two decades. However, Professor Samuel Shapiro of Johns Hopkins University School of Public Health points out that the decrease in IMR for the period 1983–84 (based on figures for the first half of each year) was only 0.9%; the comparable figure for the 1981–82 period was 4.3%. Dr. Shapiro suggests that the downward trend of the national IMR is leveling off.[40] Since the United States has a great deal of ground to cover to bring our rates down to the levels of other industrialized nations, this is a disturbing trend.

Infant mortality is not the only birth outcome that reveals poor maternal health and nutrition. As discussed earlier, most infant mortality in the United States is associated with low birth-weight. Even low-birth-weight babies who survive are subject to a wide range of impairments (see Table 6).[41] In some ways, the proportion of babies born too small is more revealing than is infant mortality. IMR reflects medical success at saving high-risk infants as well as prenatal health. Newly developed techniques in neonatal medicine save a high enough proportion of low-birth-weight babies to somewhat obscure the true impact of inadequate prenatal nutrition and care. A report by the Child Health Outcomes Project of the University of North Carolina comments:[42] "In 1982, the national LBW ratio was 6.8% (National Center for Health Statistics, 1984). The U.S. holds the best record for birth-weight-specific survival [that is, a child of a given birth-weight has a greater chance of surviving here than elsewhere]. *However, we also hold an unenviable record for having the worst birth-weight distribution of any industrialized nation* [emphasis supplied]."

Low birth-weight, like infant mortality, is distributed unevenly throughout the U.S. population. According to the Child Health Outcomes Project:[43] "Black babies are more than twice as likely as white to be born low-birth-weight [12.4% in 1982 as compared to 5.6% for whites]. In the past decade the black/white ratio for low birth-weight has increased from 2.03 in 1970 to 2.19 in 1981."

In New York City, where community figures are available for low birth-weight as well as infant mortality, the variation among communities is again quite sharp. The highest figure, 16.3% in 1982, was for Central Harlem; the lowest, 5.4% in the same year, was for the affluent East Side. In that year, the percentage of low-birth-weight babies rose in 11 out of the city's 30 health districts.[44]

In Nashville, Tennessee, the Physician Task Force was presented with a report on birth outcomes by the Maternal and Infant Care Program at Nashville General Hospital. It cited an increase from 1981 to 1982, and again from 1982 to 1983 among *both* blacks and whites in the area. (See Table 8.) Low-birth-weight rates for the hospital's own patients, poorer than the city population as a whole, were 12.9% and 14.4% for whites and blacks respectively.[45] Aside from the high rates prevalent in both racial groups, it is important to note that the difference between them is significantly reduced when poor whites are compared to poor blacks. These figures suggest that it is not some biological correlate of race, but rather income and the correlates of poverty, that explain birth outcome differences in the United States.

Data on the growth of children in the United States reveal parallel socioeconomic variation. Of the various indicators that characterize the health and nutrition status of American children, anthropometric data—measurements of height, weight, and other body dimensions—are the most widely available. Height and weight measurements are routinely performed in well-baby and well-child medical examinations. Thus, there is an enormous body of material available to researchers for analysis.

The analysis of anthropometric data depends on the existence of norms to which the findings on any individual child can be compared. When a physician takes the height and weight of a child, (s)he records these figures on a chart which graphs

Table 8. *Low-Birth-Weight Rates for Whites and Non-whites in Metropolitan Nashville, 1981–1983*

(Percent)

Population and date	Total	White	Non-white
Babies born in Davidson County (metropolitan Nashville)			
1983	9.4	7.4	14.2
1982	8.8	7.0	13.1
1981	8.5	6.7	12.7
Babies born at Metropolitan Nashville General Hospital			
1981	13.5	12.9	14.4

SOURCES: State Center for Health Statistics; Tennessee Department of Health and Environment, Metropolitan Nashville General Hospital.

growth over time (see Figure 33). The chart also permits comparison with other children of the same age and sex. A 3-year-old girl who is ranked in, say, the 50th weight percentile, is heavier than 50% of other 3-year-old girls. Extensive measurements have been done on American children to derive these norms. A physician looking at the chart of our 3-year-old wants to know two things: first, is she within the expected range for her age and sex; second, is her growth following a fairly smooth curve upward over time. While growth occurs at different rates throughout childhood, the physician would never expect to see a sustained straight line or a sharply downward curve.[46]

Generally, children falling above the 95th percentile for weight relative to height, or below the fifth percentile for either weight or height, are watched carefully. The measurements may reflect a genetically determined growth pattern that is perfectly normal for that individual child. Alternatively, it may reflect nutritional or other health problems. Examination of the child's records and life circumstances may clarify which is the case.

When growth figures are looked at for a population or subpopulation of children, much more is revealed. The larger the size of the group, the more one would expect its growth pattern to follow the normal distribution for American children as a whole. Approximately 5% of children should fall below the fifth percentile, 10% below the tenth, and so on. While some fluctuations are to be expected, two kinds of aberrations from these norms are of concern. As discussed earlier, these are:

• Wasting, defined as weight below the fifth percentile for height and age, indicative of acute and recent malnutrition.

• Stunting, which is said to occur when more than 5% of children in any sizable group fall below the fifth percentile for height. This is indicative of moderate, long-term malnutrition.

Research conducted all over the United States among children of all ethnic and racial groups reveals that poverty is associated with impaired growth. The following are summaries of the findings of several of these investigations:

Fig. 33. *Chart for Appraising Physical Growth of Girls from Birth to Six Months*

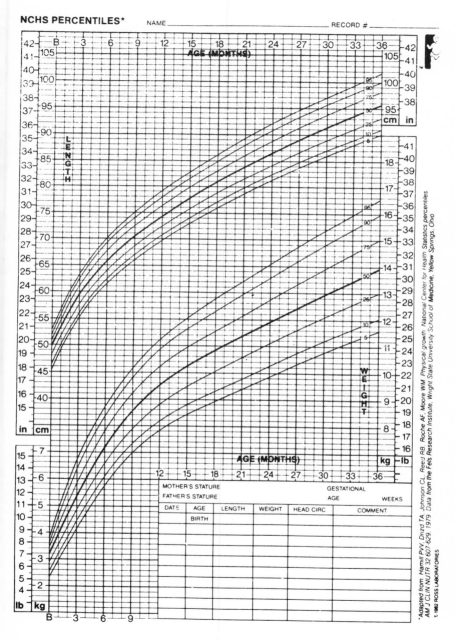

Fig. 34. *Children in the Lowest (5th) Growth Percentile, Expected vs. Observed, Boston, 1983*

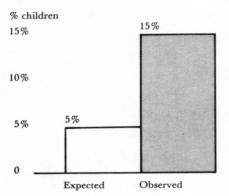

Source: Boston City Hospital.

Fig. 35. *Massachusetts Nutrition Survey, 1983: Low Height for Age by Poverty Level*

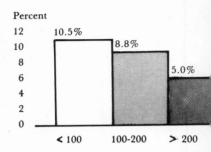

The percent of children found to be stunted the Massachusetts Nutrition Survey was hig est for those with income below the pove level.
Source: Mass. Dept. of Public Health, "19 Massachusetts Survey Final Report," Oc 1983.

• Physicians at Boston City Hospital recorded height and weight measurements for every child coming into the emergency room for a one-week period during 1983. Altogether they examined 413 children, including 231 children under the age of six. Nearly 15% were below the fifth percentile for weight or height.[47] (See Figure 34.)

• At Cook County Hospital, charts of patients in the Comprehensive Care Clinic, an outpatient pediatric program, were reviewed. Twenty-one percent were found to be below the tenth percentile for height. To follow up on the review, given this distressing finding, children under 2 who visited the clinic were measured. Of 325 children measured, 99 or 30.5% were below the tenth percentile for height or weight.[48]

• In Illinois, the state Nutrition Surveillance System indicates that among low-income children, those "under one year of age are at greatest risk of being stunted: 17.1%, representing approximately 8,100 children in Illinois."[49]

• In New Mexico, a study of the 18,000 women, infants, and children enrolled in the state WIC program revealed widespread underweight among infants and children as well as pregnant women, and stunting in infants and children.[50] (See Table 9.)

• The Massachusetts Nutrition Survey, mandated by the state's legislature to assess the health status of low-income children and carried out by the state Department of Public Health, weighed and measured 1,429 children from age 6 months to age 5 years, 11 months in 20 communities around the state. State-wide, 9.8% of the children were found to be below the fifth percentile for height. In total, 18.1% of children evaluated were found to show some indicator of chronic nutritional deficiency. Within the population, income level was inversely related to a finding of nutritional deficiency (see Figure 35). At a given income level, for reasons the researchers did not fully understand, white children were found to show greater evidence of malnutrition than non-whites.[51]

In addition to these state and local studies there is one relatively up-to-date national study of child growth. The Center for Disease Control (CDC) collects data annually on children from 32 states. These states provide information on children enrolled in publicly funded programs that involve health screening: WIC; Early Periodic Screening, Diagnosis, and

Table 9. *Percentage of Underweight Pregnant Women and of Underwight or Stunted Infant and Children Among 18,000 New Mexico WIC Participants, 1984*

Condition	Pregnant women	Infants	Children
Underweight	18%	24.6%	23%
Stunted	n.a.	13.0%	36%

SOURCE: Health Services Division, New Mexico Department of Health and Environment.

Treatment (known as EPSDT); and Maternal and Infant Health programs. The most recent data available from this system are from 1982. Findings include the following:[52] "Between 6 and 16% of children from birth to four years, depending on age and race, are below the fifth percentile in height for age. The groups at highest risk are Hispanic and Native American four-year-olds, but all racial groupings under age four showed higher than expected proportions of children below the fifth percentile for height."

These rates for malnutrition among different age and race categories of low-income children, derived from the CDC's sample population, can be applied to the entire population of low-income American children. This extrapolation results in an estimate of 500,000 children across the United States who are experiencing growth delays and other impairments generally associated with inadequate diet.

Size is not, of course, of any particular health significance in and of itself; a person who is genetically predisposed to be short is not in poor health compared to others. The significance of these findings lies not in what they reveal about height per se, but rather in what they indicate about nutritional deficits that underlie population-based stunting.

Recent studies conducted in developing countries suggest that long before a child's growth is clearly affected, his or her body begins to conserve energy stores by curtailing function.[53] This finding underlies concern expressed by many researchers that our tendency to rely on easily acquired anthropometric data for nutritional information may be obscuring the true extent of the problem. They argue that only by measuring function can we truly assess the impact of mild malnutrition on American children.

Functional indicators have been defined as "diagnostic tests to determine the sufficiency of host nutriture to permit cells, tissues, organs, and anatomical systems or the host him/herself to perform optimally the intended, nutrient-dependent biological function."[54] For a child, optimum performance includes a range of physical, socail, and intellectual activities. Function, unlike growth, is also an indicator that can give us information about adult members of the population. In adults, optimum performance includes a variety of occupational and social activities. The question before us is the extent to which function, embodied in these activities, is impaired by poor nutrition among low-income Americans.

Increasing evidence points to the impact of nutrition on function even in the earliest stages of life. One study suggests that even an infant who appears absolutely normal, who shows no overt physical signs of poor health or growth, may be harmed by poor prenatal nutrition. In Hartford, Connecticut, a study was done on the impact of poor maternal nutrition on the neurobehavioral development of newborns. The study found that: "Low maternal energy intake and weight gain were associated with poorer performance on several components of the Brazelton Neonatal Assessment Scale [a widely used instrument for evaluation of infants]. . . . It was also of interest to us that maternal weight gain in the second trimester only was associated with these changes in infant performance."[55] The variables measured on this scale include reflexes and motor performance. The cut-off point used to define "low weight gain" in the study was 15 pounds.

Another study looked at the impact of vitamin B$_6$ deficiency, very common among pregnant women in America, on infants. This Indiana study linked low Apgar scores in infants of normal birth-weight with the deficiency.[56] Apgars are measures of cardiorespiratory function used routinely to characterize infant well-being at birth.

Other research efforts assess the impact of direct nutritional deprivation of the child on his/her behavior. A 1982 study conducted in both Guatemala and the United States (in order to ensure that biological rather than cultural phenomena were measured) found that, despite some apparent differences in the way the two groups responded to cognitive challenges, iron deficiency clearly affected the performance of both groups.[57]

A study conducted in Syracuse, New York, found differences in performance measures in infants depending on iron levels, even when *none* of those tested was clinically anemic. The results were as follows:[58] "The administration of iron produced a significant increase in the Mental Development Index scores (+ 21.6) in the infants with iron deficiency but no significant change in the scores of infants with iron sufficiency (+ 6.2 points) or only iron depletion (+ 5.6 points). It is concluded that iron deficiency, even in the absence of anemia, results in biochemical alterations that impair behavior in infants."

Anemia is quite prevalent among poor children in America. This finding takes on enormous significance in light of that prevalence. It suggests that not only children diagnosed as lacking in iron, but many more who would never be designated as deficient by current medical practice, are functionally harmed by low-iron diets.

In addition to studies showing the detrimental effect of inadequate nutrition on function, children who are supplemented nutritionally fare better on functional assessments than their non-supplemented peers. Several studies conducted outside the United States support this conclusion.[59] In this country, a research project in Louisiana compared 27 pairs of siblings on a battery of cognitive and behavioral measures.[60] In each case, one of the pair had been provided with WIC supplementation during the third trimester of pregnancy and at least through the first year of life; the other in each pair received WIC supplementation only after the age of one. The researchers reported that "results indicated that the prenatally supplemented group showed significant enhancement of most intellectual and behavioral measures in the current home and school setting, including IQ, attention span, visual-motor synthesis, and school grade-point average, when compared with the group supplemented later."

Studies also reveal the functional impairment of adults who are poorly nourished. One body of research concerns work productivity in relation to nutrition status. Among groups for whom this relationship has been established are sugar cane workers, workers in an assembly plant, and farm workers. In each case, productivity or activity level increased with improved nutritional status.[61]

These findings on functional impairment are significant because they get at the low-level malnutrition some consider to be endemic among the poor in America. The studies discussed above do not, generally, compare poor and rich population groups directly. Rather, they compare function in individuals with different nutritional resources. Given what we know about the relationship between nutritional resources and income in the United States, we can extrapolate from the findings of these studies to answer the question we raised earlier. Available evidence indicates that the poor suffer functional impairment as a result of nutritional deprivation.

The most extreme expressions of malnutrition, in contrast to some of the subtle functional indicators discussed above, are disease and mortality. Data on morbidity and mortality also reveal differences between poor Americans and their better-off peers, from childhood on. Historically, studies have shown that poor children experience more illness and become more severely affected when ill than other children.[62] Among illnesses for which current data are available, findings on iron deficiency anemia are extensive.

Anemia is the term used to define a condition in which there is an abnormally low concentration of hemoglobin in the blood. Hemoglobin, the component of the red blood cell that carries oxygen throughout the body, requires iron; most anemia in children is caused by deficiency of dietary iron. Iron deficiency anemia may cause a range of effects, depending on severity. A child who is anemic may be listless and tired and may experience headache or dizziness. Chronic anemia is associated with slowed growth and weight gain, mental and physical sluggishness, palpitations and enlargement of the heart, and impaired immune response.[63] It may be, as discussed earlier, associated with distinctly impaired performance on cognitive and other functional measures.

Because anemia is one of the medical conditions that makes a low-income child eligible for WIC supplementation, WIC programs across the country have data on the prevalence of anemia among those they screen. Since any low-income woman or child may be screened for WIC, such data provide information about the prevalence of anemia generally among these high-risk groups.

The Minneapolis Health Department analyzed screening data

for their program: they found that 13% of infants, 21% of children, and 33% of pregnant women among the poor of that city were anemic.[64] The State of New Mexico, studying the state WIC population, found that 40% of pregnant women, 18% of infants, and 33% of children were anemic.[65] The Illinois Nutrition Surveillance System found that 15.8% of low-income two- to five-year-old children tested were anemic. Applying this rate to the entire population of poor children in the state, the study staff estimates that 20,000 children within that age range are at high risk in Illinois.[66] The Massachusetts Nutrition Survey ascertained hematocrits (a common means of identifying anemia) whenever possible in children they evaluated across the state. They found that more than 12% of low-income children tested were anemic.[67] This finding was, if anything, conservative given that all children tested were enrolled in preventive health programs; other low-income children in the state, lacking these services, are at greater risk.

The most significant data available on this question come from the CDC surveillance system. The CDC found that in 1982, 7% of children under 6 were anemic. While findings differed somewhat by age group and by the method of testing used to identify anemia cases, black children showed consistently higher rates of anemia than whites. For the 6- to 9-year-old age group, 18.1% of black children compared to 8.1% of whites had hemoglobin levels below the fifth percentile.[68] This is, again, a conservative finding, since all of the children in the sample were enrolled in preventive health and/or nutrition programs. They represent a relatively low-risk population compared to other poor children.

The outcomes of the CDC's 1981 survey are consistent with results of the 1976–80 NHANES. NHANES revealed that poor children generally have lower red-blood counts and lower hemoglobin levels than other American children.[69] The CDC findings indicate that this discrepancy has not been resolved since NHANES was completed.

Other, more dramatic illnesses which affect small groups of children seem to be associated with poverty and nutritional status. In 1982, a group of Boston physicians working in clinics that serve low-income children reported that they were seeing cases of failure-to-thrive, the medical term for a complex of symptoms including significant growth and developmental delays. Many of these were children from families that had recently lost benefits from one or more federal programs. Historically, failure-to-thrive has been seen as an outgrowth of severely distorted family dynamics, and in many cases as a reflection of child neglect. The Boston physicians were struck that these distorted relationships did not seem to characterize the families whose children they were treating. Lack of food was a critical problem the doctors perceived. They felt that neither medical nor psychological treatment would provide long-term solutions to these problems; restoration of benefits on which these families relied for food buying seemed to them a critical part of therapy.[70]

At Chicago's Cook County Hospital, physicians tried to quantify the increase they felt they were seeing in failure-to-thrive. They documented a 24% increase in admissions to the hospital for this condition between 1981 and 1983. They also found increased admissions for diarrhea and dehydration, both serious nutrition-related conditions in children.[71]

Another Chicago study has revealed an unexpectedly high prevalence of serious nutrition-related problems among poor children. Dr. Howard Levy, Chairman of Pediatrics at Chicago's Mt. Sinai Hospital, is the principal investigator on a long-term prospective study of children at high risk of child abuse. In the course of examining the health and the medical records of a large population of low-income children, he has found a number of "spin-offs"—conditions that are not inherently related to child abuse but are occurring in the population at risk. The first of these spin-offs is increased failure-to-thrive. The second is an increase in the number of children he sees with "water intoxication," which results from consumption of formula or milk which has been diluted to make it stretch. This is done by parents hoping to allay at least the superficial symptoms of hunger in their children. Excess water, however, is toxic to the small infant; the immature kidney is not able to handle the extra burden produced by very diluted formula, and imbalance of body chemistry results, causing illness and, potentially, death. Third, Dr. Levy notes an "inordinate incidence of sudden infant death syndrome (SIDS)" in the study population. Dr. Levy is careful to emphasize that, while SIDS is not well-understood biologically, it is not a euphemism for child abuse; medical investigation can distinguish between a SIDS death and a death by abuse. The connection Dr. Levy does perceive is between poverty and SIDS. He comments, "It is impressive that in the study population, the number of cases of sudden infant death syndrome increased significantly over the period of the project [1977–82]."[72] Nationally, the rate of SIDS deaths is twice as high among blacks (8 per thousand live births) as it is among whites (4 per thousand).[73]

Internationally, the diseases most identified with malnutrition are marasmus, which is severe protein-calorie malnutrition, and kwashiorkor, a condition caused by lack of protein but not necessarily calories. Marasmus causes a number of overt physical symptoms, most notably severe wasting.[74] The Ethiopian children seen in photographs of famine are marasmic. Children with kwashiorkor generally have thin arms and legs, revealing muscle wasting, but swollen bellies. Lack of protein causes edemic tissue swelling and the rounded abdomen reflects this. Other symptoms include loss of hair, changes in hair and skin pigmentation, skin rash, and in some cases liver enlargement. Kwashiorkor often occurs in a cycle with infection: the poorly nourished child is susceptible to infection; when infection sets in, nutritional needs are intensified while appetite and ability to absorb nutrients may be decreased. The resultant lowered intake of nutrients further increases vulnerability to disease. This cycle of disease and malnutrition is endemic and devastating in the Third World.[75]

It is not, however, typical of children, even relatively malnourished children, in the industrial world. The prevailing wisdom taught in medical schools in this country is that marasmus in the U.S. is found among adult alcoholics or others who, for individual reasons, do not take advantage of resources available to them.

Members of the Physician Task Force learned that in several parts of the country doctors observe and treat marasmus and kwashiorkor. While these reports are rare, the occurrence of these conditions at all is unexpected.

Three such reports came from the Southwest. Representatives of two Native American groups, the Navajo Nation and the Albuquerque Area Indian Council, told the Task Force that among children they serve, cases of kwashiorkor occur regularly although not frequently.[76,77] In the Rio Grande Valley of Texas, the nutritionist at Su Clinica Familiar, a highly respected health care facility, reported that she has observed both marasmus and kwashiorkor among her patients.[78] While her report was presented as personal observation rather than careful scientific study, this nutritionist has worked for several years in Third World countries and is familiar with the symptoms of the conditions she reported to the Task Force.

The best-documented evidence of profound malnutrition was presented to the Task Force by Dr. Katherine Christoffel of Northwestern University Medical School. Dr. Christoffel, who is chairperson of the committee on nutrition of the Illinois chapter of the American Academy of Pediatrics, has recently documented 16 cases of marasmus among patients under 18 months of age in the population she treats.[79] She defines the condition by the internationally accepted standard: weight less than 60% of the 50th percentile for age and sex.[80] This standard places a baby well below the fifth percentile demarcation for wasting, discussed earlier. Dr. Christoffel makes two significant points about her findings. First, diagnosis of these severely malnourished childred did not occur immediately when they came into contact with the pediatric medical care system. American physicians are not well prepared to look for conditions which are far more common in impoverished countries. Second, her hospital is only one of several in Chicago that treat poor children and it is not the hospital that treats the poorest segment of the population. She is concerned, therefore, that there may be a larger number of American children who are experiencing severe protein-calorie malnutrition while their problem goes undiagnosed.

Dr. Christoffel makes a further point, echoing Dr. Levy and others who spoke to the Task Force about low-income children experiencing diseases of deprivation. "These are not," she says, "cases of child abuse. Certainly the families in which these drastic conditions arise are troubled families. But frequently they lack the basic material supports that are absolutely necessary for raising children. A teen-aged mother with two children, no transportation, and no baby sitter, who goes to the WIC office and is told she has the wrong form and should come back in six weeks with social security cards for her babies, is hard-pressed to find a way to feed her children."[81]

Death among children is a rare event. Generally, given survival through infancy, human beings live into adulthood. So childhood mortality statistics do not provide a major body of data from which socioeconomic patterns can be discerned. A further difficulty, discussed earlier in terms of birth outcomes, is that death certificates do not include information about income directly. What data are available, however, do reveal differences in the mortality rates of children from different economic strata. These discrepancies are likely to reflect nutritional differences.

A study by Robert Mare, reported in the *American Journal of Public Health*, revealed a sharp difference in mortality rates of American children of different economic groups by examining data initially collected for other purposes. Because the data collection was not designed for research on child mortality, Mare was unable to identify the precise causes of differential rates. His own analysis suggested that most of the difference was due to deaths from accidents. However, parallel studies completed in other countries, which Mare cites, were able to identify differences for a variety of causes of death, including nutrition-related diseases, among children in different social classes.[82]

A study conducted in Maine examined death records for children in that state from 1976 to 1980. On a case-by-case basis, these records were matched with records on participation of families in government assistance programs available to the poor, so that the poverty status of every child who died could be evaluated. The finding was striking: poor children were, on the average, three times as likely to die as other children. The major difference for children under age 4 was in disease-related deaths, the category most clearly linked to nutritional status. The ratio of deaths of poor versus non-poor children in this category was 3.5 to 1. This difference did not reflect any influence of race on mortality, since the population of Maine is almost 99% white.[83]

While data on nutrition-related disease and mortality among children is relatively sparse, malnutrition among poor adults has more revealing long-term consequences. Hypertension, diabetes, and cardiovascular disease are common among poor American adults and endemic within some groups. These diseases reflect lifetime nutritional inadequacy. Research consistently reveals discrepancies in the prevalence of these conditions between income and racial groups in the United States.[84]

Confirming what is known from research in past years, the Physician Task Force visits around the country yielded a considerable body of clinical information about smaller populations of adults affected by malnutrition. Nevertheless, it is difficult to draw far-reaching conclusions from reports on small clinic populations and their disease profiles.

One of the more significant observations reported to the Task Force involved a reported increase in tuberculosis incidence in Chicago. Tuberculosis has, historically, been closely linked to poor nutrition. Dr. Jorge Prieto, Chairman of the Department of Family Practice at Cook County Hospital and President-designate of the Chicago Board of Health, presented the Task Force with both the statistics on TB in the population he serves and his own views on the recurrence of the disease:[85]

"Here at Cook County Hospital what we face daily reflects what the poor and the hungry in our city have to contend with. What we find worries us. For the year 1982, our Division of Pulmonary Medicine had a total of 280 patients admitted with tuberculosis. Of these, 168 were new cases; 82 needed admission for retreatment and 13 were repeat admissions. For the year 1983 . . . we had a total of 368 admissions for tuberculosis. That represented a 32% increase in a major disease and one that accurately reflects on the quality of life in this industrial and developed society. Of these 368 human beings, 247 were new patients."

More revealing data on adult health comes from death certificates, which tell us how many people in what segments of the population die of nutrition-related causes. Mortality statistics are useful as a direct indicator of serious nutrition problems. Since they are gathered in the same way from year to year, they allow us to explore trends in the prevalence of these diseases over time. They also provide some information on the lives and nutritional status of populations. If, for example, we learn that diabetes is a major cause of death among Native American people in their forties and fifties, we can make an educated guess that middle-aged members of this population are experiencing considerable diabetes-related disability.

Death rates are calculated annually for age, sex, and race cohorts by the National Center for Health Statistics. The preeminent causes of death for all American adults are cardiovascular diseases (heart disease and strokes), cancers, respiratory diseases, accidents, and diabetes.[86] Of these, all but accidents and some respiratory diseases which primarily reflect occupational exposures (chronic obstructive lung diseases) have some relationship to nutrition. Clearest links exist with cardiovascular disease, for which diet is often a significant risk factor; infectious respiratory disease; and diabetes.

As with infant mortality, we have no precise way of dividing Americans according to income in order to determine how different economic groups fare. We can look at the experiences of different racial groups. Since blacks are more likely than whites to be poor, differences between racial groups suggest differences between income groups. For the nutrition-related causes of death we find the following black/white ratios: cardiovascular disease, 1.47; pneumonia and influenza, 1.37; diabetes, 2.21.[87]

Black cancer rates, which may be affected by nutrition depending of the particular form of cancer, are also higher that white. These statistics, while crude indicators of economic group differences, do suggest that poverty is highly correlated with increased risk of mortality from nutrition-related disease.

We can also compare death rates of different racial groups at different ages to see how their relative risk changes throughout various stages of life. When age-specific death rates are compared, we find that the greatest differences between blacks and whites occur during the first year of life, when death rates for blacks are approximately twice those of whites. During childhood and early adulthood the differences are significantly reduced, until the ages of 35–44, when the rates are again almost double for blacks. This disparity tapers off somewhat in old age, the experience of the two groups becoming once again more similar.[88] What is striking about this pattern of differences is that blacks, the group more likely to be poor, experience higher death rates at the points in life when individuals are more vulnerable to the hazards of malnutrition. Clearly these data do not reflect poor nutrition as the only critical factor. They are, nonetheless, suggestive.

The Correlates of Poor Nutrition

Two further issues must be considered. First, coincident with changes in government programs that provide food have been changes in programs that make it possible for many to obtain medical care. Thus, in addition to finding themselves more vulnerable—more at risk of ill-health because of nutritional lacks—more Americans are going without preventive health care and are less able to pay for medical treatment when they do become sick.

Table 10 presents statistics on immunization rates among children at school entry, a major component of any adequate preventive system and therefore a good indicator of the availability of crucial programs.[89] The number of preschoolers who had been immunized against DPT in 1982, the higher year cited in Table 10, was already down 10% from 1970. A similar decline occurred for polio.

Table 10. *Percentage of U.S. Children Immunized, 1982–1983*

Immunization	1982	1983	Percent change
measles	98%	89%	−9%
rubella	97	89	−8
mumps	92	90	−2
polio	98	90	−8
diphtheria/tetanus/ pertussis	98	94	−4

Declines have occurred also in the number of children screened for lead-paint poisoning, another curcial preventive measure. Here, too, the lack of preventive care interacts synergistically with inadequate nutrition, since children with low intake of iron or calcium are at greater risk of intoxication from ingested lead. Precise data on screening is difficult to obtain, since reporting that was once obligatory became voluntary on the part of local programs just as federal funds were cut. Programs that still report to the CDC show lead screening down about 35% in the United States from 1981 to 1982.[90]

Just as birth outcomes have been associated with the qualtiy of nutrition, another important factor in infant health is availability of prenatal care. A survey conducted by the Children's Defense Fund in 1983 found that "over the past three years, there has been a disturbing nationwide decrease in the percentage of women receiving prenatal care during the first three months of pregnancy and rise in the percentage of women receiving late or no prenatal care."[91] Lack of prenatal care available to poor women was linked in a recent Boston study to increased infant mortality in some of that city's neighborhoods.[92]

Changes in Medicare and Medicaid regulations, increased health care costs, and reduced funding for local health care agencies that serve the poor at low cost have all contributed to decreased access to medical care for the poor. One final result, cited by many clinicians during Task Force field visits, is that patients seek care later in the course of illness, when their problems are more serious.

A second issue which complicates the link between nutrition and disease is the interaction of both with stress. Hunger itself can operate as a physiological stressor. It is also clear that stress can result from the efforts poor people must make to acquire food when they are destitute. Moreover, the shame experienced over the inability to provide for one's family can become a serious psychological burden with corresponding physiological consequences.

Throughout the country, the Physician Task Force heard poor people, especially parents, describe intense feelings of depression, failure, and despair. An ex-steelworker who met the Task

Force with a group of unemployed workers at its union hall outside Houston, Texas, described his feeling of hopelessness, of going to sleep at night wanting not to wake up. Unemployed men in Peoria told the Task Force they had seriously considered suicide in the face of their inability to feed their children.

While personal testimony like this is moving, it is also significant from a health perspective. The reported misery and depression are risk factors for disease. They can contribute to a range of illnesses, many of which are also associated with poor nutrition and other aspects of poverty. In many cases it is difficult to sort out the relative contribution made by overt physical impairment, and by psychosocial stress associated with hunger, in assessing disease causality.

The data we have discussed on poverty, malnutrition, and ill-health is not always easy to assess. There are gaps we would like to see filled and relationships that we can only guess at rather than prove. Lack of baseline data for many problems makes it hard to pinpoint trends over time. Nonetheless certain facts are clear:

• Infants of poor mothers die more frequently. They are at greater risk of low birth-weight and later health impairment.

• As a group, poor children are less likely to be adequately nourished and more likely to suffer growth failure than their better-off peers.

• Poor children are at greater risk of death from malnutrition-related diseases; some American children are not protected even from severe malnutrition, including marasmus and kwashiorkor.

• Low-income adults are at greater risk of certain nutrition-related diseases and face significantly greater likelihood of dying at relatively early ages than other Americans.

Given these facts, the question of appropriate response to hunger in America becomes one of policy, rather than one of science; it is for society and not researchers to resolve.

Dr. Irwin Rosenberg, Director of the Clinical Nutrition Research Center at the University of Chicago and President of the American Society for Clinical Nutrition, testified before Congress about the choices that face us given the present level of information. He asked Congress to consider at what point we should decide that the time has come to address hunger aggressively and decisively. He reviewed much of the data we have discussed and then commented that he did not think we could afford to wait, since public inaction places the health and well-being of many Americans in jeopardy.[93]

Based on the observations of the Physician Task Force all over the country, our review of medical literature, and data on the diets and health status of the poor, we share Dr. Rosenberg's perspective. There is harm being done already. As a matter of public policy, we cannot wait for the perfect study before we put an end to hunger in this country.

5. HUNGER AS THE RESULT OF GOVERNMENT POLICIES

The recent and swift return of hunger to America can be traced in substantial measure to clear and conscious policies of the federal government. Some would argue that the role of government in this regard is self-evident. Since we are a wealthy nation, and since other wealthy nations have employed the mechanism of government to eliminate hunger as a serious problem, our failure to do so speaks to the manner in which we fail to use government to address this problem in our nation.

To others the contention that government created the hunger problem we currently have runs counter to a belief that the chief responsibility of government is to promote the general welfare of people.

But whether one is shocked or complacent about the analysis, the evidence is compelling that the hunger epidemic facing our nation today is largely the result of policy decisions—some recent, some made during the past decade or earlier. In this chapter we will set out the evidence which leads to this analysis.

Three factors, each related to government policy, came into play which together precipitated and worsened the present hunger problem. The first is the weakness of America's safety net; the second is the impact of the recession, with increasing poverty and unemployment; the third is the impact of cutbacks in federal nutrition and income support programs at the time when the other two factors were having their greatest impact.

Weaknesses in America's Safety Net

America's system of aid to its more vulnerable citizens has fundamental flaws. In comparison to other industrialized nations of the world, we do not provide an adequate margin of safety and security. Examination of a variety of indices, from preventive health care to hospital coverage, from food assistance programs to income supports, reveals that economically vulnerable people in the United States do not have the protection provided by many nations which have fewer resources than our own.

Several issues will be examined which illustrate this point: many poor people in this nation receive no assistance at all; many who do are forced to survive on benefits which are grossly inadequate and sometimes overtly destructive; and finally, the assistance we provided has been diminishing for more than a decade.

Many poor households receive no assistance. Many of our poorest and most vulnerable people get no help at all. In about half the states of the nation, for example, poor families with children are not entitled to welfare assistance if both parents are in the home.

The Aid to Families with Dependent Children (AFDC) program was established by Congress to help American families through times of economic stress. Yet the federal government left to each state the option to provide AFCD assistance to children when both parents are in the home. Fewer than half the states have adopted this option, meaning that no matter how destitute a two-parent family is, the state will not assist the children unless the father leaves the home. States which require parents to break up their home in order to help the children are listed in Table 11.

Poor families in many states are denied medical coverage as well—no matter how destitute they may be. Approximately one-quarter of the states provides no Medicaid coverage for "medically needy" families. Moreover, some states provide neither medical assistance nor welfare for single individuals and childless couples, no matter how penniless they may be.

Aid to Families with Dependent Children and Medicaid are but two programs which have significant gaps in them. But because of their size and potential impact in alleviating suffering in our nation, the gaps or holes in these programs represent fundamental weaknesses in our nation's safety net.

Table 11. *States Denying AFDC to Children of Two-Parent Families, 1984*

Alabama	Indiana	New Mexico	Tennessee
Alaska	Kentucky	North Carolina	Texas
Arizona	Louisiana	North Dakota	Utah
Arkansas	Maine	Oklahoma	Virginia
Florida	Mississippi	Oregon	Washington
Georgia	Montana	South Carolina	Wyoming
Idaho	Nevada	New Hampshire	South Dakota

SOURCE: U.S. Department of Health and Human Services, December, 1984.

These safety net weaknesses are longstanding. Both Presidents Nixon and Carter, for example, proposed reforms to narrow the gaps but their proposals failed.

Benefit levels are generally inadequate—and grossly so—for most Americans who do receive help. Many safety net assistance programs are tantamount to giving a widow a supply of fruit and a space to sleep in the attic after she and her children are burned out of their home and her husband is killed in the fire. The gesture may keep them alive, but they can hardly get back on their feet.

The AFDC program, for example, is designed to help destitute families back on their feet, and to enable them to meet their basic needs until they do so. Yet it is difficult for families in most states to live on what AFDC provides.

Table 12 shows what AFDC families receive in several regions of the nation, regions which include the eight states in which we conducted field investigations. It should be noted that the benefit levels are the maximum possible; most AFDC recipients do not receive even these amounts. Moreover, AFDC is one of the more "generous" programs; those not eligible for AFDC but who live in states which provide general assistance or general relief receive only one-half to one-third of what AFDC recipients get.

According to government reports, just over half the households in poverty in the United States receive food stamp assistance.[1] This, of course, means that literally millions of im-

Table 12. *Monthly AFDC Benefits for Four-Person Family, Selected States, 1984*

State	Maximum[1]	Actual average[2]
Alabama	$147	$111
Mississippi	$120	$ 91
Tennessee	$168	$116
North Carolina	$221	$177
New Mexico	$313	$214
Texas	$201	$139
Illinois	$368	$289
Missouri	$308	$247

SOURCES: [1]Congressional Research Service, November, 1984. [2]Average family payment. Department of Health and Human Services, Office of Policy, "Monthly Benefit Statistics," April–July, 1984.
NOTE: U.S. poverty level = $850.

poverished Americans are not being helped by the food stamp program. But for those fortunate enough to receive assistance, benefits are not based on human need. In fact, the evidence is that neither food stamps nor AFDC, nor both together, provide American families with the level of support required to eat nutritiously and to maintain health.

Food stamps are not based on what it actually costs to eat. Benefits are tied to the "thrifty food plan," the cheapest food plan devised by the U.S. Department of Agriculture. Yet the Department has *never* determined that this computerized plan represents an adequate expenditure level to achieve desirable nutrition levels.

The thrifty food plan is an example of bureaucracy gone awry. A federal expenditure level was set, and a computer was programmed to design a food plan equal to that level—irrespective of human need. At the time the plan was devised, some of the Department's own researchers and nutritionists wrote that it should be used in emergencies only and was not nutritionally adequate over longer periods of time. The plan was adopted in 1975 and has been used ever since. Not surprisingly, USDA's most recent National Household Food Consumption Survey reveals that over 80% of all households whose food expenditures equal the thrifty food plan level *fail* to obtain the recommended dietary allowances for nutrients.

Many food stamp recipients do not receive even these benefits, however. Two other factors lower their effective food purchasing power. The first factor is that the thrifty food plan is based on food prices for the last quarter of the previous fiscal year. Thus, benefit levels are three months behind the rising costs of food, and by the end of the fiscal year benefits received are tied to food prices set some 15 months ago, no matter how much food prices may have inflated.

The other factor which cuts food stamp purchasing power is the state or local sales tax on food. Some 17 states have imposed sales taxes on food, further reducing what impoverished families can buy. Table 13 shows that recipients may lose up to 5% or more of their food stamp dollars. If food prices have also risen 5% since levels were set, families in such states actually have 10% less than the already inadequate food stamp level on which to try to feed themselves.

The inadequacy of food stamp assistance levels is apparent from the foregoing analysis. Yet their inadequacy has a particular twist when it comes to "new poor" families in the nation. Many of these families, particulary those who were once middle-class, find that they cannot get food stamps. They are income-eligible, but asset-ineligible. They haven't the cash to purchase food, but because they have assets such as a house or car, they are determined to be ineligible for help. This example points to the destructive nature of a number of safety net programs: families who need temporary assistance while

Table 13. *States Taxing Food Purchases*

State	Food tax	State	Food tax
Alabama	4.00%	N. Carolina	3.00%
Arkansas	4.00	Oklahoma	3.00
Georgia	3.00	S. Carolina	5.00
Hawaii	4.00	S. Dakota	4.00
Idaho	4.00	Tennessee	5.50
Kansas	3.00	Utah	4.625
Mississippi	6.00	Virginia	3.00
Missouri	4.225	Wyoming	3.00
New Mexico	3.75		

SOURCE: Congressional Budget Office.

they get back on their feet are forced to lose much of what they have worked for in order to get "help."

Under food stamp regulations, for example, a family may own a car with a market value of up to $4,500, and have additional cash assets of $1,500; assets above these amounts may make the applicants ineligible for help. The cash assets limit was set in 1971, and since that time the Consumer Price Index (CPI) has risen 160% (through November, 1984).[2] Since the car asset limit was established in 1977, the used car component of the CPI has risen 110%.[3] Thus, because assets limits have not been adjusted each year, more recently unemployed families are ineligible for food stamps than was the case in the 1970s. This, no doubt, is one of the factors which contribute to the large number of intact, formerly middle-class families appearing at soup kitchens and standing in bread lines in the nation. The assets limit on food stamps is destructive of family financial integrity, and forces families to lose in a year or so what it may have taken them a decade or two to accumulate.

The food stamps assets limit is an example of a larger problem, namely, that impoverished Americans have experienced serious income erosion during the past decade or so. AFDC benefit income for families in the nation decreased by 33% between 1970 and 1984.[4] This means that poor citizens today receive one-third less real income than they did over a decade ago, a further factor pointing to the inadequacy of key assistance programs. A similar analysis by the Congressional Research Service shows a drop of 36% nationally from 1970 to 1983.[5] Together, these governmental studies show that about one-third of the purchasing power of AFDC families was stripped away during this time because benefit levels were not tied to inflation. Consequently, no other sector of the American population has fallen so far behind inflation in recent years. Table 14 reflects this loss for AFDC families in the states where the physicians conducted their field visits.

As AFDC grants dropped so dramatically in real dollars, the cost of energy and other items which make up such a large proportion of low-income household budgets went up rapidly.

Table 14. *Percent Loss in Maximum AFDC
Benefits for Four-Person Families in
Selected States, 1970–1984*

State	Percent loss
Alabama	132.1%
Mississippi	35.9
Tennessee	51.3
N. Carolina	47.7
New Mexico	35.7
Texas	58.0
Illinois	51.2
Missouri	11.4

SOURCE: Congressional Research Service.
NOTE: Percent loss is calculated in constant dollars.

Energy Department data, for example, show that home energy costs increased several hundred percent, a rise which was off-set only minimally (one-third) by the federal low-income energy assistance program. During this same time poor households were losing in other ways.

USDA regularly computed real incomes for food stamp households during this same decade. The results show that since 1975, extremely large drops in real income occurred for food stamp recipients. In the five-year period from 1975 until the beginning of this decade, for example, recipients suffered an 18.3% loss in real income. As of December, 1981, the USDA Food and Nutrition Service calculated that food stamp recipients lost nearly a fifth of their purchasing power, calculated in constant dollars. Evidence indicates that the loss has increased since 1981, although USDA has not reported calculations since then. Table 15, showing food stamp benefit levels, lists amounts with which it is difficult, if not impossible, to provide adequate nutrition.

For the past decade and a half, then, the real income for basic necessities for America's poorest families has fallen dramatically as a result of decreased AFDC benefits and food stamp income alone. This loss reflects not only longstanding weaknesses in America's safety net, but clear decisions made through

Table 15. *Average and Maximum Federal Food Stamp Benefits, 1982 and 1984*

Number of persons in household	Average monthly benefit ('84)	Maximum monthly allowed ('82)
1	$ 43	$ 79
2	82	145
3	121	208
4	147	264
5	166	313
6	201	376

SOURCE: USDA, 1982, 1984.

government policy. Decisions were made which have driven vulnerable families well below a minimum standard of living, and often they were carried out with substantial knowledge of the consequences.

The Safety Net Rips: Poverty and Unemployment at Record Levels

The increasing economic hardship visited upon poor Americans during the decade of the 1970s reflected both gaps in coverage and declining purchasing power. Virtually no other country in the Western world permits such gaps in meeting basic human needs. Yet this situation was made worse by federal budget and tax policies enacted since 1980. Not only did policies fail to protect poor citizens from the impact of inflation and the recession, they actually made the plight of the poor worse while their suffering was greatest.

During the three-year period 1979–1981, the nation suffered unusually high rates of inflation. The lowest inflation rate during that period was 10.4% in 1981; the highest, 13.5% in 1980. Today, inflation has come down to the 3–4% range, but purchasing power for medium- and low-income American families has remained virtually unchanged.[6] This is because of several factors, one being that wages have come down as much as prices, particularly for low-income people, providing little gain in what the dollar can buy. For the poorest 40% of the population, there has been an actual loss in purchasing power.[7]

According to a recent analysis by the nonpartisan Urban Institute, the lowest fifth of the population in income lost purchasing power during the past four years. The next lowest fifth also lost, although not as much.[8] Altogether, the poorest 40% of the U.S. population lost in purchasing power from 1980 to 1984, as depicted in Figure 36.

The Institute concluded that Administration policies "helped the affluent but were detrimental to the poor and the middle class,"[9] and that the inequality which resulted would have been worse had Congress not rejected other Administration policy porposals.

THE "SAFETY NET" MYTH

The concept of a "safety net" was given prominence by members of the Reagan Administration in order to justify the major cuts in social and nutrition programs enacted in 1981. They argued that a "safety net" exists in the nation to protect vulnerable people, and that it provides adequate protection from otherwise harmful federal cutbacks.

Following substantial documentation that the 1981–1985 budget cuts had indeed harmed millions of Americans, some of these same officials acknowledged that their original "safety net" argument was a tool designed for political expediency at the time. Budget Director David Stockman later admitted:

"It [the list of safety net programs] was a happenstance list, just a spur of the moment thing that the [White House] press office wanted to put out."

In a similar vein, then White House Domestic Policy Advisor Martin Anderson dismissed the safety net as follows:

"Providing a safety net for those who cannot or are not expected to work was not really a social policy objective. The term safety net was political shorthand that only made sense for a limited period of time."

Statements made in interviews, *Washington Post*, December 4, 1983, and July 8, 1983, respectively.

Fig. 36. *Percentage Change in Real Disposable Income for U.S. Families, 1980–1984*

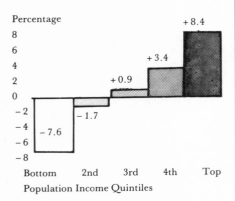

Percentage

Bottom   2nd   3rd   4th   Top
Population Income Quintiles

Source: The Urban Institute/household income model.

Fig. 37. *Long-Term Unemployed 1980–1984*

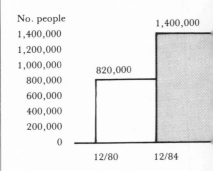

Source: Bureau of Labor Statistics.

The Institute's analysis carries significant weight not simply for the quality of its researchers, but because of their bipartisan credentials. The trustees of the Institute include five former Republican cabinet officers, and its advisory board includes several other former Republican officials, including Martin Anderson, former chief domestic policy advisor to President Reagan.

The evidence, then, clearly shows that while inflation increased, federal policies not only failed to limit its impact on low-income families, but actually further eroded their already-limited buying power. At the same time, other factors came into play which increased poverty and, ultimately, hunger.

During this period of time, unemployment in America rose from 6.2% in early 1980 to 10.7% at the end of 1982, the highest level since the Great Depression.[10] Though the rate fell to 7.2% as of December, 1984, there are still nearly 473,000 more Americans unemployed today than there were in 1980. Even these numbers do not adequately depict the severity of the unemployment problem. Long-term unemployment (workers jobless for six months or more) is worse today than four years ago. The number of long-term-unemployed Americans at the end of 1984 was up 70% over the level in 1980.[11] (See Figure 37.)

There is still more evidence on the unemployment problem. The Labor Department reports "discouraged workers" seperately from long-term unemployed. Discouraged workers are those who have been jobless so long that they have given up looking. In theory, discouraged workers reenter the labor market during economic recovery, and some indeed have done so. However, in the current recovery the number of discouraged workers remains high, evidence of the unevenness of the economic upturn.

During the first quarter of 1980 the number of discouraged

Fig. 38. *Americans Living in Poverty, 1979–1983*

millions

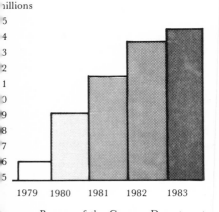

```
5
4
3
2
1
0
9
8
7
6
5
```

1979   1980   1981   1982   1983

Sources: Bureau of the Census, Department of Commerce; Economic Report of the President to the Congress.

Fig. 39. *Increasing Tax Burden on Families of Four with Poverty-Level Income, 1978–1984*

Taxes owed

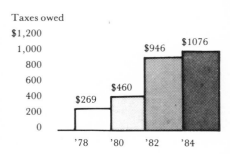

```
$1,200
 1,000
   800
   600
   400
   200
     0
```
$269 $460 $946 $1076

'78   '80   '82   '84

Source: Joint Committee on Taxation, U.S. Congress; U.S. Treasury Dept., Internal Revenue Service.

Note: Percentage of income paid in taxes each year:

1978 - 4.0%   1982 - 8.9% (est.)
1980 - 5.5%   1984 - 10.1%

workers in the U.S. was 1,055,000. During the same quarter of 1984, as the economy reportedly was improving, the number stood at 1,303,000—an increase of 23.5%.[12]

Finally, we must consider the percentage of unemployed Americans who lost their jobs permanently, as opposed to temporary lay-offs. In the previous three recessions, between 1969 and 1980, the proportion of workers permanently separated from their jobs was between 36% and 37%. In the recent recession, more than half of all unemployed workers permanently lost their jobs.[13] According to a recent study by the Bureau of Labor Statistics of 5.1 million workers whose jobs were abolished during the five-year period 1979–1984, only 60% were reemployed.[14] Many of those reemployed were working for significantly lower pay. Some 1.3 million were still looking for work, and 700,000 had left the labor force altogether.[15]

In summary, the recession brought about increased unemployment, a problem exacerbated by federal policies which, even today, have limited the number of American workers aided by the partial recovery. Today, the unemployment rate in the nation is still higher than in 1980. More Americans are unemployed on a long-term basis, and the number of discouraged workers is higher than it was four years ago.

While unemployment remains at record-high levels, another factor which compounds problems for those affected is the smaller proportion of jobless workers who receive unemployment benefits. During the 1975 recession, when unemployment was at about the same level it is today, 78% of jobless Americans received unemployment insurance benefits.[16] By contrast, the proportion of unemployed receiving such benefits toward the end of 1983 was 39%.

Throughout the last half of 1984, the proportion of unemployed people who received unemployment benefits hovered between 29% and 36%, an all-time low with unemployment at such high levels. Of the 8 million people unemployed in December, 1984, 5.1 million got no unemployment benefits, down only somewhat from the 5.9 million so affected during the height of the recession.[17] This fact reflects federal budget cuts in 1981 and the continuing high level of suffering among unemployed families.

Today, if an unemployed worker has exhausted unemployment benefits and lives with spouse and children, the family can get neither further unemployment assistance, nor AFDC, nor Medicaid in over half the states of the nation. This situation clearly reduces the likelihood that the family will have money available to feed itself.

Further exacerbating the economic problems faced by the nation's poorest families were the budget and tax acts of 1981 and 1982. These cuts had the cumulative effect of transferring billions of dollars in income from poor families to the wealthy. According to the Congressional Budget Office, the cumulative impact of budget and tax cuts enacted during 1981–1985 was to transfer some $23 billion from poorer households, and to give an additional $35 billion to those already earning over $80,000 each.[18] (See Table 16.)

While low-income families were losing income, federal policies also placed more tax burden on individuals and less on corporations. During the 1970s, the corporate sector share of the federal tax burden was 15.0%. As of fiscal year 1983, corporate sector taxes had been decreased to only 6.2%, while taxes on individual incomes had risen from 73.5% to 82.9% during the same period of time.[19]

While corporate taxes were dramatically reduced, taxes on poverty-level families were raised substantially—double and

Table 16. *Income Transfers from Poor to Wealthy Families, 1983–1985*

Year	Families under $10,000	Families above $80,000
1983	− $5.6 billion	+ $9.9 billion
1984	− $8.1 billion	+$11.9 billion
1985	− $9.4 billion	+$13.1 billion
	−$23.1 billion	+$34.9 billion

SOURCE: Congressional Budget Office, "The Combined Effects of Major Changes in Federal Taxes and Spending Programs Since 1981," April, 1984.

triple what they were several years ago. The result of this is that large numbers of those who live in poverty now have a steadily increasing portion of their meager incomes eaten up by federal taxes.

As these federal polices placed greater economic burdens on American households living at the economic margins—and largely as a direct result of these policies—poverty in America increases substantially. According to the Bureau of the Census, more than one in every seven Americans lived in poverty at the beginning of 1984, the highest poverty rate for any year since 1965.

Since 1980, poverty in America has increased 20.5%. Partly in response to the alarm expressed by some Congressional leaders about this dramatic increase, Budget Director David Stockman appeared before the House Ways and Means Committee in November 1983, to assure the Congressmen of the Administration's absolute confidence "that the poverty rate is going to decline dramatically for 1983."

Instead of declining, the Census Bureau later reported, poverty actually increased in 1983, claiming another 900,000 Americans. Today, some 35.3 million United States citizens live in poverty.[20] (See Figure 38.)

The increase in poverty does not fully reflect the increase in hardship among Americans. The sharpest increase in impoverishment has been at the bottom of the economic ladder. Many more people now have incomes which are less than half the official poverty line. Since 1980, the number of Americans living below half the poverty level has increased 38.5%.

Some critics of the poverty index claim that poverty is lower if non-cash benefits such as food stamps and health coverage are counted as income. In reality, the statistics on the increases in poverty show that no matter which way poverty is measured, the number of poor Americans grew by more than 9 million in the last four years—the largest increase since poverty figures began being compiled in 1960.[21]

It is notable that even more people would be classified as poor if the poverty level were based on take-home pay rather than gross income. Census data released in July, 1984, show that if poverty status were calculated on after-tax income more than 3 million additional people would be classified as poor.[22]

Census data also show that the number of people with gross incomes above poverty, but whose after-tax income fell below poverty, increased by 40% between 1980 and 1982. This reflects the fact that the tax burdens on the working poor have increased significantly since 1980, effectively pushing more households into poverty (see Figure 39).

The overall poverty rate masks substantial differences among population groups. For example, increasing poverty has exacted a particularly high toll among households headed by women; today over 35% of such households live in poverty.[23] For non-white households headed by women, the poverty level is 70–80%. Moreover, children are the poorest group in America today. Nearly 40% of all poor people are children, and the number is growing steadily.[24]

Among the most vulnerable children, those under the age of 6, one in five lives in poverty. One of every two black children under 6 is poor, as are two of every five Hispanic children. The growing impoverishment of children in the nation is documented by Census Bureau reports and depicted poignantly by the increasing number of children and families counted in the bread lines and soup kitchens of the nation.

Safety Net Programs Cut as Poverty and Need Peaked

Several factors converged during the past few years to place onerous burdens on American families: purchasing power decreased for low-income households; fewer and fewer unemployed workers received unemployment benefits; tax policies shifted billions of dollars from poor families to the rich; and poverty shot up by nine million more people.

As economic hardship rose to a level unparalleled since the Great Depression, more Americans were forced to rely on federal programs designed to assist them through hard times. The increasing need was largely ignored, and safety net programs were actually cut even as hardship grew.

Starting in 1981 (fiscal year 1982), changes in laws and government regulations altered eligibility standards and benefit levels for federal assistance programs. The result of these changes was to make many of the newly impoverished Americans ineligible for assistance. Many of those who were able to get assistance had their benefits cut substantially at the time that their need was increasing. The changes and budget cuts took place in both food and other assistance programs. The Congressional Budget Office calculated that for the years 1982–1985, total budget cuts in human services programs are in the vicinity of $110 billion.[25] Table 17 shows the impact of these cuts on the programs analyzed by the CBO.

The cuts in unemployment insurance and the AFDC program are especially notable, because of the unusually high level of need discussed earlier. Policy changes in unemployment insurance, as we have seen, led to the lowest coverage of unemployed workers in the history of the unemployment insurance program (29–36%). Policy changes in the AFDC program also had a severe impact on recipient families. Moreover, eligibility changes prevented many needy families from receiving any benefits at all.

As AFDC benefit levels declined in real dollars over the past several years as the cost of living increased, federal policy changes further exacerbated the burden placed on dependent

Table 17. *Other Income Security Programs: Current Baseline Percentage Changes in Outlays Resulting from Legislative Actions, Fiscal Years 1982–1985*

(Percent)

Program	1982	1983	1984	1985	Total '82–'85
Unemployment Insurance	− 4.0	+10.7	−14.8	−17.6	− 6.9
AFDC	− 9.9	−13.0	−13.5	−14.0	−12.7
Food Stamps	−12.2	− 9.7	−14.2	−14.1	−12.6
Child Nutrition	−24.3	−28.8	−29.0	−28.5	−27.7
WIC	− 4.9	+10.5	+ 7.0	+ 4.3	+ 4.4
Housing Assistance	—	+ 1.2	− 4.3	−11.5	− 4.4
Low-Income Energy Assistance	− 7.0	− 7.6	− 8.6	− 9.7	− 8.3

SOURCE: Congressional Budget Office. Reflects legislative changes made before July 31, 1983. Based on February 1983 economic assumptions. The 1981 baseline, revised to reflect current economic assumptions, is used as the base for computing percentage changes.

children and their parents. Allowances for child care and work expenses under AFDC were reduced, making it harder for the working poor to get by; AFDC benefits for the unborn child, once allowed because of the nutritional needs of the mother, were cut out; a stepparent's income was counted as income to the stepchild, whether it was or not; and the states' option to assist older students was limited.

Prior to these changes it was possible for AFDC recipients who worked to raise their income above the poverty level in 29 states. The federal budget cuts pushed substanital numbers of these families below poverty.

A study by the Congressional Research Service in July, 1984, found that federal budget reductions enacted in 1981 had the effect of pushing 560,000 persons below poverty, 325,000 of whom were children.[26] Notably, this study underestimated the impact of the budget cuts in increasing the number of people in poverty, because it did not include the impact of reductions in related programs such as unemployment insurance and social security disability.

A General Accounting Office study in April, 1984, showed that nearly 500,000 low-income working families (mostly female-headed) had their benefits terminated because of the AFDC cuts.[27] In many states, according to another study, children automatically lost Medicaid coverage when AFDC benefits were terminated, affecting an estimated 700,000 children in the nation.[28]

An additional 300,00 working families with even lower incomes remained on AFDC but had their benefits sharply reduced, losing an average of $150–200 a month.[29] So harshly did the cuts affect these families that in a number of states an AFDC mother trying to work today actually ends up with less income, owing to the cuts, than a mother who does not work.

At the same time that the AFDC cuts took effect, reductions in other critical programs compounded their impact. All low-income households in subsidized housing, for example, had their rents raised. Many families were dropped from Medicaid or had coverage cut back. And energy costs continued to rise while low-income energy assistance programs did not keep pace.

The cumulative impact of cutbacks and reductions in key programs for low-income households was substantial. They took place at the very time that need was increasing at a rate unprecedented in recent history. But it is to be noted that things did not stop here.

Cuts instituted in federal nutrition programs during the first years of this decade were the sharpest and most severe in our nation's history. Ironically, they came at a time when the programs were needed more than at any time in a decade or more.

Two of the most basic food assistance programs, food stamps and school meals, were cut substantially. Two others, elderly feeding and the Supplemental Program for Women, Infants, and Children (WIC), were saved from slated cuts by Congressional action.

In the four years 1982–1985, some $12.2 billion was cut from food stamps and child nutrition, including school breakfast and lunch programs.[30] The Congressional Budget Office calculated that $7.0 billion was cut from food stamps, and $5.2 cut from the school feeding programs. (Subsequently Congress did add back $0.2 billion of the $7.0 billion in food stamp cuts.)

The lunch and breakfast programs subsidize meals for children in their schools, providing uniform benefits nationwide through three categories of meals: free, reduced-price, and paid meals. In 1982, about 23 million children participated in school lunch, the larger of the programs. One of the significant features of this program is that it assures children at least one nutritious meal each day. School officials and teachers attest to its social and educational benefits, and a body of literature has developed supporting their observations.

Cuts imposed on the school meal programs were brought about by lowering federal meal subsidies, altering income criteria by which eligibility is determined, making many low-income families pay more for each meal, and making the application process more cumbersome.

The impact of the $5.2 billion cut was immediate. There was

a drop of 3 million children in the school lunch program, nearly 1 million of them from low-income families.[31] Some 2,700 schools had to discontinue participation in the school lunch program.[32] In addition, some 400,000 children and 800 schools stopped participating in the school breakfast program as a result of federal policy changes.[33]

Since the initial cutbacks, the number of children removed from the school lunch program has remained relatively unchanged, with some annual fluctuations. Today, about 12% fewer children are participating in the program than in 1980 (see Table 18). The drop in participation by poor children eligible for free and reduced-price meals, moreover, is in no way the result of declining school enrollments, since poverty has increased every year since the policy changes. Fewer children are served as the result of federal policy changes themselves which decreased the number of children being fed.

Monies cut in the food stamp program, which provides redeemable coupons with which low-income households purchase food, were even greater than cuts made in the school lunch and breakfast programs. Benefits of the federal program are tied to household size and are the same from state to state, based on the thrifty food plan discussed earlier in this chapter. Food stamp benefits are quite low, with the average recipient receiving about $44 per month. A three-person family with absolutely no other income is eligible for a maximum of $208

Table 18. *Participation in National School Lunch Program, Fiscal Years 1980–1984*

Fiscal year	Participation (millions)				Percent decrease from 1980
	Free	Reduced	Paid	Total	
1980	10.0	1.9	14.7	26.6	
1981	10.6	1.9	13.3	25.8	− 3.0%
1982	9.8	1.6	11.5	22.9	−13.9
1983	10.4	1.6	11.3	23.2	−12.8
1984	10.3	1.5	11.6	23.4	−12.0

SOURCE: USDA Food and Nutrition Service, August, 1984.

monthly.[34] The average benefit for all recipients in the United States is 49¢ per meal.

Federal budget and regulatory changes initially reduced benefits for all 22 million food stamp recipients at the time by delaying an inflation adjustment in 1982. In addition households with gross incomes just over 130% of the poverty line were eliminated unless they had elderly or disabled members. This particular change impacted working families with children whose gross incomes are over poverty, but whose net incomes are well below poverty. Altogether, about 1 million people were removed from the food stamp program.[35] Yet this outcome represented only a small portion of the overall impact of the cuts. The bulk of the cuts came from actually reducing benefits to poor families, at least two-thirds of them already living below the poverty line.

Even this fact fails to take into account a more significant phenomenon, namely that poverty has increased so dramatically in recent years that millions more Americans are now in need of and eligible for food stamps. At the present time, the number of citizens receiving food stamps is lower than it was four years ago, while the number in poverty has increased by several million (see Table 19).

Figure 40 shows the increasing gap between Americans in

Table 19. *Food Stamp Participation by Region, 1983–1984*

Region	Number of persons (thousands)		Percent change
	Sept. 1983	Sept. 1984	
Northeast	2,683	2,575	−4.0%
Mid-Atlantic	2,774	2,616	−5.7
Southeast	4,602	4,197	−8.8
Midwest	4,447	4,212	−5.3
Southwest	2,560	2,497	−2.5
Mountain Plains	1,262	1,144	−9.4
Western	2,709	2,500	−7.7
SSI/Elderly (national)	36	37	2.8
U.S. TOTAL	21,073	19,778	−6.1

SOURCE: USDA Food and Nutrition Service, December, 1984.

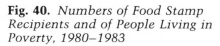

Fig. 40. *Numbers of Food Stamp Recipients and of People Living in Poverty, 1980–1983*

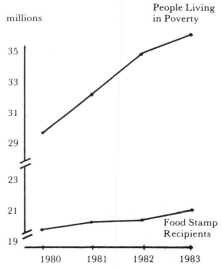

*Exclusive of Puerto Rico.
Sources: General Accounting Office; USDA.

poverty and the number receiving food stamps. For every 100 people living in poverty in September, 1980, 68 received food stamps. For the same period in 1984, only 58 of those Americans were receiving stamps.[36] Both as a proportion of people in poverty and in real terms, the number of Americans receiving food stamp assistance has declined during the past several years.

The reason that so many eligible citizens do not receive food stamp benefits is another matter, to be addressed in the following chapter. The point here is that $12.2 billion in budget cuts in critical food assistance programs took place at a time when poverty had grown to its greatest point in two decades and unemployment had risen to record levels. Moreover, these program cuts occurred at a time when the economic vulnerability of American families and individuals was probably at the highest level since the 1930s.

The substantial cuts in federal nutrition programs, coming on the heels of these other factors, caused millions of Americans to fall through a tattered safety net and land in the bread lines of this nation.

6. MEAN-SPIRITEDNESS AS GOVERNMENT POLICY

We have examined changes in programs, budgets, and taxes which increased hunger in America. Another phenomenon also contributes to hunger: the employment of administrative and bureaucratic procedures which prevent otherwise qualified people from getting the assistance they need.

For the most part the procedures are designed by the federal government, which requires state and local governments to carry them out. The resulting tension is historically interesting. A decade or two ago, the federal government often exercised its authority to ensure that states did not place impediments in the way of citizens receiving assistance for which they were qualified. Today, the federal government requires procedures which, states report, keep many qualified and needy people from getting the help they deserve.

Strong evidence supports the analysis that many qualified citizens do not receive assistance, and that a major reason they do not is the creation of bureaucratic tactics which make it unlikely that they will successfully complete the application process. Numerous individuals and American families find themselves in utterly desperate situations because of those obstacles.

Ironically, the impediments frequently are created by officials who run the programs ostensibly set up to aid needy citizens. The utilization of such procedures and practices represents, in a fundamental way, mean-spiritedness in government policy.

One of the more consistent themes found in our field investigations is that government places unnecessary impediments in the way of those who most need help. This theme, while embodied in reports from around the nation, took different forms in different places:

• "Men who worked hard all their lives suddenly find themselves out of work when their plants close. They don't want to look to the State for help. But when they finally hit bottom . . . their worst fears come true. Paperwork and red tape are stacked so high they would have to be olympic pole vaulters to get over it." *(Director, Illinois Department of Public Aid.)*[1]

• It is not unusual for people in St. Louis and Kansas City to apply for aid and wait 45–60 days before a decision is rendered. Forms are long and quite difficult to fill out. Each month many families lose benefits—not because they are ineligible but for failure to report properly." *(Worker, Lutheran Family Services, St. Louis.)*[2]

• "Many Texans with a legitimate need are being kept off, or kicked off, federal food assistance programs because of bureaucratic barriers and procedural changes." *(Chairman, Texas Senate Committee on Hunger.)*[3]

• "Why, you ask, do 280,280 Mississippians eligible for food stamps not receive these benefits? The answer . . . the hassle . . . many are physically unable to wait in long lines . . . loss of dignity and respect. It is demeaning to fill out forms which border on invasion of privacy. Some forms are even accusatory in nature. Yes, loss of dignity and respect prohibit some from applying." *(Mississippi Welfare Commissioner.)*[4]

Strong evidence exists to support the observation of Mississippi Welfare Commissioner Dr. Donald B. Roarke. In state after state, government officials report that the federal government requires them to follow procedures which are laden with unnecessary paperwork, which construct nearly impossible hurdles for applicants, and which are demeaning to those in need. All this, they report, is being done in the name of efficiency and "quality control." Actually, they say, it is a form of "expenditure control" which keeps otherwise eligible people from receiving program assistance.[5]

Both statistical evidence and experience support this analysis. "Just yesterday," reported Virginia Eldreth, a North Carolina food stamp administrator, "an elderly woman who had been hungry for weeks finally came in to apply for stamps. She was trembling as she filled out the forms. I asked her if she was all right. As it turned out, she was fearful she might make an error and be thrown in jail for fraud."[6] Ms. Eldreth's food stamp office in Buncombe County was lined with conspicuous red and white warning signs: "WARNING: We prosecute food stamp recipients . . ." It is impossible to enter the office and ignore the signs; they are noticeable and intimidating (see p. 160). The elderly woman is undoubtedly not the only person in need of help who had avoided applying; many people in that state who are eligible for food stamps are not getting them.

Poverty in North Carolina rose by 42% between 1981 and 1983. But while poverty went up, the number of poor residents receiving food stamps declined. In 1981, some 597,585 people were aided by food stamps; today that figure is down to just over 515,000.[7]

"Before 1980," reported State Senator Helen R. Marvin, "more than 60% of the poor people in North Carolina were served by the food stamp program. Today, only 40% are. More than half the people cut off are children."[8]

This phenomenon is not limited to North Carolina. We found this trend in virtually every state examined: as poverty has increased, the number of people receiving food stamps has decreased. In Texas, New Mexico, Tennessee, Illinois, and Missouri, officials pointed out that the gap is widening between the number of people receiving food stamps and the number eligible for them. But food stamps are not the only program for which this is happening. Back in North Carolina, where poverty has increased so dramatically, the number of families receiving AFDC has gone down each year since 1981, from 200,059 in 1981 to 171,705 in 1984.[9] Some of the decline in AFDC is attributed to federal budget and program changes enacted through legislation in 1981. But some of the drop, according to lawyers and officials in the state, is the result of administrative practices required by the federal government.

A number of federally required procedures have been instituted in the past several years which make it more difficult for people to receive help from various programs. They result in actual suffering, as pointed out by numerous officials and agency heads in the states across the nation. In one state we visited, a 64-year-old paralyzed man was cut off food stamps because he failed to go into the office for a recertification interview. In another state a father and his family were cut off food stamps because he had earned $22 cleaning a lot, income he reported. Because he could not produce a receipt for the cash payment his family lost food stamps for a month.

We now examine some of the procedures presently required by the federal government, in order to understand better how they work and how they harm American citizens who need help the most.

The Politics of Fraud, Waste, and Abuse

Fraud, waste, and abuse in government programs are, by definition, not in the public interest. They waste taxpayer money, and they reduce resources the nation has available to help those who need them. Political leaders who are vigilant with public dollars therefore are acting in the public interest.

Unfortunately, some political leaders take on the fraud, waste, and abuse problem seemingly more to promote their own political careers than to promote good public policy. Moreover, they go after the "little people's programs" like AFDC and food stamps, programs from which waste should be eliminated but which pale in comparison to bigger programs with far more waste. Too few political leaders have gone after the 117% cost overrun for the General Dynamics Titan Missile, for example, and too many have elected to go after the father who cannot produce proof that he was paid $22 for cleaning a lot.

The offensiveness of politicans attacking welfare recipients goes beyond their ignoring the waste among corporate contractors. The "David and Goliath" element clearly makes the beating of the little guy offensive, but other reasons exist which do as well. Evidence suggests that more public money can be saved in the defense contract arena, for example, than from among food stamp recipients. Public officials truly wanting to save public money should look at the evidence.

According to government studies, including some by the Reagan Administration, fraud, waste, and abuse in programs serving the poor is much less than commonly believed (and probably substantially less than in bigger-spending programs such as military procurements). Department of Agriculture quality control data for the food stamp program, for example, reveals a remarkably low net dollar loss due to fraud and errors. Overpayments constitute 8½% of all food stamp payments, and underpayments range between 2% and 2½%. This means that at a given time the net dollar loss for food stamps issued is 6–6½%. Moreover, the quality control studies show that this net loss includes worker error, recipient error, and fraud. Thus, if the error rate is excluded, the fraud rate would be even less than the 6–6½% range.[10] Department analysts also indicate that over 95% of households receiving food stamps are eligible for them.[11] This is a higher percentage, note some observers, than that for income tax refunds through the Internal Revenue Service.

Apparently oblivious to the facts available to them, some political leaders during the past several years have conveyed to the American public the message that social programs are fraught with fraud and waste. Extraordinary claims have been made, and unusual tactics have been employed to "get tough" and to "make government efficient."

Political rhetoric about fraud and abuse has a profound impact on people in need. Most people dislike dependency anyway, and are reluctant to ask for help in the first place. When they hear politicians lambasting programs designed to help people like themselves, they feel intimidated and embarrassed. Or, like the laid-off father in Peoria, they delay applying for help because they think that assistance is limited and that other people may need it more than they do.[12]

But political rhetoric and assumptions about fraud and abuse have also become embodied in procedures and practices followed in social welfare and nutrition programs. They result in an adversarial relationship between those in need and those who are to serve them.

Perhaps the best example of this is the situation which resulted from new procedures implemented in 1981 concerning eligibility for disabled citizens under the Social Security Disability Insurance Program (SSDI). So egregious was the administrative overreach that Congress finally stepped in to halt established practices.

The SSDI program was established to assist permanently and temporarily disabled citizens. During the past several years the number of people served annually has been between 2 and 3 million. Beginning in early 1981, administrative procedures were put in place designed to provide more "sound management" in the program. Between that time and June, 1983, many recipients were terminated from the program through the use of narrower and more arbitrary criteria. So extensive and far-reaching were these procedures that 340,000 people were cut off, a problem which quickly came to the attention of members of Congress. One Congressman referred to the SSDI case as "a budget-slashing free-for-all in which thousands of our most vulnerable citizens (disabled, handicapped, retarded) have been abandoned by the government."[13] A Maine Congressman told a Congressional hearing about a constituent hospitalized five times in one year owing to a chronic health condition. He was classified by SSDI as employable; requests for reconsideration were ignored; he and his family became destitute.[14]

Many disabled people who were cut from the program appealed their terminations and were reenrolled. Altogether a third of those cut off were reenrolled, but only after lengthy government while eligible recipients received no benefits. Altogether SSDI terminations saved an estimated $2.7 billion in four years. So pervasive was the practice of wantonly cutting disabled people from the program that the administrative law judges who heard the appeals took the unprecedented step of suing the federal government for exerting pressure on them to rule against the disabled.

In late 1984, the Department of Health and Human Services finally halted the more blatant practices which terminated benefits for the disabled, primarily as a way to keep Congress from passing legislation which would have had the same effect (it subsequently was passed anyway). But similar procedures are still being employed in other programs which serve vulnerable population groups.

Procedures have been implemented to make all school districts in the nation verify income for up to 3% of applicants for school lunch each year. The form utilized is long, similar in content to a tax form, and is mailed to the homes of school children to be filled out in addition to forms parents already complete for school officials. The new policy was referred to by one state education official as "humiliating the truly needy among us by requiring them to produce evidence that is truly demeaning."[15]

The federal government has devised similar procedures for other programs as well, including AFDC and food stamps. The commissioner of human services in one state reported that, except for devising onerous regulations, the federal government shows no interest in helping the states respond to human need,[16] a viewpoint echoed by a regional director of the Massachusetts Department of Public Welfare: "Though we try to be sensitive to clients who are so desperate, the requirements of the federal government make the process a suspicious and adversarial one."[17]

The adversarial atmosphere created by federal policies is pervasive, affecting potential recipients of a number of assistance programs. It is particularly striking in the food stamp program.

The Use of Bureaucratic Intimidation in Food Stamp Assistance

By September, 1984, participation in the food stamp program had dropped to 19.8 million people.[18] This represents the lowest participation level since 1980. Moreover, current participation trends indicate that the number will continue to decline, when seasonally compared, relative to the levels of several years ago.

This decline in participation is peculiar since the number of Americans in poverty, most of whom are eligible for food stamps, has increased dramatically during this same period. (Figure 40, p. 151, shows the growing gap between poverty, which is rising, and food stamps recipients, whose level is declining.)

WARNING:

WE PROSECUTE FOOD STAMP RECIPIENTS FOR INTENTIONALLY MAKING FALSE STATEMENTS OR FOR WITHHOLDING INFORMATION IN ORDER TO GET MORE FOOD STAMPS THAN THEY ARE ELIGIBLE TO RECEIVE.

With poverty at 35.3 million at the end of 1983, it is expected that the number may decline slightly to 34.0 million by the end of 1984, a figure which has not yet been officially calculated.[19] A poverty figure of 34.0 million in 1984 will mean that nearly 5 million more people were in poverty in 1984 than in 1980. This means many more people should be receiving food stamps.

Not all people in poverty qualify for food stamps. In 1980 and 1981, the number of people getting food stamps was about two-thirds the number of people in poverty. If we apply the same rule of thumb today, since poverty went up by 5 million, more than 3 million more people should have been added to the food stamp rolls. Instead, participation between September, 1980, and September, 1984, actually declined by 300,000 people.[20] Moreover, if one uses 1981 as the base year to compare with 1984, the year during which new policies were just being implemented, the decline in food stamp participants is actually 500,000.[21]

The obvious question is why fewer people receive food stamp assistance at a time in which poverty has skyrocketed. One obvious factor is the Omnibus Budget and Reconciliation Act (OBRA) of 1981, which restricted food stamp eligibility criteria. Both the Department of Agriculture and the Congressional Budget Office estimate that OBRA eliminated about 1 million people from the food stamp program. What then accounts for the other 2 million or more people?

We believe that a number of new policies and practices instituted after passage of OBRA have had the effect of keeping otherwise eligible people from receiving food stamps. Many of these same practices have resulted in food stamp recipients being terminated.

The politics of fraud, waste, and abuse described earlier in this chapter were played out perhaps most visibly in the area of food stamps. Public statements by political leaders about fraud and abuse in food stamps, whatever their motivation, establish a climate of belief first, that the problem is somehow of large scope and second, that any recipient is a potential crook. Clearly the climate has changed in the past several years, and the mood created by political manipulation of public attitude has been extensive. In every state, government officials and program administrators speak of this change of attitude and the impact it is having both on their ability to serve the poor, and on the lives of the poor. The warning signs in the Buncombe County food stamp office did not just appear. They are a direct result of a political climate established in Washington.

Seldom, if ever, are American citizens singled out for such social stigma and ridicule as are the poor, especially poor food stamp recipients. Imagine, for example, bold, brightly colored signs in every Internal Revenue Service office in the nation: "WARNING: We prosecute taxpayers . . ." The public would be outraged.

It is not because some citizens do not cheat on taxes. They do and they should be prosecuted. It is because most citizens do not cheat that we do not expect to be treated as cheaters. We expect our government, including the IRS, to carry out the law, but to treat us with dignity and respect. Dignity and respect are often lacking in the way citizens are treated in "poor people's" programs, especially in food stamps. Ironically, as we have seen, the evidence is that fewer food stamp recipients cheat than do taxpayers paying their bills.

Despite the evidence, some politicians continually attack food stamp "fraud," and create in the public mind an image of recipients which is stigmatizing. One cannot easily measure the direct impact of this factor on recipients and potential recipients themselves, but from all indications it is serious. So serious in fact that the negative image created may actually prevent many needy and eligible people from even applying for assistance.

The stigma factor, we learned from food stamp officials in the regions of the nation we visited, is especially serious among the elderly and recently unemployed or "new poor" families. But it extends to other population groups as well. People's natural pride, and the reluctance to admit dependence, is great. If, in addition, politicians are depicting them as crooks and freeloaders, many people will simply suffer rather than request the help that they and their children need.

Yet, many citizens, driven by hunger, desperation, or chronic need, still apply for food stamp assistance. Newly instituted practices in the process of application and determination of eligibility serve to keep many of them out of the program. These practices, we believe, along with the political climate which has been created, are among the reasons that food stamp participation has gone down while poverty has gone up.

A growing phenomenon in programs serving the poor is that of "procedural denials." A procedural denial is the denial of program assistance for an applicant not because the applicant is not needy and qualified for help, but because he or she has somehow failed to pass all the procedures by which eligibility is determined. For example, a disabled or elderly woman whose ride did not arrive on time to take her to the food stamp office may arrive the next day to find her application has been denied and her case closed because she was unable to come on the scheduled day. Or, as another example, a father working at a sub-minimum wage cannot verify his income because the employer, fearful of being caught for paying below federal standards, refuses to give pay verification. The father's food stamp application for his family is denied since he cannot verify income, even though the family is otherwise eligible and needy.

Procedural denials are not limited to the application process, however. Once recipients are determined to be eligible for assistance, they may be terminated for procedural reasons. For example, a semi-literate mother having difficulty filling out a monthly reporting form may be terminated because she ignored a section of the form or filled it out improperly.

Procedural denials occur in many programs, but appear to be serious problems especially in AFDC and food stamps. We will examine the problem with respect to this latter program, and the manner in which bureaucratic requirements greatly complicate the goal of getting help to those who need it.

New application and paperwork procedures required of food stamp applicants are onerous, prompting the Illinois welfare director's remark that applicants must be "olympic pole vaulters" just to get over the red tape.[22] So many forms and

so much documentation are required that a number of officials observed that filling out a food stamp application is more
difficult than filling out the long form for the Internal Revenue Service. Not only are there numerous forms, but they are
frequently changed or revised. In fact, new policies keep the
food stamp program—for administrators and recipients alike—
in a constant state of turmoil. In one state, as an example, the
food stamp manual in 1965 contained 40 pages; as of 1983, the
manual had grown to 978 pages.[23] While the length varies from
state to state, this example fairly reflects the burgeoning com-
plexity confronting program workers and administrators.

In addition, the Food and Nutrition Service of the Department of Agriculture, which oversees the program at the federal level, initiated *ninety regulatory changes in a 30-month
period.*[24] These changes apply to all states, and serve to promote constant turmoil in the program: workers are uncertain
what rules apply when, and applicants are caught in the mo-
rass created by the Washington bureaucracy. "Never in my
twenty years in the food stamp field," one administrator told
us, "have I seen such a bureaucratic jumble."[25]

The state of Mississippi, for example, has 21 forms some 35
pages in length for the food stamp application process (see Table 20). Some are internal forms for workers to process;[26] others are for applicants to fill out, the latter requiring up to 18
different kinds of documentation on past and present salaries,
utilities, medical care, bank accounts, social security status,
relatives in household, citizenship, and so on.

Each time a new regulation is issued—every ten days on the
average—new forms may have to be created. State computers
may need to be reprogrammed, local procedures reanalyzed,
staff retrained, and applicants re-educated about the procedures. The process is "an administrative nightmare, a need-
less jungle of paperwork," damaging the workers and the people they try to serve, according to the Chairman of Food Stamps
of the National Council of State Public Welfare Administrators.[27]

The damage is not only widely reported by professionals in
the program, but obvious to observers who look into the matter. Some people no doubt are too intimidated to even try ap-

Table 20. *Forms Required for Food Stamp Application,*
State of Mississippi, 1984

Form number	Description or contingency	Form number	Description or contingency
500	Application.	522	Social security enumeration.
500-A	Application separate first page.	522-A	SS-5 form.
530	Rights and Responsibilities.	559	FACS form.
		509	Change report form.
520	Workers supplement.	504	Work registration.
521	Food Stamp budget.	533	Notice of action.
528	Route and instruction sheet.	514	If any bank account.
		513	If receiving unemployment.
501	Monthly reporting form (requires detailed explanation.)	MBR	If receiving Social Security or SSI.
525-A	Notice to issuance unit.	517	If receiving ADC.
531	Request for information (more often than not requires two).	502	If authorized representative.
			Daysheets.

plying. It is difficult for well-educated people to complete the forms, let alone the less well-educated who comprise the majority of the poor. One can only speculate how imposing a packet of forms is to one who can hardly read. In addition, forms usually are only in English, making it very difficult for refugees and non-English-speaking American citizens to apply for aid.

The point is not that the application process is impossible, but that it is so onerous that it acts as a barrier, a screening device, in and of itself—irrespective of whether people are eligible for help. Many people get screened out by the application process alone.

Physician George Pickett, a member of the Physician Task Force and formerly director of the California Department of Welfare, observed that the federal food stamp procedures now used are more difficult than income tax documents:[28] "The forms and procedures for food stamps are more onerous than tax forms. I have given food stamp forms to legislators, along with instructions which are given to applicants, and they have been unable to complete the forms accurately."

Dr. Pickett went on to note that the difficult application process, along with the constant program turmoil created by changing regulations, "artfully produces an adversarial relationship between workers and clients resulting in denials of eligibility."[29] This adversarial relationship is real, and of great concern to many food stamp administrators.

With the ever-changing regulations, increasing paperwork, and decreasing staff levels, food stamp workers are indeed placed in an adversarial relationship with people they otherwise would wish to help.

For the elderly couple raising their grandson, the decision to apply for food stamps may be traumatic in itself. To be told, however, that despite lack of food in the house they will first have to prove that they are the child's legal guardians may lead to stress that is exhibited in the food stamp office. Or for other adults applying for food stamps to be told that they must first apply for social security numbers for their children may seem an infuriating obstacle, a delay which can lead hungry people to be less than understanding toward the bureaucrats they see standing between their families and food.

But the nastiness of the adversarial relationship goes both ways. "We noted abrupt and basically nasty treatment of clients, and little expression of sympathy," reported Dr. Joyce Lashoff, dean of the University of California School of Public Health, following state field visits. "Supervisors state that newly-instituted procedural requirements place a burden on staff and clients alike."[30] In other instances, we learned from food stamp supervisors that they instruct workers during their training "not to take the time to go into the details of benefits and so on with clients."[31]

The onerousness and adversarial nature of the process is largely a result of the new paperwork requirements imposed on the states from Washington. But other changes contribute to the tensions created, and to the likelihood that increasing numbers of eligible applicants will not make it through the application process successfully. The requirements which contribute to this outcome are numerous, but we will discuss two examples.

The first is the elimination of all food stamp outreach

workers by the federal government. In 1982, the Department of Agriculture ordered every state to stop using federal funds for food stamp outreach efforts. Outreach workers previously worked with people during the application process, helping them complete forms and obtain necessary documents to help determine eligibility, and, in the case of disabled and elderly applicants, bringing them in for office visits or, alternatively, meeting with them in their homes. In addition, one of the responsibilities of the outreach workers was to locate people who were in need of food stamps but who did not know about the program or had never applied. An example would be to identify illiterate people or recent immigrants who are poor and hungry and who, because they do not know of the program or do not know how to apply, are not receiving assistance. In 1982, all outreach activities were terminated.

Another example concerns one of the functions previously performed by some outreach workers—transportation. With no outreach workers, and with new procedural requirements, transportation has become a reason many recipients are terminated from the rolls.

"We have many old people, some with arthritis or otherwise incapacitated, who were dropped from food stamps because they had no way to get to the office," reported home health nurse Joyce Stancil of Greenwood, Mississippi. "The food stamp program," reported another worker, "is not designed to reach people [who] must travel 20 to 40 miles round trip."[32]

The transportation problem is particularly difficult for the disabled and rural elderly, not only because the offices may be up to 25 miles away, but because newly complicated procedures may require multiple office visits. For many elderly who receive social security, food stamp benefits may be as little as $10 a month—an amount that may be important to them and their diet but is more than used up by car or cab fare during one trip to the food stamp office. Many drop out as a result.

Transportation during the application process is one obstacle; another is transportation once eligibility is determined. The federal government, by placing stringent restrictions on state food stamps, leads some states to require recipients to pick up their stamps each month instead of getting them through the mail. Some states, in particular, have experienced postal thefts of food stamps. The Department of Agriculture has, through excessive pressure on the states, placed on recipients the burden of coming to get the stamps each month.

In state after state we learned from workers and recipients alike that this practice causes many needy people to go without their food stamps. Social security recipients who have made it through the application process to be awarded $10 monthly in food stamps then find that they spend at least that amount each month in transportation to and from the food stamp office. Once there, many have to wait in long lines, sometimes for hours at a time. Some states permit mailing of food stamps, but require recipients to sign for them upon receipt. In rural areas, we learned, many people, again primarily the elderly, often wait an hour or two, at mail boxes some distance from their homes, for the postman to arrive. The nearest post office is miles away, and should they miss the delivery, they must travel that distance or go without food.

Many state and local governments object to the obstacles which the federal government places in the way of food stamp recipients, and to the hardship created as a result. The federal government, however, has the power to see that the other levels of government adhere to these obstacles.

The Department of Agriculture created error rate targets to which the states must adhere each year. States with error rates above the target are sanctioned by loss of federal funds, which can be substantial. The fear of losing this federal reimbursement makes states comply with every new mandate that comes from the Department.

The imposition of error rates is ironic because, as we will see, the new policies and procedures required by the Department of Agriculture create even more paperwork. With fewer staff to do it, it becomes more likely that errors will occur. But the greater impact is on the recipients themselves. The Department ignores errors which hurt clients, penalizing states only for errors in favor of clients.

Since error rates ultimately reflect individual cases, let us take one case to examine the impact of the policy. Mrs. Jones comes to the food stamp office for a required review of her case. During the interview the worker notes that an employer has reported income paid to Mrs. Jones (through her computerized social security number). Mrs. Jones, as a result, is terminated from the food stamp program for unreported earnings, even though she did not work or receive any income. Several weeks later, it is found that the social security number linking the income to her was in fact a keypunch error. Even though Mrs. Jones is still eligible for food stamps, she and her family have been cut off the program for weeks and will have to go through the laborious application process all over again.

Even though this impoverished American family was denied an entitlement which was legally its right, the Department of Agriculture does not consider it an error. In fact the Department does not count this as an error even if the family never recoups what it lost while terminated from the program. If Mrs. Smith, on the other hand, had mistakenly been given an extra five dollars a month in food stamp benefits through a calculation error by her worker, the Department would count that as part of the state's overall error rate, which could result in sanctions for the state.

By imposing the error rate system as it does, the Department insures that states follow its dictates, regardless of the consequences to recipients. And by imposing sanctions only for errors in favor of the client, the Department creates an explicit bias against applicants. Because states and workers can be penalized only for giving assistance when they should not, but not for not giving it when they should, the bias is to deny.

"When in doubt, deny," stated one administrator. "That's what the government is making us do. Do we hurt a lot of people this way? You bet! Do we mean to? No. But the federal government wants to create an anti-recipient system and they have it. There's nothing we can do about it because they hold the purse strings."[33]

Other officials find the system of sanctions against the states, and the bias against clients, unfair in other ways. "What error rate sanctions have been applied to the Defense Department?" asked one state welfare commissioner. "Why have social programs become the target of error rates and sanctions? Why aren't error rate sanctions applied where the big bucks are in trying to reduce deficits?"[34]

Getting Food Stamp Beneficiaries Off the Program

To this point, many of the new practices discussed serve to prevent needy people from applying for or receiving food stamps in the first place. Yet, those who do make it through the application and verification process face constant hurdles in order to continue receiving stamps for food. Failure to leap any one of them can lead to termination from the program and serious problems for the family.

The practices employed are required by the Department of Agriculture. While unique to the Department and the food stamp program, they have the same effect that the SSDI eligibility redeterminations had on disabled recipients of that program before Congress forced discontinuation of the practices. We turn now to the practices which result in many food stamp families being denied benefits—again, even though they are eligible.

Under the OBRA budget act of 1981, states were required to begin a mandatory monthly reporting and retrospective budgeting (MRRB) program for food stamp recipients. Recently modified somewhat, the MRRB system was established because of its presumed efficiency and because it was supposed to reduce errors and save money. It originally was based on the first year of a two-year MRRB demonstration program in Boulder, Colorado.

The monthly reporting component requires that food stamp households receiving any income have their eligibility redetermined every month rather than every several months, as had been the case previously. This means that every month, for example, a father who earns from $50 to $60 a week doing odd jobs has to complete a report or come to the food stamp office to report his earnings. Moreover, he must have verification of all earnings; otherwise he and his family may be terminated.

Retrospective budgeting, on the other hand, is an accounting procedure used to determine the amount of food stamps a family with some income is to get. The level of stamps for a given month is based on the family's average income during the second preceding month. Retrospective budgeting often has a devastating impact on marginally employed families. A family may have a steady income, but so small that it is eligible for food stamps each month to supplement the income. Yet, with retrospective budgeting, their food stamp allotment will always be based on what the family earned two months before. If the family suddenly loses its entire income, it may be weeks before the food stamp allotment is adjusted upward. Examples of families suffering as a result, going extended periods of time without food, are provided by program administrators, emergency food providers, and clergy in every state.

Both retrospective budgeting and monthly reporting are procedures which enormously increase the paperwork for food stamp workers, place inordinate burdens on families with few resources, and frequently result in their being terminated from the program for mistakes or minor infractions. A Mississippi father was terminated from food stamps because he forgot to report that he earned $5 several weeks before by hauling wood for a neighbor. The father who earned $22 cleaning a vacant lot, and who did report it but had no receipt to verify the amount and was cut off as a result, is another example.

The practice of terminating clients for the smallest of bureaucratic reasons is common in food stamp programs throughout the nation. Ministers and doctors report it among their congregations and patients. Poor families report being cut off. Elderly get cut off, many never knowing why. And program administrators themselves acknowledge the practice. But, they say, it is required by the Department of Agriculture and if they do not terminate the recipients, the states stand to be penalized.

Without question MRRB hurts recipients. It causes absolute anguish in many families. Over and over we found hungry people who had been terminated from food stamps for reasons relating to MRRB. But, it might be asked, while MRRB hurts clients, does it in fact reduce error rates as it was intended to do? Since 1981, extensive research on MRRB has been done, including experiments in Michigan, New York, and Illinois. None of the new studies shows the same encouraging, money-saving results as the first year of the Colorado demonstration program upon which the MRRB requirements were based.[35] In fact, the second year of the Colorado program actually led to an *increase* in costs. The first-year savings were an artifact of comparing the new system to a poorly run conventional system; when the latter was updated, it actually performed better than MRRB.

In Michigan, MRRB resulted in a savings of 0.2%, defined as statistically insignificant, and resulted in increased administrative costs. In the Illinois program, administrative costs rose with no reduction in error rate.

Data from the states where MRRB has been closely monitored shows that MRRB is not only costly, but generally ineffective in reducing error rates. While some of the MRRB demonstration projects have been in the AFDC program (both AFDC and food stamps require MRRB under certain circumstances), several studies specifically tested MRRB in the food stamps program. One such study, done by John Bayne, analyzed MRRB research for the U.S. Department of Health and Human Services from 1978 to 1982. He concluded that MRRB, as required in the food stamp program, "may well increase some types of errors and overall program costs." One is forced to conclude, Bayne noted, "that regular quarterly redeterminations can be a much more effective method of caseload management than monthly reporting."[36]

The Deficit Reduction Act of 1984 partially repealed some of the MRRB requirements for AFDC households (ironically bringing about yet another change in administration of the food stamp program with which workers and recipients of both AFDC and food stamps must contend). But administrators still report that the burden placed on them and the recipients is not worth it. "Monthly reporting," stated Alabama supervisor Sarah Lunn, "does not save money. It increases errors by requiring more paperwork."[37]

"MRRB is a lot of work for nothing," added Chris Murphree, administrator of the food stamp office in Greenwood, Mississippi.[38] And, noted Virginia Eldreth, administrator in Buncombe County, North Carolina, "it is causing so much attention to paperwork that we are serving fewer people as a result."[39]

"Workers in food stamp offices are being put in the position of being an accountant, real estate agent, and lawyer," observed Wanda Jackson Speights, herself a paralegal whose clients include food stamp recipients. "It's no wonder they're not nice sometimes."[40]

Concluding Statement

It may be little wonder that the food stamp program is not nice to clients at times. But nice or not, the issue is why any government program embodies procedures and practices overtly harmful to large numbers of people it is supposed to help. And, of course, the question is why the program was changed in the past few years in such a way as to have a profoundly harmful impact on families and individuals.

One scholar of federal programs sees these new policies and their effects as more than mistakes:[41] "There is a saying in the motor vehicle field that 'staying alive is no accident.' Hunger is no accident either. The policies of denying assistance to many of the neediest people are for the most part the result of deliberate efforts at the federal and state levels to discourage otherwise eligible people from qualifying or staying on public assistance."

Few citizens, no doubt, would like to believe that their government purposely designs schemes which harm other citizens, particularly the most vulnerable population groups. But the question of deliberateness may not be the central point. Whether by design or grossly insensitive administration, several of the most important federal programs serving the poor are often unresponsive to human need. Not infrequently they are overtly hostile and destructive. Whether by intent or incompetence, the impact on the needy is the same.

One year ago, for example, the President's Task Force on Food Assistance (hunger) pointed out that many homeless people in the nation are not getting food stamps because of an Agriculture Department regulation requiring all recipients to have a mailing address.[42] The Administration promised to move on this problem immediately—a relatively simple problem which could be solved in a few days. Yet more than a year later the Department still has not taken effective steps to insure that states discontinue the use of this requirement. One example of a problem, admittedly, but a clear one: irrespective of intent, hungry people who are eligible for food stamps are not getting them directly because of governmental action.

Unfortunately, the system of bureaucratic obstacles and overt hostility we have examined is altogether consistent with available data and our field experience. Food stamp recipients are decreasing in number as poverty and, therefore, eligibility for food stamps increases. We believe that this phenomenon is due in large part to the policies and practices which we found in the field, and which we have described here.

Bureaucratic practices are being employed which require Americans with the fewest resources to be the most resourceful in feeding their families. It does not make sense as a matter of logic or public policy. As a consequence, many hungry citizens are getting no help at all.

7. ELIMINATING HUNGER IN AMERICA

As a body of doctors and health care professionals, we believe it is time to end hunger in America.

It is our judgment that hunger and related ill-health have no place in a democratic society, especially one with the resources of the United States.

This nation has the resources and ability to end hunger. We have heard no one deny that this is true. America is not a poverty-stricken Third World nation caught between the pincers of a poor economy and inadequate food supply. To the contrary, we produce enough food to feed our people probably several times over. Our nation's warehouses bulge with food, so much food that each year thousands of tons are wasted or destroyed. Clearly lack of food is not the cause of hunger in America.

Neither do we lack the financial resources to end hunger in this land. Ours is perhaps the strongest economy in the world. We cannot maintain that we lack the resources to end hunger when numerous other industrialized nations have done so. That is illogical. In fact, by increasing annual federal food programs just by the amount we spend on two CVN Nuclear Attack Carriers, we could probably eliminate hunger in the nation. No, lack of money is not the cause of hunger in America.

Neither do we have hunger because we don't know how to end it. Through very recent experience, we are certain that we can end hunger if we wish to do so. Hunger and malnutrition were serious problems in this country in 1968. Then as today, national organizations, church groups, and universities investigated and found hunger. Government agencies, as today, found hunger. And as today, doctors went into regions of the country and reported that it was a widespread and serious problem.

The nation responded to that problem. In the decade between 1970 and 1980 we extended the food stamp program from the 2 million poor Americans which it covered at the time to some 20 million people. While this did not cover all Americans living in poverty, other nutrition programs provided assistance. We expanded the free school lunch and breakfast programs. We established elderly feeding programs (congregate meal sites and Meals-on-Wheels for shut-ins) to insure that our senior citizens did not go hungry. And we established the Women, Infants, and Children (WIC) program to insure adequate nourishment for low-income pregnant women and their infants.

These programs were established in response to hunger among American people, and they worked. Teams of doctors in 1977 retraced the routes they had covered the previous decade when they found serious hunger and malnutrition. Summarizing their findings, the medical teams stated: [1]

Our first and overwhelming impression is that there are far fewer grossly malnourished people in this country today than there were ten years ago . . . many poor people now have food and look better off. This does not appear to be due to an overall improvement in living standards. In fact, the facts of life for Americans living in poverty remain as dark or darker than they were ten years ago.

But in the area of food there is a difference. The food stamp program, the nutritional component of Head Start, school lunch and breakfast programs, and to a lesser extent the Women, Infants, and Children (WIC) program have made the difference.

In a few years this nation basically eliminated hunger as a problem. The success was relatively swift and not difficult to see. So, clearly, we do not lack the experience or the knowhow to end hunger in America. We have enough food to end hunger in this land. We have enough wealth to end hunger. And we have recent experience upon which to rely. All that remains is the political will.

Immediate Steps to End Hunger

Today we have a public health crisis which threatens a significant segment of our population. We must respond to it as we would any other problem of epidemic proportions.

We would not permit other health crises to become so widespread before acting. Yet hunger afflicts more of our citizens than do AIDS or Legionnaires Disease. In fact it constitutes one of the more serious problems imperiling the health and well-being of our people today.

But while hunger is a health epidemic, it cannot be ended by those in the medical profession. Like most public health problems it must be addressed in the political and public policy arena. In short, our political leaders must be responsible for ending hunger. The essence of political leadership is to lead—to respond to problems. That, in part, is why we have government. Today, we need leadership from our political leaders. It is time to end the contrived befuddlement of some who wring their hands wondering what to do about hunger.

It is time to stop responding to hunger by cutting children's school lunches. It is time to show more compassion for hungry families than by reducing their food stamps even as they become poorer. And it is time to set aside compassionate platitudes and political rhetoric about how loving a people we are.

Let us feed the hungry of our nation.

We call upon Republicans and Democrats in the United States Congress to take immediate action to feed the hungry.

We ask that the leadership of the House and Senate, on a bipartisan basis, announce that it will prepare an emergency legislative package to respond to the hunger crisis. The components of the plan should include:

- *Strengthening the food stamp program*

Increase food stamp benefits to American families and individuals by a minimum of 25%, to the level of the USDA low-cost food plan.

Remove restrictive food stamp measures which eliminated the "new poor" and working poor from the program; families with gross incomes of up to 150% of poverty, but whose disposable income is below poverty, should be assisted.

Alter asset restrictions so families experiencing temporary economic hardship are not driven further into poverty as a condition for getting food stamps.

Alter restrictive deductions such as those for shelter, child care, and residency requirements in the food stamp program.

Take immediate legislative action (similar to that enacted recently for Social Security Disability Insurance) to terminate administrative policies which harass and otherwise prevent needy eligible citizens from receiving food stamp assistance.

- *Strengthening school and other meals programs for children*

Restore eligibility for free and reduced-price meals for children recently removed from the programs.

Increase the federal subsidy for free and reduced-price meals to enable more children from families living on the economic margins to participate in the program.

Restore the child care, milk, and summer feeding programs for children whose family incomes previously permitted them to participate.

- *Utilizing the WIC and Medicaid programs more fully to protect high-risk children*

Expand the WIC (Women, Infants, and Children Supplemental Feeding Program) to cover all currently eligible mothers who wish to participate.

Extend Medicaid benefits to all pregnant women and children under 18 living below the federal poverty level, to insure better health care and birth outcomes.

- *Expanding elderly meals programs to be certain that all low-income elderly have access to congregate meals or the Meals-on-Wheels program*

- *Protecting families by strengthening income support programs*

Expand unemployment benefits for unemployed families left without work so that the two-thirds of the unemployed now with no benefits are covered by the program.

Expand AFDC assistance by federal legislation to bring children above the poverty level; this should include coverage for the unborn child to insure adequate nutrition, and should include mandatory coverage in all states for fathers in the home so that federal and state policy no longer forces families to break apart to become eligible for help.

Congress should pass legislation to create a permanent and independent body to monitor the nutritional status of the population.
Our nation should have on-going access to current data on the nutritional status of its people, particularly high-risk populations such as children, pregnant women, and the elderly. This proposal was made by the 1969 White House Conference on Food, Nutrition, and Health convened by President Nixon. It should be established without further delay.

We ask that appropriate Congressional committees direct responsible administrative agencies to report on a quarterly basis progress made in eliminating hunger, until such time as it has been ended in America.
We believe that, based on past experience and the fact that we have the programmatic vehicles still in place, our nation can eliminate hunger within six months. Such a time frame, however, will require continuing oversight by appropriate Congressional committees to be certain that administrative departments and agencies are carrying out the will of the Congress.

Longer-Term Steps to Prevent the Return of Hunger

If the Congress agrees to undertake the above plan of action, it will end the present hunger crisis. But the proposed plan alone may be insufficient to end poverty in America.

The fact that hunger, once nearly ended in the nation, returned as such a serious problem clearly points to the need to undertake more serious and far-reaching policies to eliminate the poverty which underlies hunger. We would do well to address this more fundamental problem.

We ask the United States Congress to establish a Bipartisan Study Commission to recommend legislative changes to protect all our citizens from the ravages of poverty and its attendant ills in the future.

As a body of physicians and other health professionals, we believe it is unwise to permit hunger and malnutrition to exist in this nation. We believe not only that these problems must be eradicated, but that our country can and should address the underlying poverty which victimizes so many of our citizens.

We would not tell sick patients that they might improve without medical treatment if we have the means to treat them and limit their present pain and discomfort. Neither should our political leaders hope that hungry Americans will one day be less hungry when our nation now has the means to respond to their suffering and its underlying cause.

APPENDICES

A. The Extent of Hunger in America

No official "hunger count" exists in the United States, so we have no precise way of knowing how many hungry people there are. But methods exist by which we can estimate the dimensions of the problem and, based on these, we believe that some 20,000,000 Americans suffer from hunger.

The majority of this number, over 15 million, are people who live below the poverty line but who receive no food stamp assistance. The remainder are income groups below poverty who receive food stamps but for whom the program is inadequate; they are joined by near-poor families whose economic circumstances make adequate food purchases impossible. These groups and the manner in which we estimate their numbers are detailed in this appendix.

Approximately 35.3 million Americans live below the official government poverty level.[1] In the United States poverty is defined by a construct based specifically on the ability to purchase a minimal diet.[2] As a matter of policy, families living at or below the poverty level do not have sufficient income to purchase a nutritionally adequate diet.[3]

Of the 35.3 million people in poverty, most are eligible for food stamps. Many, however, do not receive food stamp assistance. Some of them are eligible but get no help for various reasons. Others are in need but technically are ineligible. By their income they are eligible, but because they have assets (such as the new poor who may own cars) they cannot get food stamps even when they have no food.

With this information in mind, we can then calculate the number of people below poverty who cannot purchase the food they need.

A. *People in poverty who receive no food stamps.* While 35.3 million Americans are in poverty, only 19.8 million receive food stamps.[4] It is possible to receive food stamps with an income up to 130% of poverty, so all food stamps recipients do not live below the poverty level. But since there are no current data available on the percentage of food stamp recipients in poverty, we will assume for the purposes of our calculations that all food stamps go to people below the poverty level. (By assuming that more poor people get food stamps than actually do, this calculations is unduly conservative.)

Even so, we see that more than 15 million impoverished Americans have an inadequate food supply:

$$35,300,000 - 19,800,000 = 15,500,000.$$

B. *People in poverty who do receive food stamps.* The evidence cited in this report, as well as from numerous other sources, shows that food stamp benefit levels are not adequate for a large proportion of recipients. Thus, some recipients experience hunger as a result.

We know in several ways that benefit levels are nutritionally inadequate: a) the thrifty food plan, upon which food stamp benefit levels are based, is by definition nutritionally inadequate;[5] b) food stamp families have lost purchasing power over the years; c) food stamps, even in combination with AFDC, yield a monthly income well below the poverty level in every state;[6] d) national and state survey data show that a large proportion of food stamp recipients run out of food the third to fourth week of the month; and e) emergency food programs throughout the nation report that a large proportion of the people they try to help are food stamp recipients who run out of food.

Despite this evidence, there is no definitive basis upon which to calculate the number of below-poverty food stamp recipients who at times experience hunger. One national survey found that 96% of food stamp recipients interviewed at emergency food programs consistently run out of food stamps each month.[7] Given the bias of the sample, however (it being administered among recipients at emergency programs), the figure cannot be applied to the general food stamp population.

State and local food stamp recipient surveys have found that, depending on the survey, from 50% to 90% of recipients run out of food each month. Again, however, problems of small sample size and bias make it difficult to generalize to the larger recipient population.

Taking into account our own investigation and the survey data available, we believe that most people living below the poverty line on a food stamp budget are unable to purchase a nutritionally adequate diet. But in order to provide a conservative estimate of people in this category, we will calculate their numbers by taking the lowest survey finding (50%), and then reduce that by half:

$$.50 \times .50 \times 19,800,000 = 4,950,000.$$

People below the poverty level are not the only Americans vulnerable to hunger. Food stamp eligibility extends to households with gross income up to 130% of poverty, so long as net income is below poverty. The individuals exposed to hunger within this income category fall into two more groups: those eligible for food stamps and those who are not.

C. People at 100–130% poverty who are food stamp eligible/ineligible. Census data provide no precise count of people whose incomes range between 100% and 130% of poverty. We do, however, know that there are 11.9 million people with household incomes between 100% and 125% of poverty. For purposes of simplicity we will assume that these 11.9 million people constitute the total near-poor population.[8]

We have no good way of determining how many of these people may be hungry. Some who receive food stamps, and who experience hunger when their inadequate allotments run out, have been implicitly counted in category B above (when we made the conservative assumption that all food stamp recipients are below poverty). Others within this income class are not eligible for food stamps for technical reasons: assets above eligibility guidelines, net income above poverty level, and related reasons.

Many within these near-poor groups (those eligible and those ineligible for food stamps) clearly experience hunger, but we have no way of quantifying that number.

D. People above 130% poverty who are in need but ineligible. Until the passage of OBRA, the 1981 federal budget act, food stamp eligibility extended to households with incomes up to 150% of poverty. Before OBRA, government policy acknowledged need among certain households with high child care costs or other expenses which brought net income to a level which makes adequate food purchases impossible.

With OBRA, the policy changed but the need did not. The census reports that the number of people between 125% and 150% of poverty is 12.2 million.[9] Unfortunately, no way exists to determine how many people in this group experience hunger. In categories C and D, therefore, we have 24.1 million people whose incomes make many of them vulnerable to an inadequate food supply. Let us assume that of all the people living in both groups (100–150% of poverty), only 10% experience hunger. This assumption would yield the following calculation:

$$.10(11,900,000 + 12,200,000) = 2,410,000.$$

Based on these calculations, we estimate that somewhat over 20 million Americans experience hunger. Because we have made conservative assumptions whenever presented with the choice, we believe the actual number may be higher. There is some independent confirmation of our estimate. In January, 1984, the Harris Survey interviewed a sample of 1,251 adults throughout the United States. Each interview subject was asked about first-hand knowledge of hunger (Do you know anyone who is hungry? Is that someone close to you or not?). According to the Harris Survey outcome:[10] "A substantial 7.6 million households report that members of their families are hungry and do not get enough to eat. This translates into close to 21 million Americans who can reasonably be classified as suffering from hunger."

Nearly 80% of respondents agreed with the statement that because the number of homeless is increasing, and because the number of soup kitchen lines is increasing, there can be no doubt that there are many hungry people in America today. Concluded the Harris Survey:[11] "By any count it is obvious that the vast majority of the American people are convinced that hunger is a problem in this country, that it is a matter which touches the vast majority deeply, and that in actual measurement hunger indeed is a highly serious matter, even in affluent America."

We realize that reasonable people may disagree with our calculations, or with the results of the national Harris Survey. Some, for instance, might argue that hunger cannot be equated with a nutritionally inadequate diet. Others might argue that the poor spend more of their income on food than is assumed by the government in constructing the federal poverty level. Some may raise yet other issues. Nevertheless, we feel confident in the methodology and reasonableness of our conservative calculations. Moreover, we believe they help us to understand the dimensions of domestic hunger.

While it is helpful to understand the dimensions of the hunger problem in America, in a fundamental sense it is not necessary to know the number of hungry people before we take steps to feed them. Protracted debate over numbers can delay dealing with the problem. Clearly this must not happen.

We would not expect our political leaders and government agencies to respond to a major earthquake by saying that nothing can be done until the casualties are counted. Neither is it appropriate to first count the number of hungry Americans, a problem of even larger dimensions, before we take immediate steps to end their suffering.

B. AFDC and Food Stamp Benefits as a Percent of Poverty for a Family of Four

The federal poverty level for a family of four is $10,608. As has been established, even this income level is not adequate for a family to provide for basic necessities and to purchase food supplies necessary to meet minimum nutritional requirements.

In no state in the nation, however, does the combined income from food stamps and AFDC (two major safety net programs) even bring a family up to the poverty level.

In Alaska, the state with the highest combined benefits, family income is 89.3% of poverty. In Mississippi, the state with the lowest benefit levels, the combination of these two programs yields a family income of less than half the poverty level (43.4%).

An examination of state-by-state benefit levels for these two programs helps one to understand the contribution which their combined inadequacy makes to the national hunger problem.

State	AFDC benefit	AFDC as a percent of poverty	Food stamps benefit	Total benefit	Total benefit as a percent of poverty	Rank of state
Alabama	$147	16.6%	$264	$411	46.5%	50
Alaska	775	70.1	212	987	89.3	1
Arizona	282	31.9	256	538	60.9	38
Arkansas	191	21.6	264	455	51.5	48
California	660	74.7	143	803	90.8	3
Colorado	420	47.5	215	635	71.8	21
Connecticut	549	62.1	176	725	82.0	8
Delaware	336	38.0	240	576	65.2	33
Dist. of Columbia	366	41.4	231	597	67.5	29
Florida	273	30.9	259	532	60.2	39
Georgia	245	27.7	264	509	57.6	43
Hawaii	546	53.7	318	864	85.0	9
Idaho	344	38.9	238	582	65.8	31
Illinois	368	41.6	230	598	67.7	28
Indiana	316	35.7	246	562	63.6	35
Iowa	419	47.4	215	634	71.7	22
Kansas	396	44.8	222	618	69.9	24

State	AFDC benefit	AFDC as a percent of poverty	Food stamps benefit	Total benefit	Total benefit as a percent of poverty	Rank of state
Kentucky	$246	27.8%	$264	$510	57.7%	42
Louisiana	234	26.5	264	498	56.3	44
Maine	452	51.1	205	657	74.3	12
Maryland	376	42.5	228	604	68.3	26
Massachusetts	463	52.4	202	665	75.2	10
Michigan	441	49.9	209	650	73.5	15
Minnesota	611	69.1	158	769	86.9	5
Mississippi	120	13.6	264	384	43.4	51
Missouri	308	34.8	248	556	62.9	37
Montana	425	48.1	213	638	72.2	19
Nebraska	420	47.5	215	635	71.8	20
Nevada	272	30.8	259	531	60.1	40
New Hampshire	429	48.5	212	641	72.5	17
New Jersey	443	50.1	208	651	73.6	14
New Mexico	313	35.4	247	560	63.3	36
New York	566	64.0	171	737	83.4	6
North Carolina	221	25.0	264	485	54.9	45
North Dakota	454	51.4	205	659	74.5	11
Ohio	343	38.8	238	581	65.7	32
Oklahoma	349	39.5	236	585	66.2	30
Oregon	446	50.5	207	653	73.9	13
Pennsylvania	401	45.4	221	622	70.3	23
Rhode Island	440	49.8	209	649	73.4	16
South Carolina	206	23.3	264	470	53.2	46
South Dakota	371	42.0	230	601	67.9	27
Tennessee	168	19.0	264	432	48.9	49
Texas	201	22.7	264	465	52.6	47
Utah	425	48.1	213	638	72.2	18
Vermont	688	77.8	134	822	93.0	2
Virginia	321	36.3	245	566	64.0	34
Washington	561	63.5	173	734	83.0	7
West Virginia	249	28.2	264	513	58.0	41
Wisconsin	612	69.2	157	769	87.0	4
Wyoming	390	44.1	224	614	69.4	25

SOURCE: Center on Budget and Policy Priorities, Washington, D.C., February, 1985.

NOTE: AFDC benefit is as of November 1984. Poverty line has been projected to be $10,608 for calendar year 1984, for a family of four. Food stamp benefits are as of November 1, 1984.

C. Impact of Inadequate Programs
on Dependence

This morning I got pretty scared . . . unusual things happen to your body when you're old. I needed to go to the doctor but the new rules [federal regulations] say you can go just so many times. It reminds me of how we used to have to get permission from the boss man' before the doctor would see us. It's sort of like the old days again.

Mr. Campbell, Greenwood, Mississippi

The rural counties of the Mississippi Delta are in many ways reminiscent of a system of race and class which vanished decades ago from most other parts of the nation. Poor tenant farmers are at the mercy of landowners who still maintain plantations proudly marked by signs along the roads. The families live in primitive, unheated shacks often in exchange for their continued labor. Wages are insufficient to maintain even minimal needs, so the tenants are heavily dependent on the food stamp program.

In order to use the stamps at a store, tenants frequently have to sell them at black market rates as a way to obtain transportation to town, often in the back of the boss's truck.

Having violated the rules of the food stamp program by this transaction, tenants are subject to blackmail by the landowner. At any time, disclosure that the recipient has sold some stamps can result in sanctions by the food stamp office, including a complete cut-off of food stamps for 90 days.

For unemployed families, AFDC is not available if the father stays with his family and Medicaid benefits are not available. During a pregnancy, if the mother wishes to go to a private physician, the family must pay first. Often it borrows from the landowner. Loans of $1,500 are not uncommon and are deducted from whatever monthly wages the borrower receives, at such a rate that it may take a decade or more to pay off the loan. This places the family in servitude to the landowner.

A climate of fear is apparent. On our trip poor families frequently were afraid to speak about their problems until they understood that their visitors were doctors, many from outside the state. Even at public meetings there was some concern that people who spoke up might lose their jobs or be reported to an employer, not for political discourse but for talking about the food stamp system.

So striking is this fear in the Delta that a number of the physicians who visited the area raised the problem in their individual field reports. "People are kept in bondage," one doctor reported. "Getting and staying on food stamps seems almost a full-time occupation," observed another.

Dr. William Beardslee has traveled to the Mississippi Delta on several occasions to investigate hunger and health conditions among the residents. "This time," he reported, "I am angry, saddened, deeply troubled by what I saw. The lives of individuals reflect the reemergence of armored racism and governmental meanness disguised as bureaucracy. Bureaucratic red tape of the food stamp program is like confirmation of life's hopelessness for the poor. Rather than offering hope, the program makes it almost impossible for them to get what they need."

This is not a problem unique to Mississippi. Perhaps for historical reasons it is clearer there, possibly more dramatic. But other physicians observed the hopelessness and sense of powerlessness which come as byproducts of programs which perpetuate poverty and dependence rather than permit citizens the possibility of independence.

Dr. Stanley Gershoff, Dean of the Tufts University School of Nutrition, observed that governmental aid programs are administered in ways which tend to institutionalize poverty. They often penalize people who find low-paying work. Program benefits are lessened and medical care is lost as the result of a father trying to get his family on its feet.

"Federal program regulations for food stamps and AFDC contain serious disincentives for trying to become self-sufficient," notes Dr. David Satcher, President of Meharry Medical College. "A low-paying job means losing Medicaid, and moving in with parents to try to save on rent may mean losing food stamps. This is the result of a family's trying to become independent of government programs."

In Tennessee Dr. Tom Yeager found the same phenomenon operating: "Federal programs interact in such a way that an increase in one results in a decrease in another. Families can never increase the total amount they have in order to become independent. In the words of an eastern Tennessee father, 'you never get ahead.' Governmental programs seem set up to keep people in poverty rather than getting them out."

So pervasive is the intimidation and miserliness within some programs that they have, in the eyes of some observers, become a substitute plantation system. People receive some assistance, but in such a way that it promotes servitude and dependence.

Dr. Aaron Shirley, a Mississippi native, eloquently makes this point in the following field observation report:

This observer has had the opportunity to participate in previous studies of hunger among poor residents of the Mississippi Delta. However, my first-hand experience with hunger and malnutrition is not limited to the days and weeks spent participating in studies such as this. Mine is an everyday experience of attempting to provide health care and nutritional support and counseling in Jackson, the state capital.

While I agreed to participate in this particular study, there was considerable doubt in my mind as to any meaningful improvement that might result from our documentation of this problem, given the attitude that prevails in Washington. My general feeling was, "Why another study?" It is general knowledge among most knowledgeable people that hunger is a problem. I reluctantly agreed after realizing that to do nothing assured no action, while there is a remote possibility that just one more try might do some good.

As a life-long resident of this state and as a practicing physician among the poor for 25 years, I have on a day-to-day basis come to realize that the problems of hunger are related not just to poverty, but to a system so imbedded in our society that any attempt to alleviate hunger will have only a marginal impact unless there are more basic changes in:

A. An economic system which perpetuates a plantation mode of operation for those in power, which in turn fosters a plantation mentality among the poor, especially in the Mississippi Delta.
B. A food stamp distribution system which reinforces "A," above.
C. A political system which reinforces "A" and "B."
D. A criminal justice system which supports all three.

A description of several encounters with families which we had in Leflore and Holmes might best illustrate what I mean. In one household on a plantation in Itta Bena, only a stone's throw from Mississippi Valley State University (a predominantly black institution), a family consisted of four generations of plantation life with all evidence of future generations of the same. There was an elderly lady of 74 years; her 44-year-old daughter; the daughter's 19-year-old daughter, who had dropped out of 11th grade; and the granddaughter's 18-month-old child.

In the Mississippi Delta this all too often is the case. Generation after generation is found where family members are ill-housed, overworked, underpaid, and with little or no formal education, Because of isolation and lack of knowledge there is very little opportunity to escape this vicious cycle of deprivation. Thus, when we physicians and others visit this area at ten-year intervals, it is little wonder that we often find the same conditions over and over again.

This particular family was hungry. There was no food in the house. It was towards the end of the month and the food stamps always run out before the month ends. Thanks to the WIC Program, the 18-month-old had formula, but the older woman, the daughter, and the granddaughter were cold and hungry. How does the food stamp program reinforce the conditions just described? One has to fully understand the plantation system in order to make the connection.

On the typical plantation there is the white owner, the white overseer, and the black tenant farmer. The tenant farmer and his family are at the complete mercy of the overseer, who reports directly to the owner. The owner's interest is best served by a docile tenant, and in order to assure this state of mind it is better to discourage education and knowledge. The owner controls the local public schools that the tenant farmer's children attend (if they attend at all; the owner's children attend private segregated academies). The overseer is frequently the tenant farmer's major contact with creditors, places of business, legal assistance, etc. Thus the overseer exerts considerable influence over the tenant farmer and family—influences such as to discourage them from voting, seeking justice, or petitioning for better schools and educational opportunities.

Now comes the food stamp program with its organizational structure and administration. What we have is the white county welfare director (plantation owner), the white welfare case worker (overseer), and the black food stamp recipient (tenant farmer). The same conditions and forces prevail, with all the attending adverse effects as exist on the plantation farm itself.

This may best be illustrated by an interview with a pregnant girl waiting in the line outside the food stamp office at 7 in the morning in Greenwood. She already had one child and was expecting another any day. Her food stamps had run out about a week before and she and her child were hungry. She was anxiously waiting to receive her allotment of $90.00 worth of stamps, which would be for the month of May. She had experienced several humiliating encounters with her welfare case worker (overseer) over her second pregnancy. Who was the father? Was she still sexually active? When the new baby arrived, copies of the infant's footprint would have to be provided to the case worker before the food stamp allotment could be increased by another few dollars. In any case there would be a 30-day waiting period no matter what. Neighbors of the young mother were constantly queried about who visited her, and how often. All of this bothered the young food stamp recipient (tenant) but she felt powerless and helpless. As a child she had been raised on a plantation farm with her parents. This "way of life" had been imbedded in her mind and even though she had escaped physical contact with the farm plantation the system outside was the same. She, like her parents, wouldn't dare challenge the overseer (case worker) or the plantation owner (county welfare director).

The criminal justice system as applied also perpetuates this system system. On the real plantation, as the tenant becomes more enlightened and attempts to exert himself as a free individual, the overseer is responsible for keeping him in his place. We frequently see assertive black tenant farmers accused of stealing some item from their bosses such as a battery or tractor part, indicted and convicted by an all-white jury or a jury made up of mostly whites and some ill-informed and intimidated blacks, many of whom are themselves tenant farmers. How does this relate to the food stamp program? Families we interviewed in Holmes County revealed this connection. For historical reasons, Holmes County blacks are more assertive. They have traditionally owned land and have been politically active over the past two decades. Time after time there were statements from Holmes County food stamp recipients relating to prosecution for abuse of the food stamp program. Selective prosecution, as it is referred to in legal circles, is used to control assertive blacks who are legally entitled to food stamps. Holmes County perhaps has one of the highest percentages of this type of intimidation of any county in the state.

Why have I taken this approach in my report on hunger? Wasn't it after all our task simply to investigate the existence of hunger and malnutrition? As I have lived in this area all my life and as I have been confronted with the problems of malnutrition and its adverse effects on health, particularly among children, my reaction is different from that of an occasional observer. My overriding concern is why do these conditions have to persist. Certainly the food stamp and other food assistance programs have made the difference between the outright starvation which we observed in the 1960s and the conditions we are seeing today.

I feel compelled, however, to expand on the issue of hunger in this country, especially aiming the most vulnerable and most powerless population groups, and to raise a critical issue about one of the basic food assistance components, the food stamp program. This program, with all its proven effectiveness and benefits, is being administered in some ways in a manner which perpetuates the root causes of people being hungry in the first place. As we address the obvious need for increased appropriations for this program, very strong consideration must be given to the manner in which it is being administered. Lessons could be learned from the Head Start programs, where the administration is left to community-based, non-profit sponsors. This mechanism eliminates the white landowner / white overseer / black tenant family syndrome. The products are more compassionate administrators; Head Start teachers and social workers who instill into the children and their parents a feeling of self-worth; and, most important, a generation of enlightened children whose minds have been freed from the plantation mentality which has enslaved so many of those currently in need of food assistance. Would it be such a bad idea to place the administration of food stamp programs in the hands of Head Start programs and maybe community-based health programs? I think it deserves serious consideration.

NOTES

Notes

Foreword

1. Drew, Elizabeth, "Going Hungry in America: Government's Failure," *Atlantic Monthly,* December, 1968 (article based on report of physicians to the Senate Subcommittee on Poverty, 1967).

1. Task Force Purposes and Findings

1. Shirley, Aaron, M.D., letter of June 13, 1984, based on field investigation report covering Leflore and Holmes Counties, Mississipi, April 30, May 1, 1984.
2. April 29, 30, 1984, Harvard School of Public Health, Boston, Massachusetts.
3. Citizens' Commission on Hunger in New England, *American Hunger Crisis: Poverty and Health in New England,* Harvard School of Public Health, February, 1984.

2. Hunger as a Well-Documented Phenomenon

1. United States Conference of Mayors, *Human Services in FY82,* Washington, D.C., October, 1982.
2. United States Conference of Mayors, *Hunger in American Cities,* Washington, D.C., June, 1983, p. 3.
3. ibid.
4. ibid.
5. "Report on Nine Case Studies of Emergency Food Assistance Programs," submitted by Social and Scientific Systems, Inc. to the United States Department of Agriculture, Washington, D.C., May, 1983.
6. Center on Budget and Policy Priorities, *Soup Lines and Food Baskets,* Washington, D.C., May, 1983.
7. U.S. General Accounting Office (GAO), *Public and Private Efforts to Feed America's Poor,* Washington, D.C., June, 1983.
8. United Church of Christ, *World Hunger Action Program Report,* January, 1983.
9. Salvation Army of America, *Report,* New York, New York, June, 1983.
10. National Council of Churches, *Work Group on Hunger and Poverty Report,* August, 1983.
11. Bread For the World, *Hunger Watch,* Washington, D.C., September, 1983.

12. Food Research and Action Center (FRAC), *Still Hungry*, New York, New York, November, 1983.
13. Citizens' Commission on Hunger in New England, *American Hunger Crisis: Poverty and Health in New England*, Boston, February, 1984.
14. Save the Children and American Can Company, *Hard Choices*, September, 1984.
15. United States Conference of Mayors, *The Urban Poor and the Economic Recovery*, Washington, D.C., September, 1984.
16. Food Research and Action Center, *Bitter Harvest*, Washington, D.C., November, 1984.
17. Texas Senate Interim Committee on Hunger, Executive Summary of Final Report, Austin, Texas, 1984.
18. Ohio Senate Task Force on Hunger, personal communications with Jill Poppe, September, 1984.
19. New Orleans Nutrition Task Force, "Third Draft Report on Nutrition in the City of New Orleans," New Orleans, August 30, 1984.
20. Florida IMPACT, *Hunger in the Community.* September, 1981.
21. Interfaith Hunger Coalition of Southern California, *Report*, Los Angeles, April 30, 1983.
22. Oklahoma Conference of Churches, *Hunger and Malnutrition in Oklahoma*, Oklahoma City, Winter 1982–83.
23. Walker, Bailus, Ph.D., "The Impact of Unemployment on the Health of Mothers and Children in Michigan, Recommendations for the Nation," Michigan Department of Public Health, January 31, 1983.
24. Sidel, Victor, M.D., Montefiore Medical College, New York City, Testimony before Agriculture Subcommittee on Nutrition, U.S. Congress, Washington, D.C., October 20, 1983.
25. Governor's Task Force on Food and Nutrition, *Interim Report*, Baltimore, Maryland, November, 1984.
26. Virginia Forum, *Report*, Urbanne, Virginia, November, 1984.
27. Wisconsin Nutrition Project, *Report*, Madison, Wisconsin, December, 1984.
28. Rutgers University School of Social Work, *Report*, New Brunswick, New Jersey, 1982.
29. Legislative Advisory Committee on Public Aid, *A Review of Studies: The Impact of Federal Budget Cuts in Illinois*, Chicago, May, 1984.
30. Kentucky Task Force on Hunger, *Report*, July, 1984.
31. Boulder County Department of Community Action Programs, *Food Needs in Boulder County*, Boulder, December, 1983.
32. Northern California Anti-Hunger Coalition, *Survey of Reports of Emergency Food Assistance in Three Counties*, Sacramento, December, 1984.

33. Hunger Action Center, *Tucson Hunger Survey*, Tucson, December, 1983.
34. Food Conservers, Inc., *Delaware Hunger Watch Report*, April, 1984.
35. Eccher, JoAnn, Project Bread Hunger Hotline, statistics from ongoing monitoring system, Boston, Massachusetts, January, 1985.
36. ibid.
37. Rhode Island Community Food Bank, telephoned report of statistics, Providence, January, 1985.
38. Rhode Island Community Food Bank, *Hunger in Rhode Island II*, Providence, May, 1984.
39. Ramsey, Jack, Second Harvest, Chicago, Illinois, personal communication, January 19, 1985.

3. The Increase of Hunger in America

1. Raff, Michael, Director, Governor's Office of Human Development, Mississippi, testimony and documents presented to Physician Task Force, May 2, 1984.
2. ibid.
3. Field hearing, House Subcommittee on Domestic Marketing, Consumer Relations and Nutrition, Greenwood, Mississippi, June 29, 1984.
4. Interview, May 1, 1984.
5. Interview with agency workers, Jackson, Mississippi, May 2, 1984.
6. Interview with County Extension Office social workers at Tutwiler health center, May 1, 1984.
7. Stancil, Joyce, RN, testimony before Physician Task Force, Greenwood, Mississippi, May 1, 1984.
8. Levy, David, M.D., Jackson, Mississippi, report of observations and findings to the Physician Task force, May, 1984.
9. Frazier, Leon, Commissioner, Alabama Dept. of Pensions and Securities, testimony before Physician Task Force, May 4, 1984.
10. U.S. Dept. of Labor, Bureau of Labor Statistics, November, 1984.
11. Extrapolation based on annual average household(s) food tax as a proportion of annual average income for food stamp household(s) of same size.
12. Alabama Vital Statistics records, 1981, 1982, 1983.
13. Data presented by staff, Western Health Center, Ensley, Alabama, to Physician Task Force on Hunger, May 3, 1984.
14. Pickett, George, M.D., Birmingham, Alabama, report of observations and findings to Physician Task Force, May, 1984.
15. Starnes, Paul, Tennessee State Representative, testimony before the Physician Task Force, Nashville, June 5, 1984.
16. Perrin, James, M.D., Nashville, Tennessee, report of observations and findings to Physician Task Force, June, 1984.
17. ibid.

18. Interview, June 4, 1984.
19. Zee, Paul, M.D., Memphis, TN, report of observations and findings to Physician Task Force, May, 1984.
20. Satcher, David, M.D., Ph.D., Nashville, TN, report of observations and findings to the Physician Task Force, June, 1984.
21. Petrey, Dixie, Director, Nutrition Project, Knoxville/Knox County Community Action Agency, testimony before Physician Task Force, June 4, 1984.
22. Interview with Mrs. Otis, Nashville daycare center operator, June 4, 1984.
23. Hudgins, Daniel, Dir., Durham Cty., Dept. of Soc. Ser., testimony before the Physician Task Force on Hunger, Raleigh, NC, June 8, 1984.
24. ibid.
25. In 1981 the IMR was 13.2; in 1982 it rose to 13.7.
26. Based on statistical data compiled from individual WIC records, April, 1984, and May, 1984.
27. ibid.
28. Interview conducted by Evelyn Schmidt, MD, Project Director, Lincoln Community Health Center, Durham, NC, June 7, 1984.
29. Adkins, interview, September 4, 1984.
30. Parmer, Hugh, Chmn., Texas Senate Interim Committee on Hunger and Nutrition, testimony before Physician Task Force, Houston, Sept. 6, 1984.
31. ibid.
32. Based on union records, as of August, 1984.
33. Interviews with emergency food providers, Presbyterian Center, Houston, TX, September 7, 1984.
34. Parmer, ibid.
35. ibid.
36. ibid.
37. Su Clinica, Harlingen, TX, testimony before the Physician Task Force, September 5, 1984.
38. DiFerrante, M.T., nutritionist, Houston Health Department, Houston, TX, September 7, 1984.
39. Personal interview conducted by Aaron Shirley, M.D. with physicians and staff at Clinica La Fe, El Paso, TX, September 5, 1984.
40. ibid.
41. Guerra, Fernando, M.D., San Antonio, TX, report of observations and findings to the Physician Task Force, September 1984.
42. Brahmin, A.P., M.D., Medical Director, Hidalgo County Clinic, testimony before Physician Task Force, September 5, 1984.
43. Chicago Hunger Watch, *Hunger in Chicago: Summary*, Chicago, 1983, p. xiii.
44. Ahrens, Robert, Chicago Office for Senior Citizens, testimony before the Senate Budget Committee, March 2, 1984.

45. Davis, Merry Jo, M.P.H., RD, Chief Clinical Dietitian, Cook County Hospital, testimony before the Physician Task Force, October 1, 1984.
46. Levy, Howard, M.D., Chicago, IL, testimony before House Subcommittee on Domestic Marketing, Consumer Relations and Nutrition, Chicago, IL, March 2, 1984.
47. Cranston, Linda, testimony before the Physician Task Force, Peoria, IL, October 2, 1984.
48. Interviews with health care administrator and WIC nutritionist, October 3, 1984.
49. Huneke, Diane, Director, Central Missouri Food Bank, Columbia, MO, personal communication summarizing results of survey of Community Action agencies in eight Missouri counties, January, 1985.
50. Jones, Evelyn, Community Services worker, Lutheran Family Services, St. Louis, MO, testimony before Physician Task Force, October 4, 1984.
51. Caneen, Edith, St. Patrick's Center, St. Louis, MO, interview, October 4, 1984.
52. Mayor's Task Force on Food and Hunger, *Task Force Report: Hunger in Kansas City*, presented to Mayor R.L. Berkley, November 10, 1984.
53. Spatti, Raymond J., Ph.D., Central Missouri State University, testimony before Physician Task Force, St. Louis, MO, October 4, 1984.

4. Malnutrition, Ill-Health, and Hunger

1. Several systems do exist which provide some relevant information: the Nationwide Food Consumption Survey, the National Health and Nutrition Examination Survey and the Centers for Disease Control Pediatric Nutrition Surveillance System all gather data on health and nutrition of some segments of the U.S. population. No one of these alone constitutes an adequate surveillance system, however, and they are not currently administered so that their findings can easily be linked. Further information on each of these systems appears later in this chapter.
2. Ciba Foundation, *Symposium on Size at Birth*, Symposium Number 27, Amsterdam, 1974.
3. University of North Carolina—Child Health Outcomes Project, "Monitoring the Health of America's Children: Ten Key Indicators," September, 1984.
4. Hoekelman, R.A., Blatman, S., Brunell, P., Friedman, S., Sidel, H., *Principles of Pediatrics: Health Care for the Young*, New York, 1978.
5. UNC—Child Health Outcomes Project, ibid.
6. Office of Policy, Planning and Evaluation, Food and Nutrition

Service, United States Department of Agriculture, "Evaluation of the Effectiveness of WIC," 1980.

7. Kotelchuk, Milton, Testimony Concerning the Special Supplemental Food Program for Women, Infants and Children, Subcommittee on Nutrition, U.S. Senate Committee on Agriculture, Nutrition and Forestry, April 6, 1983.

8. ibid.

9. Dobbing, J., "Rate of Brain Growth," in M.S. Scrimshaw and J.E. Gordon, eds., *Malnutrition, Learning and Behavior,* Cambridge, 1968.

10. Stock, M.D., Smythe, T.M., Moody, A.D, and Bradshaw, D., "Psycho-Social Outcome and C.T. Findings After Gross Malnourishment During Infancy: A 20 Year Developmental Study," *Developmental Medicine and Child Neurology,* 24:419, 1982.

11. UNC—Child Health Outcomes Project, ibid.

12. Mahaffey, K.R. and Vanderveen, J.E., "Nutrient-Toxicant Interactions: Susceptible Populations," *Environmental Health Perspectives,* 29:81, 1979, and Ziegler, E.E., et al., "Absorption and Retention of Lead by Infants," *Pediatric Research,* 12:29, 1978.

13. Chandra, R.K., "Interactions of Nutrition, Infection and Immune Response," *Acta Paediatrica Scandinavia,* 68:137, 1979.

14. Beaton, George H., "Evaluation of Nutrition Inverventions: Methodologic Considerations," *American Journal of Clinical Nutrition,* 35:May, 1982.

15. Robinson, Corinne H., and Lawler, Marilyn R., *Normal and Therapeutic Nutrition, 15th Ed.,* New York, 1977.

16. Franz, Marion, "Nutritional Requirements of the Elderly," *Journal of Nutrition for the Elderly,* 1(2), 1981.

17. Administration on Aging, U.S. Department of Health and Human Services, "Aging: Nutrition and the Elderly," September-October, 1980.

18. Posner, Barbara M., *Nutrition and the Elderly,* Lexington, MA, 1979.

19. ibid.

20. Food and Nutrition Board, National Research Council, National Academy of Sciences, *Recommended Dietary Allowances: Revised, 1980,* Washington, D.C., 1980.

21. Schaefer, Arnold, "Why Are We Still Debating the Issue," *Hunger Notes,* Vol. 9, No. 8, March, 1984.

22. Abraham, Sidney, "Preliminary Findings of the First Health and Nutrition Examination Survey, United States, 1971–1972: Dietary Intake and Biochemical Findings," DHEW Publication No. (HRA) 74-1219-1, Rockville, MD, 1974.

23. National Center for Health Statistics, Dept. of Health and Human Services, "Dietary Intake Source Data: United States (1976–1980)," Vital and Health Statistics Series 11, No. 231 and "He-

matological and Nutritional Biochemistry Reference Data for Persons 6 months–74 Years of Age: United States 1976–1980," Vital and Health Statistics Series 11, No. 232; Washington, D.C., 1983.

24. Science and Education Administration, Department of Agriculture, "Food Consumption and Dietary Levels of Low-Income Households, Nov., 1977–March, 1978," Nationwide Food Consumption Survey, 1977–78: Preliminary Report, No. 8, Washington, D.C., 1981.

25. U.S. Senate, Select Committee on Hunger Report, Washington, D.C., 1977.

26. Peterkin, B., Kerr, R.L., and Hama, M.Y., "Nutritional Adequacy of Diets of Low-Income Households," *Journal of Nutrition Education* 14(3):102, 1982.

27. Leard, Robert, Administrator, Food and Nutrition Service, USDA, comments on the "Today" show, NBC News, October 16, 1984.

28. Science and Education Administration, Department of Agriculture, ibid.

29. Social Security Administration, Department of Health and Human Services, *Social Security Bulletin*, Vol. 47, No. 12, December, 1984.

30. Public Health Service, Department of Health and Human Services, *Health United States, 1980*, MD, 1980.

31. Wegman, Myron E., "Annual Summary of Vital Statistics—1983," *Pediatrics*, Vol. 74, Performance in Nonanemic, Iron-Deficient Infants," *Pediatrics* Vol. 71, No. 6, June, 1982.

32. UNC—Child Health Outcomes Project, ibid.

33. Wegman, ibid.

34. World Health Organization, *World Health Statistics Annual*, Geneva, 1983.

35. Public Interest Health Consortium for New York City, "Prenatal Care in New York City," *City Health Report*, No. 1, September, 1984.

36. M.T. DiFerrante, "Health Data on Houston Residents," Presentation to Physician Task Force, Houston, September 7, 1984.

37. Dept. of Health and Human Services, *Healthy People: The Surgeon General's Report on Health Promotion and Disease Prevention*, Washington, D.C., 1979.

38. Data from research by Dr. Penny Feldman, Harvard University School of Public Health.

39. Lewis, Angela D., "Saving Our Babies: Black Infant Mortality Reviewed," Pittsburgh Black Women's Health Network, Pittsburgh, PA, April, 1984.

40. Shapiro, Sam, Presentation on Infant Mortality and the Poor, Harvard University School of Public Health, October 15, 1984.

41. UNC—Child Health Outcomes Project, ibid.

42. ibid.
43. ibid.
44. Public Interest Health Consortium for New York City, ibid.
45. McLaughlin, F. Joseph, Report to the Physician Task Force on Hunger in America, Metropolitan Nashville General Hospital, June 5, 1984. Data from State Center for Health Statistics, Tennessee Department of Health and Environment, and Metropolitan Health Department.
46. Valadian, I., Porter, D., *Physical Growth and Development from Conception to Maturity*, Boston, 1977.
47. Spivak, H., unpublished data.
48. Lattimer, Agnes, Testimony before House Agriculture Committee, Subcommittee on Nutrition, October 20, 1983.
49. Nutrition Services Section, Illinois Department of Public Health, Illinois Nutrition Surveillance System: 1984 Update, Springfield, Illinois, 1984.
50. Mullan, Fitzhugh, Presentation to the Physician Task Force on Hunger in America, Albuquerque, New Mexico, September 5, 1984.
51. Massachusetts Department of Public Health, "1983 Massachusetts Nutrition Survey," Boston, 1983.
52. Centers for Disease Control, "Prevalence of Growth Stunting and Obesity: Pediatric Nutrition Surveillance System," *Morbidity and Mortality Weekly Report*, Vol. 32, No. 4ss.
53. Allen, Lindsay, "Functional Assessment of Nutritional Status: Its Potential for Program Evaluation in the U.S.A.," Presentation to conference on Nutrition Monitoring in the 1980's, Washington, D.C., December 7, 1984.
54. ibid.
55. Picone, T.A., Allen, L.H., Olsen, P.N., Ferris, M.E., "Pregnancy Outcome in North American Women: Effects of Diet, Cigarette Smoking, Stress and Weight Gain on Neonatal Physical and Behavioral Characteristics," *American Journal of Clinical Nutrition*, 36:1214–1224, 1982.
56. Roepke, J.L.B., Kirksey, A., "Vitamin B-6 Nutriture During Pregnancy and Lactation," "Vitamin B-6 Intake, Levels of Vitamin in Biological Fluids, and Condition of the Infant at Birth," *American Journal of Clinical Nutrition* 32:1211–1221, 1982.
57. Liebel, R.L., Pollitt, E., Kim, I., Viteri, F., "Studies Regarding the Impact of Micronutrient Status on Behavior in Man: Iron Deficiency as a Model," *American Journal of Clinical Nutrition*, 35:1211–1221, 1982.
58. Oski, F.A., Honig, A.S., Helu, B., Howanitz, P., "Effect of Iron Therapy on Behavior Performance in Nonanemic, Iron-Deficient Infants," *Pediatrics* Vol. 71, No. 6, June, 1982.

59. See for example, Barrett, D.E., Radke-Yarrow, M., Klein, R.E., "Chronic Malnutrition and Child Behavior: Effects of Early Caloric Supplementation on Social and Emotional Functioning at School Age," *Developmental Psychology*, Vol. 18, No. 4, 1982.

60. Hicks, L.E., Langham, R.A., Takenaka, J., "Cognitive and Health Measures Following Early Nutritional Supplementation: A Sibling Study," *American Journal of Public Health*, Vol. 72, No. 10, 1982.

61. For review of relevant literature see, Allen, Lindsay, "Functional Indicators of Nutritional Status of the Whole Individual or the Community," *Clinical Nutrition*, Vol. 3:169–175, 1985.

62. For discussion see Starfield, Barbara, "Family Income, Ill Health and Medical Care of Investigation on Hunger in America, U.S. Senate, Minneapolis, MN, Nov. 19, 1983.

63. UNC—Child Health Outcomes Project, ibid.

64. Milhous, P., Testimony before Committee on Labor and Human Resources, Field Investigation on Hunger in America, U.S. Senate, Minneapolis, MN, Nov. 19, 1983.

65. Mullan, ibid.

66. Illinois Department of Public Health, ibid.

67. Massachusetts Department of Public Health, ibid.

68. Centers for Disease Control, "Nutrition Surveillance: Annual Summary 1981," DHHS Publication No. (CDC) 34-8295, Washington, D.C., 1983.

69. National Center for Health Statistics, Department of Health and Human Services, "Hematological and Nutritional Biochemistry Reference Data for Persons 6 Months–74 Years of Age: United States 1976–1980 " Vital and Health Statistics, Series II, No. 232, Washington, D.C., 1983.

70. Spivak, H., Testimony before the Citizens' Commission on Hunger in New England, Boston, MA, Oct. 31, 1983.

71. Lattimer, Agnes, ibid.

72. Levy, H.B., Testimony before Subcommittee on Domestic Marketing, Consumer Relations and Nutrition of the House Committee on Agriculture, Chicago, Ill., March 2, 1984.

73. March of Dimes Birth Defects Foundation, "Despite Infant Mortality Decline Black Infants Still Die at Twice the Rate of Whites," *Maternal/Newborn Advocate*, Vol. II, No. 3, November, 1984.

74. "Glossary of Nutritional Terms," *American Journal of Public Health Supplement*, Vol. 63, November, 1973; adapted from Todhunter, E.N., "A Guide to Nutrition Terminology for Indexing and Retrieval," DHEW/PHS/NIH Publication, Washington, D.C., 1970.

75. Chandra, R.K., ibid.

76. Wilson, Roger, personal communication with members of the Physician Task Force on Hunger in America, Windowrock, AZ, Sept. 3, 1984.
77. Porter, Ona, Testimony before hearing of Physician Task Force on Hunger in America, Albuquerque, NM, Sept. 4, 1984.
78. Olson, Gwenn, Discussion with members of Physician Task Force on Hunger in America, Su Clinica Familiar, Harlingen, TX, Sept. 5, 1984.
79. Christoffel, K.K., Presentation at meeting with Physician Task Force on Hunger in America, Chicago, Ill., Oct. 1, 1984; Based on material from Listernack, R., Pace, J.J., Chiaramone, J.P. and Christoffel, K.K., "Severe Protein Calorie Malnutrition in Patients with 'Non-Organic' Failure to Thrive," unpublished paper, Chicago, 1984.
80. Shaper, A.G., Kibukamusoke, J.W., Hutt, M.S.R., *Medicine in a Tropical Environment,* London, 1972.
81. Christoffel, K.K., ibid.
82. Mare, Robert D., "Socioeconomic Effects on Child Mortality in the United States," *American Journal of Public Health,* Vol. 72, No. 6, June, 1982.
83. Maine Department of Human Services, "Children's Deaths in Maine: 1976–1980, Final Report," Augusta, ME, April, 1983.
84. Kitagawa, E.M., Hauser, P.M., *Differential Mortality in the U.S.: A Study in Socioeconomic Epidemiology,* Cambridge, MA, 1973.
85. Prieto, Jorge, Presentation to Physician Task Force on Hunger in America, Chicago, Oct. 1, 1984.
86. Wegman, ibid.
87. ibid.
88. National Center for Health Statistics, Department of Health and Human Services, *Monthly Vital Statistics Report,* Vol. 32, No. 13, Sept. 21, 1984.
89. UNC—Child Health Outcomes Project, ibid.; based on data from Centers for Disease Control, "Data from the U.S. Immunization Survey, 1982," Atlanta, 1983.
90. Centers for Disease Control, "Surveillance of Childhood Lead Poisoning—United States," *Morbidity and Mortality Weekly Report,* Vol. 32, July 16, 1982.
91. Children's Defense Fund, *American Children in Poverty,* Washington, D.C., 1984.
92. "Studies on Health Effects of Program Cutbacks," *Focus* (Journal of Harvard Medical Area), Nov. 8, 1984; Data from research by Dr. Penny Feldman, Harvard University School of Public Health.
93. Rosenberg I.H., Testimony before Subcommittee on Domestic Marketing, Consumer Relations and Nutrition of the House Committee on Agriculture, Chicago, Ill., March 2, 1984.

5. Hunger as the Result of Government Policies

1. Based on number of food stamp recipients compared to number of Americans living below federal poverty level, December, 1983.
2. Bureau of Labor Statistics, Washington, D.C.
3. ibid.
4. Congressional Research Service based on data from U.S. Department of Health and Human Services, Washington, D.C.
5. Congressional Research Service, ibid.
6. Palmer, J.L. and Sawhill, I.V., *The Reagan Record: An Assessment of America's Changing Domestic Priorities*, An Urban Institute Study, Ballinger, Cambridge, MA, 1984, comparison of 1980 and 1984 data.
7. ibid.
8. ibid.
9. ibid.
10. *Monthly Economic Indicators*, U.S. Govt. Printing Office, Washington, DC, 1980 through January, 1984.
11. Bureau of Labor Statistics, Washington, DC.
12. ibid.
13. Bednarzik, Robert W., "Layoffs and Job Losses," *Monthly Labor Review*, Washington, DC, September, 1983, pp. 3–11.
14. United States Department of Labor, Bureau of Labor Statistics, Washington, DC, November 11, 1984.
15. ibid.
16. U.S. Department of Labor, Bureau of Labor Statistics, *News*, "State and Metropolitan Area Employment and Unemployment: October and November, 1983," and U.S. Dept. of Labor, Employment and Training Administration, *Unemployment Insurance Claims: Reference Week of October 22, 1983 and November 19, 1983*.
17. Bureau of Labor Statistics, Washington, DC, and Center on Budget and Policy Priorities, Washington, DC.
18. Congressional Budget Office, "The Combined Effects of Major Changes in Federal Taxes and Spending Programs Since 1981," Washington, DC, April, 1984.
19. Center on Budget and Policy Priorities, *End Results: The Impact of Federal Policies Since 1980 on Low Income Americans*, Washington, DC, September, 1984, p. 11.
20. U.S. Dept. of Labor, Bureau of Labor Statistics, May, 1984.
21. Center on Budget and Policy Priorities, *End Results*, ibid.
22. Based on data provided by the U.S. Bureau of the Census to the Committee on Ways and Means, House of Representatives, July, 1984.
23. Children's Defense Fund, *American Children in Poverty*, Washington, DC, 1984.

24. ibid.
25. Congressional Budget Office (CBO), Congress of the United States, "Major Legislative Changes in Human Resource Programs Since January, 1981," Washington, DC, August, 1983.
26. Congressional Research Service, "Effects of OBRA, Welfare Changes and the Recession on Poverty," Washington, DC, July 25, 1984.
27. Center on Budget and Policy Priorities, *End Results: The Impact of Federal Policies Since 1980 on Low Income Americans,* Washington, DC, September, 1984.
28. ibid.
29. ibid.
30. CBO, ibid.
31. Center on Budget and Policy Priorities; Food Research and Action Center, Washington, DC; data based on U.S.D.A. records.
32. ibid.
33. ibid.
34. United States Department of Agriculture, Food Stamp Eligibility Schedule, 1984–85.
35. Center on Budget and Policy Priorities, ibid.
36. United States Department of Agriculture data.

6. Mean-Spiritedness as Government Policy

1. Coler, Gregory L., Director, IL Dept. of Pub. Aid, testimony before House Subcommittee on Domestic Marketing Consumer Relations and Nutrition, March 2, 1984.
2. Barwinski, Sally, Lutheran Family and Childrens Services, St. Louis, Missouri, testimony before the Physician Task Force in St. Louis, October 4, 1984.
3. Parmer, Hugh, Chmn., Texas Senate Interim Committee on Hunger and Nutrition, testimony before Physician Task Force, Houston, Sept. 6, 1984.
4. Roark, Dr. D.B., Commissioner, MS Dept. of Welfare, testimony before President's Task Force on Food Assistance, Nov. 18, 1983.
5. ibid.
6. Eldreth, Virginia, Administrator, Buncombe County Food Stamp Office, Asheville, North Carolina, information reported to field investigation team of Physician Task Force, June 6, 1984.
7. Hudgins, Daniel, Dir., Durham City, Dept. of Soc. Ser., testimony before the Physician Task Force on Hunger, Raleigh, NC, June 8, 1984.
8. Marvin, Helen R., N.C. State Senator, testimony before Physician Task Force on Hunger, June 8, 1984.
9. Silberman, Pamela, N.C. Legal Services Resource Center, Raleigh, N.C., testimony before the Physician Task Force in Raleigh, NC, June 8, 1984.

10. U.S. Department of Agriculture, Review of Quality Control Data, FY 1983.
11. ibid.
12. Interviews with laid-off workers, Labor Temple, Peoria, IL, October 2, 1984.
13. Vento, Rep. Bruce F., reprinted from "Social Security Disability Reviews: A Federally Created State Problem," Select Committee on Aging, Washington, DC, June 20, 1983, p. 6.
14. Snowe, Rep. Olympia J., ibid., p. 13.
15. Petit, Michael R., Commissioner of Human Services, Augusta, Maine, interview with Citizens' Commission physicians, January 10, 1984, Augusta, Maine.
16. ibid.
17. Greenleaf, James, Regional Director, MA Department of Public Welfare, Greenfield, MA, testimony before Citizens' Commission, Greenfield, MA, December 20, 1983.
18. U.S. Dept. of Agriculture, Food and Nutrition Service, December, 1984.
19. Projections by Dr. Peter Gottschalk, Bowdoin College, Maine, a leading authority in the field.
20. USDA, Food and Nutrition Service: 9/80-20.1 million recipients; 9/81-20.3 million recipients; 9/84-19.8 million recipients.
21. ibid.
22. Coler, ibid.
23. Roark, ibid.
24. ibid.
25. Murphree, Chris, Mississippi food stamp administrator, interview with Physician Task Force, May 1, 1984.
26. Review of forms used in Leflore County, MS, food stamp office, May 1, 1984.
27. Roark, ibid.
28. Pickett, ibid.
29. ibid.
30. Lashoff, Joyce, M.D., Berkeley, California, report of observations and findings on Southwest field investigations to the Physician Task Force, September, 1984.
31. Beardslee, William, M.D., Boston, MA, report of observations and findings on Southwest to the Physician Task Force, September, 1984.
32. Gort, Samuel Jr., Exec. Sec., Tallahatchie Development League, American Baptist Churches USA, testimony before President's Task Force, November 18, 1983.
33. Interview with food stamp administrators, Chicago, IL, October 1, 1984.
34. Roark, ibid.
35. Based on an MRRB analysis conducted by the Center on Budget and Policy Priorities, Washington, DC, Nov., 1983, and Jan., 1985.

36. ibid.
37. Lunn, Sarah, food stamp supervisor, Montgomery County, Alabama, interview with Physician Task Force, May 3, 1984.
38. Murphree, ibid.
39. Eldreth, ibid.
40. Kisten, Naomi, M.D., Chicago, IL, report of observations and findings on Alabama and Mississippi to the Physician Task Force, May, 1984.
41. Rogers, Allen, Director, Massachusetts Law Reform Institute, Boston, MA, testimony before the Citizens' Commission, October 31, 1983, Boston, MA.
42. *Report of the President's Task Force on Food Assistance*, Washington, DC, January, 1984.

7. Eliminating Hunger in America

1. Kotz, Nick, *Hunger in America: The Federal Response*, The Field Foundation, New York, 1979.

Appendix A

1. U.S. Census Bureau data for 1983, released August, 1984.
2. See Chapter 5.
3. ibid.
4. U.S. Department of Agriculture, Food and Nutrition Service, September, 1984.
5. See Chapter 5.
6. See Appendix B.
7. Food Research and Action Center, *Still Hungry*, November, 1983, Washington, D.C.
8. U.S. Census Bureau, 1981.
9. ibid.
10. Louis Harris Survey, "One In Eleven American Families Suffering From Hunger," February 2, 1984, Tribune Company Syndicate, New York.

GLOSSARY

Glossary

Health-Related Terms

Deficiency disease

A disorder or disease condition with characteristic clinical and laboratory signs caused by dietary deficiency of specific nutrients. Deficiency diseases may be prevented or cured by supplying the nutrients that are lacking. Some deficiency diseases are iron deficiency, anemia, rickets, osteoporosis, and scurvy.

Failure-to-thrive syndrome

Failure of a child to develop physically and/or mentally. The syndrome is attributed to a number of causes, among them inadequate nutrition and a disturbed mother-child relationship. It is observed among infants and toddlers.

Growth failure

Failure of the infant or child to grow in weight and/or stature at a normal, predicted rate for age and sex.

Hunger

For the purposes of this report, hunger is defined as the chronic underconsumption of food and nutrients.

Infant Mortality Rate

The number of deaths of infants under 1 year old per thousand live births in a given population.

Kwashiorkor

A severe clinical condition resulting from a deficiency of protein (and other nutrients), often in the face of a relative excess of calories. Occurring most frequently in children 1 to 3 years old, kwashiorkor is characterized by growth failure, edema, and muscle wasting. There is usually a preceding or accompanying infection such as diarrhea, respiratory infection, or measles.

Low birth-weight

Low-birth-weight infants are those weighing 2,500 grams or less at birth. They fall into two categories: those who are born prematurely (less than 37 weeks of gestation), and those who are full-term babies but are small for their gestational age.

Malnutrition	A broad term indicating an impairment to physical and/or mental health resulting from failure to meet nutrient requirements. The insufficiency of nutrients may result from inadequate intake or from interference with the body's ability to process and utilize nutrients. Malnutrition is most often clinically observed as stunting, tissue wasting, cognitive and behavioral deficits, or, in extreme form, a disease of starvation (e.g., kwashiorkor, marasmus).

Mild malnutrition, sometimes called *undernutrition,* may not present any clinical or laboratory symptoms, though the affected individual may suffer a loss of vitality and reduced ability to function physically and mentally.

Marasmus	A severe clinical condition resulting from a gross deficiency of calories over a period of time, as well as a lack of protein and other nutrients. The condition usually occurs in infants aged 3 to 18 months and is characterized by low body weight, loss of subcutaneous fat, and wasting of muscle tissue.
Neonatal Mortality Rate	The number of deaths of infants aged 28 days or under per thousand live births in a given population.
Nutrients	One of the components of food: for example, protein, fat, carbohydrate, minerals, vitamins, water.
Nutritional status	The overall health condition of an individual as influenced by the intake and utilization of nutrients. Nutritional status is determined by the correlation of information from physical, biochemical, and dietary studies.
Premature infant	An infant born before full gestation (37 weeks).
Prevalence	The number of cases of a disease or a particular condition occurring in a particular group or region and during a specific period of time. No distinction is made between new

and old cases; prevalence is the count of all cases at the time the count is made.

Recommended Dietary Allowances (RDA's)

The term used by the Food and Nutrition Board of the National Research Council of the National Academy of Sciences for recommendations for daily intake of specific nutrients. The intake recommendations, based on healthy individuals according to age and sex, are designed to be adequate for good health, allowing a margin of safety for individual variation.

Emergency Food Terms

Bread line

A term popularized during the Depression of the 1930s, it depicts lines of people waiting to receive bread or other minimal food from charities and relief organizations. Though bread lines as such still exist, the term is now also commonly used to describe people waiting to receive a bag of groceries, surplus commodities, or a box lunch.

Commodities

Commodities are surplus agricultural products acquired by the government under the Price Support Program of the Commodities Credit Corporation. Commodities are stored in government warehouses. There are two categories of commodities: Title I and Title II. Title I commodities may include such items as powdered eggs, canned meats and fruits, and dried beans; they are used in the school lunch program and are currently available to larger soup kitchens and congregate meal programs. Title II commodities may include rice, flour, honey, corn meal, non-fat dry milk, butter, and cheese. The foods are packaged in family-sized quantities and are currently available for distribution by food banks and social service agencies.

Food bank

A non-profit corporation that serves as a clearinghouse for soliciting, receiving, storing, and redistributing surplus or salvage foods from growers, processors, markets, and restaurants to other groups. A food bank offers food at low cost (usually about 10–20¢ a pound to cover bank operating costs) to non-profit organizations feeding those in need.

Food pantry

Food pantries are predominantly voluntary efforts by churches and social service agencies to provide an emergency bag of groceries to people in need. Pantries typically range from a corner in a church rectory to a well-stocked room of food in a community center. The diversity of the programs and the charitable nature of the effort account for extreme differences in the variety of food, the availability of food, the eligibility requirements for receiving food, and the distribution schedule from one pantry to the next. Pantries typically provide an individual or family with a three-day supply of non-perishable groceries (usually canned or dry goods). Food pantries obtain their food from food banks, churches, community food drives, and local solicitation from stores. What food a pantry can offer frequently changes according to supply. Many pantries set a limit on the number of times they will help someone in a given period of time.

Good Samaritan laws

Good Samaritan laws, enacted by individual states, provide incentive to the food industry to donate food to non-profit food banks and pantries. The laws protect the donor from liability concerning the donated food. Currently 48 states have such laws, and there is variation among the states as to rights and responsibilities under the law.

Soup kitchen

Soup kitchens are places where a meal, usually lunch or dinner, is served on a regular basis (daily or weekly). Kitchens are typically located in churches, shelters for the homeless, or community centers. They are staffed by volunteers who plan, prepare, and serve a full meal at little or no cost to as many as several hundred people. Meals range from soup or a sandwich and beverage to a full-course hot dinner. Soup kitchens obtain their food in much the same way food pantries do.

Publicly Funded Program Terms

AFDC

Aid to Families with Dependent Children, enacted in 1962, is an outgrowth of the Aid to Dependent Children (ADC) provision of the 1935 Social Security Act. In order for a family to qualify for AFDC cash assistance, there must be children who are deprived of the financial support of one of their parents owing to death, disability, absence from the home, or unemployment (this last program is called AFDC/U). Also, the family's income must fall below a predetermined needs standard. The actual amount of the AFDC payment depends on the number of persons in the household and the amount of other income and assets. AFDC recipients may be eligible to receive medical services under the Medicaid program (Title IX of the Social Security Act) and other services, such as food stamps.

AFDC is funded jointly through the Social Security Act, Title IV-A, and matching state funds. The match is 50-50. Medicaid and social services are funded through the Social Security Administration.

Child nutrition programs

These include the National School Lunch Program, the School Breakfast Program, the Child Care Food Program (CCFP), the Summer Food Program for Children (SFP), the Special Milk Program (SMP), and the Nutrition Education and Training Program (NET).

Elderly nutrition programs

The Older Americans Act (OAA) of 1965 was amended in 1972 to provide congregate (on-site) meals service for people over 60 years of age. In 1978 OAA was again amended to include a system of home-delivered meals called Meals-on-Wheels. The elderly nutrition program is in operation in all 50 states.

Funding for elderly nutrition comes from a variety of sources: Title II of the Older Americans Act; USDA; Title XX of the Social Security Act; state and local funds.

Food stamps

The Family Nutrition Program, widely called the Food Stamp Program, was begun in 1961 under the U.S. Department of Agriculture (USDA). It is now in effect in all 50 states, usually administered by state departments of welfare or social services. Under the Food Stamp Act of 1964, food stamp eligibility was tagged to the USDA poverty level, with semi-annual adjustments for inflation and allowable deductions for household living expenses. Once eligibility was proved, a family could purchase stamps from a local office, up to a maximum amount based on family size. The cost of the stamps to the family was variable, depending on the family's net income. The difference between the actual value of the food stamps and the cost to the family was called the Bonus Value. Stamp allotments per family were based on the USDA's Thrifty Food Plan.

The Food Stamp Act of 1977 mandated that free food stamps be made available to low-income households lacking the cash to buy stamps. To determine the amount of stamps available to a family, 30% of its net monthly income was subtracted from the Thrifty Food Plan cost for a family of its size, and the balance was allotted in free coupons. Coupons were issued directly to eligible households, eliminating the purchase step.

The USDA pays the full value of food stamps and provides states with half of the costs of administering the program.

Monthly Reporting and Retrospective Budgeting (MRRB)

MRRB encompasses two procedural requirements of certain governmental assistance programs such as food stamps. MRRB was first included in the 1980 amendments to the Food Stamp Act, which made these procedures optional for the states to enact. The Omnibus Budget Reconciliation Act (OBRA) and the Food Stamp Act Amendments of 1981 made these procedures mandatory in all 50 states. Through MRRB, the eligibility and benefit levels of certain food stamp households are redetermined every month.

Monthly Reporting requires that certain food stamp recipients receiving any income report that income, with documentation, to the food stamp office each month. Failure to report or to produce detailed documentation may result in immediate termination.

Retrospective Budgeting requires states to use a food stamp recipient's past income (the income two months before the present) as the basis for determining current benefit levels. In effect, a recipient's benefit level, thus determined, reflects past rather than present need.

Procedural denial

Denial of program assistance on the basis of incomplete information and procedural errors, regardless of the applicant's financial eligibility and need.

School meals

The National School Lunch Program (NSLP) was started in 1946 in response to widespread evidence of malnutrition among young men examined for the draft during World War II. Congress mandated free and reduced-price lunches to needy children and full-price meals for non-needy children. Schools can receive cash reimbursement for each meal served, as well as government surplus food and funds for food service equipment.

The School Breakfast Program was begun in 1966. At first it was targeted to low-income children. However, in 1972 it was revised and made available to all participating schools. The breakfast program also provides meal subsidies and equipment money.

The two programs are run by the School Programs Division of the Food and Nutrition Service (FNS) of the USDA. FNS administers the federal law on a national level. On the state level, the programs are run by the state education agency, operating under a contract with FNS. On the school level, public school districts are responsible for the programs; the local school board signs a contract with the state. Private schools may participate in the meals program if a given proportion of their students are low-income.

The USDA funds school meals by providing some commodities and per-meal reimbursement to local programs.

Supplemental Security Income (SSI)

A federal cash benefit program for the aged, blind, and disabled. Eligibility is based on a determination of need.

WIC

The Special Supplemental Program for Women, Infants, and Children (WIC) was established by Congress on a pilot basis in 1972, and made permanent in 1974. The program improves the health of low-income people by providing vouchers for the purchase of prescribed foods for pregnant and nursing women and children under five years of age. WIC is administered by the USDA nationally and by state governments and Native American tribes locally. These intermediaries allocate funds among health centers and clinics, which in turn distribute vouchers to clients. Women and children qualifying for WIC must be recertified at a health center every six months. Without recertification, eligibility is automatically terminated.

WIC is funded entirely by the USDA. Local funds are distributed according to a needs assessment formula, which must include at least one economic indicator (e.g., unemployment rate) and one health indicator (e.g., Infant Mortality Rate). Eligibility criteria differ among the states, but must fall within federal guidelines.

INDEX

Index